ENDING
SPOUSE / PARTNER ABUSE

Robert Geffner, PhD, ABPN, is the Founder and President of the Family Violence and Sexual Assault Institute now located in Fort Worth, TX, and San Diego, CA, he is a Licensed Psychologist and a Licensed Marriage, Family & Child Counselor who was the clinical director of a large private-practice mental health clinic in Texas for 15 years, and is a former Professor of Psychology at the University of Texas at Tyler. Dr. Geffner is currently a Clinical Research Professor of Psychology at the California School of Professional Psychology in San Diego. He is also the editor of the *Journal of Child Sexual Abuse, Aggression, Maltreatment & Trauma,* and the *Family Violence & Sexual Assault Bulletin,* and co-editor of the *Journal of Emotional Abuse,* all internationally disseminated. He has a doctorate in psychology and postdoctorate training in clinical psychology, neuropsychology, child psychology, family violence, child maltreatment, forensic psychology, and diagnostic assessment. He has a Diplomate in Clinical Neuropsychology from the American Board of Professional Neuropsychology. He has served as an adjunct faculty member for the National Judicial College since 1990. His publications include treatment manuals and books concerning family violence, and numerous book chapters and journal articles concerning spouse/partner abuse, child abuse, child psychology, forensic issues, neuropsychology and psychological assessment. He has served as a consultant and grant reviewer for the National Center for Child Abuse and Neglect, the Department of Health and Human Services, the National Institutes of Mental Health, and other national and state agencies, and has served on various national and state committees dealing with various aspects of family psychology, family violence, and child abuse. He was a founding member and former President of the Board of the East Texas Crisis Center and Shelter for Battered Women and their Children in Tyler, TX. He has been involved in teaching, training, research, and private practice for over 22 years.

Carol M. Mantooth, MS, is the Director of Psychoeducational and Case Worker Services at the Andrews Center, a community mental health agency in Tyler, TX. She has been employed in various clinical capacities for Andrews Center for seven years. She is a former Director of Client Services at the East Texas Crisis Center where much of this treatment program was developed. She has also been employed by Tyler Junior College as a Psychology Instructor. She has a Master of Science degree in Psychology from the University of Texas at Tyler. She assisted in developing the couple counseling program at the Crisis Center, and she helped develop and implement the counseling program for couples in groups, for battered and formerly battered women in groups, and for batterers in groups.

ENDING
SPOUSE / PARTNER ABUSE

*A Psychoeducational
Approach for Individuals
and Couples*

Robert Geffner
with Carol Mantooth

 Springer Publishing Company
New York

Springer Publish Co.
536 Broadway
New York NY 10012
Dorothy Kouwenberg ~~Kotz~~
Workbook to Accomp
Ending Spouse / Partner Abuse
bettaver

Springer Publishing Company, Inc.
536 Broadway
New York, NY 10012-3955

Acquisitions Editor: Bill Tucker
Production Editor: Pamela Lankas
Cover design by James Scott-Lavino

00 01 02 03 04 / 5 4 3 2 1

ISBN   0-8261-1271-4

Printed in the United States of America

Contents

IV Intimacy Issues and Relapse Prevention

Preface

The treatment program and this manual were developed to provide alternatives in the efforts to reduce the national epidemic of wife/partner abuse. It has become clear that the more options that are available for clinicians, the more likely the impact we will have on eliminating the violence that occurs in too many relationships. With this in mind, we developed a model that incorporates many other theories and approaches of psychotherapy, while focusing on the abuse as a primary issue. The assumptions of the therapy program described are based on modified cognitive-behavioral, psychoeducational, and systems approaches in general, and these are elaborated in the manual. In addition, our model allows for treating individual men who abuse or batter their partners, groups of men, individual couples, and groups of couples. The latter two conjoint approaches still focus on the abuse of the perpetrator, but also helps improve skills and the relationship when both partners desire such an approach. Conjoint therapy groups, by their nature, involve both men and women attending therapy groups together. In some cases the individuals attending groups do so: with spouses with whom they are still living; sometimes with spouses from whom they have separated; and in some cases they do so without their spouses, if they have chosen to discontinue the program. When the term "spouse" is used in this manual it does not, therefore, assume that group participants are limited to intact couples, or those who are married. In no case is a person who has been abused required to attend conjoint groups. Descriptions of the criteria used for choosing the appropriate treatment program are provided in this manual.

The advantage of our treatment program is its flexibility. Modifications in the order and materials can be made by trained clinicians to fit the needs of their clients. The ordering of sessions listed in this manual is the one we found most beneficial for couples and conjoint groups. When the treatment program has been used for gender-specific groups, however, the ordering may be more flexible. For example, some clinicians use the same order for both types of groups whereas others have exchanged some sessions in Modules II (Communicating and Expressing Feelings) and III (Self-Management and Assertiveness). We generally recommend following the order in a sequential manner.

The forms, questionnaires, and handouts for the treatment program are available as a complete package in a separate workbook that can be obtained in multiple copies for clients or group members. This workbook is also available in a Spanish translation. In addition, the flexibility of this model and program enable other materials to be added by clinicians and group facilitators that they have found to be successful in working with these clients.

Acknowledgments

Part of the curriculum contained in this manual was adapted from *Family Preservation: A Treatment Program for Reducing Couple Violence* by C. Mantooth, R. Geffner, J. Patrick and D. Franks (1987). The original program was used to treat couples and groups of couples in Tyler, TX. The program has been expanded and modified over the past 12 years to include gender-specific groups for batterers only, as well as conjoint groups for couples when spouse or partner abuse has occurred. The treatment described in this manual can be used with either gender-specific groups, gender-mixed groups, individual batterers, individual couples, or groups of couples throughout the country. The original program would not have been possible without the support and efforts of Dawn Franks, MPPA, Former Executive Director of the East Texas Crisis Center, and John Patrick, MS, the first Director of Clinical Services at the Center. They both were instrumental in the development of the original treatment program. Without their hard work and insight, our treatment program would never have been developed nor been able to evolve.

In our work during the past 18 years, we were helped by many other people who shared in planning, implementing, and improving the original counseling program. These have included Kathryn Avilla, Ann Buchanan, Trent Goodwin, William Grant, Stephen Hidalgo, Tamma Holmes Isabell, Nancy Laney, and Martha McGowen. Many intern and practicum psychology students from the University of Texas at Tyler, as well as volunteers, assisted in scoring assessments, screening couples, and helped with a multitude of other jobs.

The Community Involvement Team of the now closed Levi Strauss plant in Tyler, and Tom Harris at the Levi Strauss Foundation in San Francisco, deserve special recognition for providing support and funding for the initial counseling program. We are also grateful to Anson Schupe, PhD, and William Stacy, PhD, of the University of Texas at Arlington, coauthors of *Violent Men, Violent Couples*, for including our initial program in their evaluation of treatment programs for abusive men in Texas. Through the independent follow-up study conducted by these sociologists and their assistants, we received vital feedback concerning our program and its effectiveness.

Over the past 8 years, many others have contributed ideas and feedback that enabled the current treatment program to be developed. We deeply appreciate the efforts of Dan Saunders, PhD, in Michigan and David Wexler, PhD, in California. They provided considerable feedback as well as allowed us to used or adapt some of their materials in this manual. Their help and efforts were instrumental in the refining of the treatment program. They were consultants, along with the senior author of this manual, for a major research project for the United States Navy Family Advocacy Program in San Diego, CA. Frank Dunford, PhD, from Colorado was the principal investigator who conducted the project in San Diego. The feedback from all the clinicians who conducted the groups for the navy was also valuable in improving and refining the current program. We would like to express our gratitude to these clinicians: Tony Salkas, LCSW, Cindy Lochtefeld, LCSW, Ken Marlow, LCSW, Steve Tess, PhD, Delores Jacobs, PhD, Michele Koonin, LCSW, Bob Bray, PhD, Sheila Stittiams, LCSW, Paul Sussman, PhD, Gene Batalia, LCSW, Jerry Gold, PhD, and Ana DeSoto, PhD.

The support and contributions of Lt. Pamela Murphy, the Director of the Family Advocacy Center at the time the development of this revised manual began, and Lt. Commander Elizabeth

Burns, the Director of the Family Advocacy Center during much of the adaptation and implementation of the curriculum for the navy, were invaluable and essential to the successful development of our treatment program at the Family Advocacy Center. Lt. Commander Norma "Cindy" Jones was also involved in the latter period of the project, and her leadership is appreciated. The project in San Diego was under the overall supervision of Sandra Rosswork, PhD, who directs the Family Advocacy Program for the United States Navy. We appreciate her support and leadership during the navy project.

Others who conducted the treatment groups at the East Texas Crisis Center in Tyler, TX at various times deserve special mention as well. Ken Elliott, MEd, and Tim Coody, MA, provided feedback based on their experience treating batterers, and their comments were appreciated and incorporated into the present manual.

In addition, we would like to acknowledge the hours of patient and helpful editorial assistance provided by Teri Geffner. Finally, we would like to thank the many men, women, and couples who entrusted us with their experiences and feelings without whom we could not have developed this program. Thus, this treatment manual represents the combined efforts of many clinicians and clients accumulated over the past 18 years. We continually strive to improve the model as more research and knowledge becomes available.

Handouts and Forms

Introduction

This manual is the result of 18 years of planning, implementing, retrenching, and reimplementing. There were times when our work with those who abused their partners and the partners who were victimized was tremendously rewarding, and there were times when frustration left us wondering if we would still be working with these clients the following month. In most of the cases we treated, the men were the abusers and the women who were their partners or spouses were the victims.

There were some cases, though, in which the woman was the abuser and her partner (male or female) was the victim. In some other cases, we also treated men who were abusing their male partners, or women who were abusing their female partners.

Through all of this, we gained a great deal of insight about working with those in violent relationships. At times, our goals were reached, would then shift, and then the process would repeat itself. Eventually, we realized the importance of sharing what we had learned with others in the clinical fields and in the battered-women/shelter movement. This manual is designed to provide practical information that can be immediately applied to counseling abusers and those who have been abused.

For those who already work with abusers and couples in abusive relationships, some of the information in this manual will not be new, and for experienced clinicians, the general techniques may already be familiar. It is hoped, however, that our perspectives, how we have used different counseling techniques, and the specific procedures, materials, handouts, and assignments will be helpful. For other counselors who are beginning work with clients involved in wife/partner abuse, information concerning appropriate counseling techniques as well as accompanying educational material is provided in this manual in the format used in our treatment program.

This introduction describes the initial development of our program. This section is central to the perspectives presented in the rest of this manual because they have developed over time and were well honed by our clinical experiences and evolving research. The second chapter then describes general counseling techniques that may be used in working with abusers or couples. The third chapter describes assessment and screening issues and techniques. The remainder of the manual is divided into 26 sessions, each dealing with specific issues that we feel the clients need to work on. The order in which they are presented is the one most highly recommended, as stated above. They should be used to meet the needs of the men or the couples, however. Some men and couples need to spend more time on certain sections, others less. Our program is divided into these 26 sessions, one per week, followed by monthly sessions for 6 months. Each session is divided into four subsections: Objectives, Materials, Tasks, and Procedures; the latter includes counseling, education, and homework. The materials and handouts needed for each session are clearly outlined. The sessions themselves are divided into counseling and education for the clients, hence ours is a psychoeducational approach. The combination of these two elements are the basis of our program. They build on each other. Homework assignments help the clients use what they are learning and prepare for the next session in an active, participatory manner. The educational material that is presented with each section has been developed for that particular session.

Material that was borrowed, adapted, or modified from other sources has been so noted and credit has been given to the source. This manual would not have been possible without the contributions of many other programs, clinicians, and researchers. The reader will find a list of resources at the end of most chapters to identify many of these important contributors.

Over the years, considerable dialogue has taken place during office coffee breaks, at conferences, and in various journals and newsletters concerning the possible success rates of different treatment and educational approaches, as well as the pros and cons of various methods. This treatment program is offered in an effort to encourage more research and dialogue. It should be noted that research is currently being conducted at several sites and programs, and their results should be published during the coming years. It appears that mere education may not be sufficient for many abusers, especially if it is offered in a shame-based, punitive manner, and that many approaches may be effective with certain groups of abusers. There is no research to date that indicates one approach is "better" or "correct" for all abusers. In fact, there is also no research that indicates or even suggests that conjoint programs that focus on the abuse in conjunction with other areas in an approach that does not place blame is less successful or more dangerous than other methods, despite media statements to the contrary. Clinical experience and reports from those trained to work with abusers and couples suggests that this model may be quite successful with many abusers in gender-specific or in couples groups. The important components include clinical training of the therapists, training concerning family-violence dynamics, established criteria for determining who may be included in the different types of treatment, and assessment to provide information in making these decisions.

Ending domestic violence is the obvious goal for all of us who are working in this field. It appears to us that it is time to integrate and unite those using various approaches, as most methods provide important information and are successful with certain people. Some abusers volunteer for treatment on their own, whereas others may not even participate with court or military mandate.

Similarly, some battered women find shelters empowering, whereas others merely use them as emergency stops before returning to their abusive husbands. It is clear that many abusers enter treatment based on "partner mandate" (i.e., the abuser enters treatment or the partner will leave and end the relationship). The fear of loss is a very strong motivating factor for many abusers.

This could also have negative ramifications, however, because the time when a spouse/partner leaves a relationship can also be the most dangerous. This is a sensitive time and many battered women face a fine line when making these decisions.

The advantage of our program and similar ones is that for abusers and couples who do participate, the family system can also be changed. This helps create a functional family (which is often what both the spouses or partners desire), as well as reduces the likelihood of a generational perpetuation of violence, especially if the family is involved in treatment. There are cases in which a systems approach is not feasible; in these situations, using gender-specific methods for the battered woman and the abusive man is required. To eliminate any method or technique without research evidence seems counterproductive. We hope that this manual, therefore, will add to the repertoire of the various practitioners working with clients who have or are abusing their partners and those who have been abused.

PERSPECTIVE: HISTORY AND FUTURE

In the fall of 1981, the East Texas Crisis Center in Tyler, Texas embarked on a very ambitious project. With the goal of ending violence in families, the center created a counseling program that combined education, home visits, and therapy. Some of the key people involved in developing this project had considerable counseling experience in varied areas. They were relatively new to the field of family violence at the time, however. The program developers designed and implemented a conservative counseling program attempting to meet the needs of their community. Because there had been virtually no involvement on a national level by any of these people, many of the feminist issues that have now been incorporated in the issues of family violence did not appear significant then.

Almost all of the people involved in developing this program definitely call themselves feminists, yet we saw no contradictions in developing a counseling program that would be able to include couples. Our belief in this idea was reinforced by a large percentage of the battered women who left our shelter only to return home. There were many reasons they returned. Often it was for financial reasons or out of fear, but shelter and counseling staff also recognized that many times a woman chose to go home because she loved her partner. The message seemed loud and clear.

Couples needed a way to help them end the violence together. Frequently, when a woman came to the shelter, the staff would hear from her partner within a few days. As the counselors listened to his side of the story, and to hers, they began to get a glimpse of what binds a man and a woman in a violent relationship, and how many abusers convince or force a woman to remain or to return. Clearly, the world was not full of violent men getting their kicks hurting the women they loved.

Nor were women asking to be abused and beaten. In addition, some of these men wanted help to change their behavior as they did not know how to stop on their own. It was clear that most of these women did not want to leave their husbands, but they did want the abuse and violence to stop.

One of our project developers had read about a child-abuse project in Arkansas that was using a combined therapy/visitation program to stop child abuse. Additionally, some staff had been involved with in-home programs and were aware of how effective they could be. It seemed feasible that an adaptation of such a model could be useful with violent couples. Thanks to the foresight of the Community Involvement Team (CIT) at the local Levi Strauss plant, the vision became reality. The CIT supported the Levi Strauss Foundation in funding what became known as the Family Preservation Project (FPP). This was a 2-year pilot project that combined a male/female counseling team and a male/female family consulting team. In its original form, a batterer and a battered woman would come to the Center's office for weekly counseling sessions and the family consultants would make weekly visits to the family home. This combined education, counseling, and home interventions in order to eliminate the violence and improve the family relationship.

COUNSELING

In the early years of the project, the counseling team worked with individual batterers and also with individual couples. A commitment to the male/female cotherapy-team approach for the abusers and for the couples was made and kept in those early years. The staff had a strong belief that the role models the team provided to the men or to the couple would be helpful to the counseling, as well as preventing either individual in couples from feeling "ganged up on" by two members of the other gender. That philosophy remains even though other changes have been made. Counseling issues were based on the needs of the batterer for gender-specific treatment and on the couple for conjoint treatment. These needs were determined by completion of an extensive social history, questionnaires, and several psychological tests. Various counseling techniques were used and they are described in the next chapter of this manual. The initial program in the early 1980s included 10 weeks of treatment. A few years later, the program was increased to 12 and then to 16 weeks, plus intake and assessment.

FAMILY CONSULTANTS

Originally the family consultants had a twofold purpose. The first goal was to educate the couple, if they remained in the relationship, about various issues, including family violence, communication, and parenting skills. The education lessons were designed to complement the counseling that took place each week. The second goal was to allow project staff a glimpse into the family's personal world, as it was believed that violent family members may exhibit different behaviors in their own home compared to meeting in a public place or office. It was also hoped that consultants and counseling staff would have a more rounded picture of the family, and more success with intervening in such a dysfunctional system in a relatively brief time period.

Individual family-education plans were jointly developed by the counseling team and family consultants. During the period that family consultants made home visits, no violent incidents occurred in our program.

SOCIAL AND PSYCHOLOGICAL ASSESSMENT

From the beginning, social and psychological assessment were used as a method of aiding the counseling. Not only did it help the counselors to identify problem areas for the clients, but the assessment was interpreted in general to the individuals alone or to the couples in joint sessions, which often increased the partners' understanding of each other. The use of assessment with battered women has long been criticized because of the fear that it would increase the general perception that she has personality or other psychological disorders. With the use of the assessment, however, significant knowledge was gained concerning the dynamics of the personalities, attitudes, and behaviors of the clients. Many battered women were indeed significantly depressed, had low self-esteem, were hostile, and may have been using alcohol excessively to escape the pain. It was common for many of the battered women to have posttraumatic stress disorder from years of abuse.

In general, a pilot study indicated similar profiles for both the battered females and male batterers on the various inventories and questionnaires (Geffner, Jordan, Hicks, & Cook, 1985). It was also clear that in most of the cases, however, the men were the abusers and the women were the victims (this is similar to many research reports). Pre- and postquestionnaires were also given to determine any changes in personality, attitudes, behaviors, and levels of abuse. Again, the assessment was interpreted to the clients and used to reinforce the changes and improvements they had made. In addition, a modified version (the *Weekly Behavior Inventory*) of the Conflict Tactics Scales (Straus, 1979) was used throughout the counseling to measure abusive incidents. Again, this was very useful in plotting the change in behavior patterns during the program.

SELF-REFERRED VERSUS COURT REFERRED

Throughout the initial years of the treatment project, participating clients and families were often self-referred. The rate of self-referrals increased as the public became aware of the program. It was common for either partner to make initial contact, later bringing the other one into the counseling. Both men and women exhibited initiative in seeking help to end the violence. Often the first visit to the center was by both partners together. Because the East Texas Crisis Center operated a shelter for battered women and children, it was assumed that many women choosing to return home would arrange to participate in the program. Although many women tried to get their husbands to come to the couples-treatment program, however, it is estimated that fewer than 25% of these couples actually did complete the program.

It is unclear how the issue of being self-referred versus court referred affected the success rate of eliminating violence. Clearly, all the clients who initially completed the counseling program were self-motivated, which would affect the outcome. Motivation levels of the individual partners frequently differed.

Future studies need to assess the significance of varying motivation levels in conjunction with court referrals versus self-referred couples. The techniques used in our program would apply to either group, however. In fact, in recent years the majority of referrals have been court ordered rather than self-referred. This may be a result of the increased awareness and recognition of the problem, and quicker involvement from law enforcement and the criminal-justice system. The rate of completion of the treatment program has varied over the years. In the beginning, nearly 75% of the clients and couples who began the program finished it. As court referrals became prevalent, the dropout rate actually increased. During certain years, when the courts tended not to have good follow-up and enforced consequences, the dropout rate approached 50%. The current program with its options for treatment tends to have a 60%–70% completion rate. The dropouts include those who withdraw (some remain in denial or attempt to manipulate the system, and some feel they have received sufficient treatment to handle the problem on their own; the latter may also include denial at times), as well as those who are dismissed because of failure to participate or benefit from the treatment. Attrition issues are in need of further research, both for our program as well as for others. Obviously, the higher the completion rate, the more successful the program will likely be. When there is a court order for specified treatment in conjunction with tight controls of monitoring and legal enforcement of the consequences for dropping out, the completion rates are much higher. However, the program has also been used successfully in states that require up to 52 sessions (each of the current sessions were increased from 1 to 2 weeks). It is possible, though, that all abusers and couples may not need the same length or type of treatment, and some may actually benefit from shorter term programs. This also needs more research. Our recommendation, in general, is for a 6-month program in order to be able to deal with the complex combination of issues and attitudes involved in abusive relationships.

FROM ELIMINATION TO PROGRESS

Inevitably the question arises: Was the counseling program successful? Indeed, at the outset of the program the intent was to help abusive men end the violence. Frequently, the staff found that they were being far too idealistic in their goal of ending violence completely. Not surprisingly, it was discovered that the staff's definition of violence was broader and far more encompassing than the one used by the women in the couples. For instance, many women were shoved or occasionally slapped, yet these events were not registered as violence or abuse by them. Sometimes the men would say, "I only hit her with an open hand. I didn't use my fist."

The counselors recognized that a great deal of education about the dynamics and definition of family violence was needed. During the reeducation process, the counselors discovered that it was possible to get a man and woman to negotiate the level of violence that was acceptable to each individual. At first this seemed like "copping out" and giving up the idealistic goal of eliminating violence. We found, however, that many battered women became alienated from us when we tried to impose a strict no-abuse rule using our definition. We therefore began to gradually change the woman's definition so that all abuse could be eliminated, but this took some time. With gender-specific groups, we were quite strong and committed to our requirement of no abuse. With the couples, starting with the woman's definition eventually became a useful tool in helping the couple communicate and increase respect for each other's needs, and this then would lead to the elimination of the violence and abuse as their definitions changed over time with the treatment.

PROGRESS LEADS TO SUCCESS

So again the question is faced: Was the program successful? Only the clients and couples could truly answer that question. In the summer of 1984, Anson Schupe and William Stacey of the Center for Social Research at the University of Texas at Arlington conducted an independent extensive follow-up of couples and clients who had participated in our program. The following statistics were a result of that independent 1-year follow-up survey. The men reported the following:

72% said the violence had stopped;
16% said the violence was less severe.

The women reported the following:

47% said the violence had stopped;
31% said the violence was less severe.

The above statistics show a variation between male and female groups. Shupe and Stacey account for this variation resulting from the batterers perceiving the violence as less severe than that perceived by the victim. Additional statistics compiled by the researchers showed that of the 78% of women surveyed who reported less or no violence at all 1 year after the counseling program, 79% of them remained married. In addition, findings showed that 100% of the clients and couples surveyed would recommend our program to others (Riza, Stacey, & Shupe, 1985). Thus, although the results were positive, improvement was still needed, and it was obvious that modifications in the treatment program were necessary. Eight years ago, the program was expanded to 26 weeks, and several new topics were added based on feedback from clinicians using the treatment program in various locations and settings, new research, and pilot testing with the United States Navy. The current manual represents the improvements that have been incorporated during the past 8 years.

GENDER-SPECIFIC VERSUS COUPLES TREATMENT

There has been much controversy in the battered women/shelter movement regarding programs that counsel with couples. Generally, there is concern that such programs will shift the responsibility of the violence from the batterer to the victim, and that such programs may even escalate the level of violence. Contrary to these concerns, we and others have not found that violence escalated as a result of our counseling, but seemed to be a continuation of previous patterns. In fact, the essential ingredients of our program include: holding the abuser personally responsible for his or her violent actions and stressing that he or she is not powerless to stop it; trying to obtain objective, independent information about the violent persons and monitoring their behavior during the time they are in counseling; and creating an atmosphere in counseling sessions that physical violence and emotional abuse are neither appropriate nor excused.

The staff believed in couple counseling as an *option* because of our experiences and the reports of the clients, both men and women. Obviously, it is not the answer for every situation, but in cases where there is self-motivation on the part of both partners, it is believed that violence can be significantly reduced and then eliminated. It should be noted that, contrary to popular opinion, many batterers and battered women do want to change their situation, end the violence, and improve their relationship. Unfortunately, they often do not know how to do this, may be in denial, or may not realize there are other ways to respond. There are definitely those abusers who do not want to change, and some who would rather go to jail, murder their spouse, and/or commit suicide rather than try do so. They are not appropriate for most treatment programs, including ours.

Fortunately, these batterers are in the minority. The important point, though, is that the more options we have, the more likely that treatment will be successful. Using gender-specific treatment, couples treatment, or a combination of the two are all worthwhile depending on the specific treatment, the clients, and the situation (i.e., some programs require completion of gender-specific groups before couples counseling, and others begin in a parallel approach with the men and women separated but then joined after some time period and treatment). It should be pointed out, though, that the couples program is abuse-specific counseling, not traditional marital therapy.

We have used all of the preceding modalities at different times, and all have advantages and disadvantages. It is important to note, however, that we have treated many couples with our treatment program without them having received prior treatment. They were screened first as will be described in the third chapter. We should also note that in 18 years of conducting couples treatment with this program, we have not had one fatality or any life-threatening or severe injuries of women in the program. We have had a few such injuries and two deaths over this

18-year period with a few men who dropped out of gender-specific treatment. This has also been reported unfortunately in other treatment programs using different models. Our couples program has actually been the safest of all the treatment options we have available.

PROGRAM CHANGES

As the years passed, our treatment program underwent changes as a result of our experience working with clients. Currently, the program presented in this manual is used in a group format.

Additionally, the family consultant has been eliminated, leaving the counselors to provide both the therapy and the education. Home visits have also been eliminated. The primary reason for this last change was budgetary, because the Center could not maintain the cost of cotherapists and co-consultants. Eventually, education and therapy were combined into single sessions with one building on the other. This adaptation has been very successful. The group format has provided peer support to the participating men and couples, as well as allowing more men and couples to be admitted to the program. This format is still appropriate, however, with individual batterers and individual couples in therapy, and many of the techniques are also used with individual women and groups of battered women.

The program continues the tradition of a male/female co-counseling team. Although this can be costly budget-wise, it is believed that the counseling team approach is very important to the success of the program. We have been told, though, that individual clinicians have been successful in using our treatment program without a co-therapy team.

LOOKING AHEAD

Future possibilities for the treatment program include the use of marathon counseling sessions, offering follow-up relationship-enhancement courses, and conducting all-day relationship-enhancement seminars for the general public using the same program material. The marathon counseling sessions have been successfully used by the Center in its counseling program for incest survivors and formerly battered women. Although this requires a large investment of time by the counselors, it has been a very effective method of supplementing the counseling process.

Offering relationship-enhancement courses as a follow-up to the initial program has grown from the realization that ending abuse and violence in a relationship may be achieved in incremental stages. In a number of cases, men and couples have returned either after completing the program, or perhaps after dropping out, with the need to again work on several problem areas. When given an open-door policy with encouragement to return when they feel the need, some men and couples will continue to reduce abuse, intimidation, and violence to the zero level over a period of a few years.

Initially, counselors conducting treatment in our program envisioned ending abuse and violence during the course of the original 10-week counseling program. Experience has taught the staff that the dynamics of violence in relationships are complex and the wounds mutual as well as deep. A commitment from counseling staff to work with a batterer or a couple through these different stages over a long period of time can be very productive. Wife/partner abuse is an area that we are still attempting to better understand. Shelters have provided emergency housing for the short term; now we must learn to deal with the complexities of guiding abusive men and abused women to a healthy, stable situation individually or in the relationship for the long term. This work takes time.

As stated previously, the counseling program presented here is one method of working with abusers and couples. It is not the answer for all situations, but it will work with those who have a reasonable level of motivation (either personal, self-referred, or externally mandated). The strategies, techniques, and homework outlined in this manual may be adapted to fit your program's needs. It is offered as one of many building blocks that will be necessary in ending violence in the family in the future.

RESOURCES

Ammerman, R., & Hersen, M. (1991). *Case studies in family violence.* New York: Plenum.

Ammerman, R. T., & Hersen, M. (1990). *Treatment of family violence.* New York: Wiley.

Ammerman, R. T., & Hersen, M. (1992). *Assessment of family violence: A clinical and legal sourcebook.* New York: Wiley.

Barnett, O. W., & LaViolette, A. D. (1993). *It could happen to anyone: Why battered women stay.* Newbury Park, CA: Sage.

Barnett, O. W., Miller-Perrin, C. L., & Perrin, R. D. (1997). *Family violence across the lifespan: An introduction.* Thousand Oaks, CA: Sage Press.

Bolton, F. G., & Bolton, S. R. (1987). *Working with violent families: A guide for clinical and legal practitioners.* Newbury Park, CA: Sage.

Brinegar, J. (1992). *Breaking free from domestic violence.* Minneapolis, MN: CompCare.

Caesar, P. L., & Hamberger, L. K. (1989). *Treating men who batter.* New York: Springer Publishing Co.

Crowell, N. A., & Burgess, A. W. (Eds.). (1996). *Understanding violence against women.* Washington, DC: National Research Council, National Academy Press.

Dutton, D. (1998). *The abusive personality: Violence and control in intimate relationships.* New York: Guilford.

Dutton, M. A. (1992). *Empowering and healing the battered woman: A model for assessment and intervention.* New York: Springer Publishing Co.

Edleson, J. L., & Tolman, R. M. (1992). *Intervention for men who batter: An ecological approach.* Newbury Park, CA: Sage.

Finkelhor, D., Hotaling, G. T., & Yllo, K. (1988). *Stopping family violence: Research priorities for the coming decade.* Newbury Park, CA: Sage.

Garbarino, J., & Gilliam, G. (1980). *Understanding abusive families.* Lexington, MA: Lexington Books.

Geller, J. A. (1992). *Breaking destructive patterns: Multiple strategies for treating partner abuse.* New York: Free Press.

Gelles, R. (1997). *Intimate violence in families* (3rd ed.). Newbury Park, CA: Sage.

Giles-Sims, J. (1983). *Wife battering: A systems theory approach.* New York: Guilford.

Gondolf, E. W. (1985). *Men who batter: An integrated approach for stopping wife abuse.* Holmes Beach, FL: Learning Publications.

Hamberger, L. K., & Renzetti, C. (1996). *Domestic partner abuse.* New York: Springer Publishing Co.

Hanson, M., & Harway, M. (1993). *Battering and family therapy: A feminist perspective.* Newbury Park, CA: Sage.

Harway, M., & Hanson, M. (1994). *Spouse abuse: Assessing and treating battered women, batterers, and their children.* Sarasota, FL: Professional Resource Exchange.

Hotaling, G. T., Finkelhor, D., Kirkpatrick, J. T., & Straus, M. A. (1988). *Family abuse and its consequences: New directions in research.* Newbury Park, CA: Sage.

Jaffe, P., Wolfe, D., & Wilson, S. (1990). *Children of battered women.* Newbury Park, CA: Sage.

Kivel, P. (1992). *Men's work: How to stop the violence that tears our lives apart.* Center City, MN: Hazeldon Press.

Mills, L. G. (1998). *The heart of intimate abuse: New interventions in child welfare, criminal justice, and health settings.* New York: Springer Publishing Co.

Neidig, P. H., & Friedman, D. H. (1984). *Spouse abuse: A treatment program for couples.* Champaign, IL: Research Press.

Pagelow, M. D. (1984). *Family violence.* New York: Praeger.

Paymar, M. (1993). *Violent no more: Helping men end domestic abuse.* Alameda, CA: Hunter House.

Paymar, M., & Pence, E. (1993). *Education groups for men who batter: The Duluth model.* New York: Springer Publishing Co.

Peled, E., & Davis, D. (1995). *Groupwork with children of battered women: A practitioner's manual.* Newbury Park, CA: Sage.

Renzetti, C. M. (1992). *Violent betrayal: Partner abuse in lesbian relationships.* Newbury Park, CA: Sage.

Roberts, A. R. (Ed.). (1998). *Battered women and their families: Intervention strategies and treatment programs* (2nd ed.). New York: Springer Publishing Co.

Salber, P., & Taliaferro, E. (1995). *Physicians guide to domestic violence: How to ask the right questions and recognize abuse.* Volcano, CA: Volcano Press.

Sonkin, D. J. (1995). *Counselor's guide to learning to live without violence.* Volcano, CA: Volcano Press.

Sonkin, D. J., & Durphy, M. (1997). *Learning to live without violence: A handbook for men* (rev. ed.). Volcano, CA: Volcano Press.

Stacey, W. A., & Shupe, A. (1983). *The family secret: Domestic violence in America.* Boston: Beacon Press.

Stordeur, R. A., & Stille, R. (1989). *Ending men's violence against their partners: One road to peace.* Newbury Park, CA: Sage.

Straus, M. A. (1979). Measuring intrafamily conflict and violence: The Conflict Tactics (CT) Scales. *Journal of Marriage and the Family, 41,* 75–88.

Van Hasselt, V. B., Morrison, R. L., Bellack, A. S., & Hersen, M. (1988). *Handbook of family violence.* New York: Plenum.

Walker, L. E. (1984). *The battered women syndrome.* New York: Springer Publishing Co.

General Counseling Techniques

Overall the counseling approach that is used with men, couples, and groups of couples is an eclectic approach. The counselors basically assess the individual's or couples' needs, the group members' needs, and the marital situations. The two main approaches are behavioral and cognitive, or a combination of the two. Many of Albert Ellis' rational emotive behavior therapy (REBT) (Ellis & Harper, 1975) techniques are very effective in dealing with distorted and irrational thinking patterns. Behavior-modification techniques are effective in changing specific behavior patterns. Other specific approaches that are an integral part of the counseling are the reality therapy model, which overlaps with REBT in many ways, the Rogerian model, and some transactional analysis (TA) techniques. In the 18 years that we have counseled abusers and couples, numerous techniques and materials have been used. (Note: Some materials were borrowed from unknown sources. If another author or counselors' ideas were included and not acknowledged in the reference section, please let us know so proper credit can be given.)

The approaches we used will be addressed in this section in general. Because combinations of these techniques were employed, some procedures may fall into more than one specific theory. There are also some miscellaneous techniques from other approaches that have not been classified as a specific theory, but they will also be presented in this chapter.

This treatment manual was not intended to be a volume on new research, nor was it intended to specify which theory or techniques are most effective. Its specific purpose is to describe the techniques that are being used in the treatment program. Books are available with more detail about the theories and techniques of counseling in general as well as other approaches to batterer treatment and couples counseling for batterers and their spouses. References are listed at the end of the book, and other resources are listed at the end of most chapters to provide further instruction if needed.

GENERAL GUIDELINES AND PHILOSOPHY

The Counselors' Training and Experience

It is obvious that counselors using a treatment program such as ours need a solid educational and clinical background, as well as training in family-violence dynamics. If couples counseling is also to be conducted, then substantial training in marital and relationship counseling is also required. In addition these clinicians should also be knowledgeable regarding domestic violence and related issues.

There are many aspects to being a competent therapist in this program. It is important to be able to maintain task structure, handle conflicts calmly, engage all members of the group, facilitate rather than dominate, intervene to point out and promote insight during group interactions and role play, enforce group ground rules, be able to note improvement and progress, reinforce the clients and reframe negative statements, model appropriate behaviors, balance power issues, and adhere to the treatment program. The therapist should be able to switch smoothly from education to counseling, discuss and assign homework, maintain objectivity without bias, and explain the generalizability of the responses in sessions to the clients' behaviors in general. In addition to all of the preceding qualities, the clinician must be sensitive to cultural and ethnic issues and differences.

Finally, the counselor should be aware of any unresolved conflicts within himself or herself regarding domestic violence in general. The issues surrounding the battering of women are likely to stimulate a wide range of emotions within the counselor, depending on his/her own background and personal experience with family violence. An ongoing dialogue with a supportive co-therapist or team is an appropriate means to monitor and assist with any difficulties that may arise.

Developmental Therapy Process or Developmental Intervention

Experience suggests that the timing of intervention and confrontation should be considered in relation to the length of time a client has been in counseling. For example, it is usually not a good idea to encourage clients to give unbridled vent to their emotions early in therapy. Our experience is that emotional catharsis is easier to handle after clients/couples have learned communication techniques or have learned some method of constructively dealing with their emotions. We have also found that confrontation is best postponed until sufficient rapport has been established. Therefore, the counselors need to be adaptable and flexible, as well as sensitive to what a client/couple can tolerate at any given session.

Male/Female Counseling Team

In counseling with clients/couples, whether in groups or individually, it is very effective to use a male/female counseling team. As stated previously, there are various reasons for the effectiveness of this approach. One reason is that both a male and a female point of view are contributed in the counseling session. Another reason is that with couples, neither feels "ganged up on." The counseling team can also contribute much to the sessions by being role models as well as doing actual role plays to emphasize major points in the session. There are times when the women in couples groups feel more comfortable talking to the male counselor. Some men feel safer expressing some feelings to a female counselor. Men may feel that talking about feelings to another man may make them look less masculine or weak.

Gender-Specific and Couples Group Counseling

As stated in the previous chapter, treatment can be accomplished in gender-specific groups with batterers and battered women separately, or in conjoint groups with the couples together. When abusers are being treated in gender-specific groups, it is important to obtain feedback from their partners, and to watch that woman bashing does not occur. In these groups, it is hoped that the skills and attitudes emphasized in treatment are being practiced in the home, and that the changes will generalize outside the treatment into the relationship. Therefore, it is important to role play behaviors and situations in the treatment. Gender-specific treatment assumes that the abused partner may not be safe in a session with the abuser, and that the victim may even feel revictimized by being placed in a counseling situation with her partner. There is also a possible presumption that the victim may feel partially to blame for the abuse if she is also in treatment. Safety and blame are important issues to deal with in any treatment program that involves domestic violence.

Couples treatment has been quite controversial, as stated previously. Counseling with couples or groups of couples can be effective, however, because both spouses are being taught the same educational materials simultaneously. They also have the opportunity to express their feelings and perceptions of the problem areas in the relationship. By agreeing on the problem areas, it is much easier to work toward solutions. The clients also have the opportunity to talk with their spouses in a safe environment without the fear of things getting out of control. The counselors are there to help keep the anxiety and emotional level under control. The counselors can also get both to agree to deal with these emotional issues only during the counseling sessions, not outside the program, until they have learned more effective communication and anger-management skills.

Another advantage of working with couples is that the counselors get a more accurate view of what is actually happening in the relationship. Couples counseling may keep the batterer "honest."

Working with the couple together also eliminates some of the paranoia that is usually present if the couple goes for counseling separately. Neither has to wonder what his or her spouse has said to the counselor about them. In addition, there is immediate feedback from the partners when both are in the session, and numerous opportunities arise for role play and to direct feedback to them. Some advocates believe, however, that couples work puts the woman in more danger after there is an increase in the anxiety level as a result of problems coming to the surface. One way of decreasing the possibility of a violent incident after the counseling session is to directly address the issue. Let the couples know that there will be issues discussed in the sessions that may be upsetting to them.

If the counselors feel there is a potential for a violent incident, they should get the batterer to sign a nonviolence contract. This contract states that he will not harm his partner in any way, and if he feels that he is going to be violent he will immediately seek assistance. Just the promise not to be violent can sometimes be a deterrent. The counselor can also decrease the risk of a violent incident by briefly teaching some specific techniques that the batterer can use if he starts getting angry. In addition, strong statements concerning the consequences of violence, including reports to legal authorities, should be emphasized at the beginning of the treatment.

Counselor accessibility is also a deterrent to violence. Emergency procedures that allow the clients to contact the counselors or on-call professionals must be established. Not only does the batterer have someone to turn to in this situation, but just the idea of the behavior being monitored decreases the risk. The woman also has constant support and access to the counselors. She is encouraged to deal with relationship issues during the regular counseling sessions with her spouse present if she is in a couples group. She is given information about shelters and other alternatives in case a violent incident or the threat of such should occur, however. At the beginning of treatment, safety plans for the victims and control plans for the abusers are developed and emphasized.

Behavior Accountability with a No-Blame Approach

Our counseling style has been a "no-blame" approach. Occasionally, various individuals have questioned this phrase, fearing that the counselors are not holding the male batterer accountable for his behavior. This, of course, is not the case. The counselors actively work to have both partners accept responsibility for their own behavior. Rational emotive therapy techniques, as well as cognitive therapy approaches in general, have been effectively used to promote accountability and acceptance of responsibility. The counselors have used "no blame" as a description of their attempts to minimize fault-finding, blaming, and the making of accusations. These types of behavior are especially evident during the initial counseling sessions. The male blames the female, stating that it is her fault that he hit her. If she had not done what she did, or said what she said, the violence would not have occurred. The wife then blames him for saying what she said, or doing what she did. They both fault the other for the state of the relationship. The counselors have found that abusers and couples can, and do, engage in this seemingly endless cycle of blaming and fault-finding without any impact on the violence or the relationship unless the counselors take an active role in confronting this unproductive behavior. It is also clear that a shame-based, punitive program has a negative impact on abusers and may increase attrition. Usually the counselors allow some of the "fault-finding discussions" and interactions to occur, with little interference for a while before they intervene. The counselors then explain the futility of this behavior to the abusers or the couple and the almost impossible and time-consuming task the counselors would face in trying to determine who is to blame. They further point out their reluctance to help with this, to be "lawyers" and "judges," as they have no training in this area. Instead, counselors encourage the abusers or couples to join them in ending the violence and improving the overall relationship as quickly as possible. Sometimes counselors tell the clients they will get to blame and fault later. Responsibility for behavior can be more easily discussed after the clients have been introduced to REBT and cognitive concepts, learn some basic communication skills, begin to get more in touch with their feelings, and learn more about their own identity.

Each client is then directed toward accepting responsibility for his/her own feelings, emotions, and behavior. If the man is violent, he is held accountable for his reactions or behaviors. The woman is also held accountable for her reactions or behaviors in the situation. Violence is never an acceptable option. Counselors, however, avoid pointing a finger at either client and saying "How awful that you did this to your partner." The abuse is never acceptable, and this is emphasized, with the abuser being held responsible for the behavior. This type of approach usually breaks down the rapport and reinforces the low self-esteem that is already a major factor in the clients.

"No blame" further suggests that the counselors are not punitive agents. Counselors do not seek to punish the violent male or the abused female. We are adamant in our belief that counselors should not become punishing agents. Many of the male clients have told clinicians of their anxiety and reluctance to enter into counseling fearing that the counselors would verbally attack them or "put them down." They usually tell the counselors this as a prelude to reporting how relieved they were to find their preconceptions unfounded. The counselors have found that this "no-blame" approach reduces resistance and promotes cooperation in the men and women. Thus, when each is held accountable in a nonblaming way by the group, counselors, and their partners, the bonding and trust tends to increase and the counseling process is enhanced.

A positive way of encouraging accountability of actions is to let the client talk about what happened and how things got out of control. If the abuser tries to blame the partner, the counselors could provide some brief education about "ownership" of emotions and behaviors. After there is a strong bond between the group members and with the counselors, there is more positive effect from confronting the abusers' rationalizations and projections. If there is little bonding, however, this approach will not be very effective.

Counselors also work hard at not taking sides, unconsciously or covertly, especially when working with couples. It is important, however, for the counselors to ensure a balance of power when working with couples during therapy. They must intervene any time the batterer attempts to intimidate his partner, and model appropriate assertive and communication techniques. This will occur more often at the beginning of the program. The unconscious aligning with the male or female partner is difficult to control but is greatly reduced with the use of a male/female co-therapist team. The therapists can monitor one another and discuss the counseling process regularly, minimizing or becoming aware of any unconscious alignments before they interfere with the counseling. Sometimes this can be very difficult, especially when a client is being particularly difficult to deal with. Occasionally, counselors do openly take sides. For example, one counselor may take the position of one of the relationship partners to help that partner articulate his or her position better or to assist him or her in some way. Another example would be when one counselor focuses on one partner for a while during a session or during role playing. In either case, the individuals are told clearly what the counselors are doing.

Counselors try to remain as objective as possible. This is often most difficult in the early stages of intervention. Clients will often relate very shocking and disturbing events involving violence and abuse of some kind. It is important that the counselors strike a balance between listening, being concerned, and showing respect for the seriousness of the events related while not allowing themselves to become overly emotional or overreacting in some way. Obviously, a certain amount of control of both verbal and nonverbal communication on the part of the counselors is necessary. Experience has taught us that if too much emotion is shown, the clients are likely to retreat and be reluctant to reveal further "secrets." As the counseling relationship progresses, it may be possible, and often is appropriate for the counselor to reveal his or her affect more openly.

The counselors are usually very supportive of the clients. They openly express their appreciation for the clients' efforts in counseling and commend them for getting involved in counseling, no matter how they came into the program. The clinicians encourage them and reinforce their progress. The counselors attempt to be warm and friendly and most clients seem to respond to this. The counselors try to convey a sense of hope, attempting to be enthusiastic, cheerful, and positive. Many of the Rogerian theories of unconditional positive regard enter in this phase of the counseling.

Peer Counseling

A major emphasis through the counseling sessions is to teach the clients to be peer counselors for each other. The counselors do this by continually encouraging the clients to be supportive and help each other learn and implement what they learn in the sessions in their own relationships. The emphasis is on listening to each other, giving feedback, and bringing it to each other's attention when an unwanted behavior or nonverbal cue is occurring that the client had agreed to change. An example might be the use of the "fair fighting" rules in Session 7. If one partner starts calling his or her spouse's mother names, the clinician, or the other partner if it is in a couples group, can remind the client that when they had talked about the fair-fight rules they had agreed that name-calling had been a problem. One hopes that at this point the client would agree and apologize.

Another part of the peer counseling is for the clients to learn to listen to what is going on and give each other permission (freedom) to talk about a wide range of emotions. This will increase the probability of the clients or couples dealing with problems as they come up rather than keeping them inside until they blow up in an abusive situation. Just the process of clients learning to better understand what's going on with themselves or their partners can decrease the tension in the relationship and often gives clients a different perception of events that occur in their relationship.

Counseling and Education

Using a combination of counseling and education is effective. During the counseling segment of the session, the counselor can deal with specific relationship problems. The education segment can be used to teach the clients specific skills in communication, assertion, anger management, and so on. What is learned during the education segment can be applied during the next counseling segment. The use of education can be a way of restructuring some of the beliefs that abusers and couples have about gender roles, violence, and irrational beliefs in general. When applied during counseling, the information will be reinforced and directly associated with a problem area relevant to the clients. Each session is divided equally into counseling (or "processing") and education. Some of the handouts will be discussed during the sessions as noted, and others will be provided to the clients for additional education.

It is appropriate to begin each session with a brief relaxation exercise and completion of any homework assignments. Then general counseling and processing of the previous week's events, other situations, or problem areas occur. During this counseling, prior skills and educational information can be brought in and applied to the particular problems. At the half-way point in the session, there is a change to the didactic educational material. The session would then end with the homework assignments for the next week.

Nonviolence Contract

The use of a verbal or written agreement for the clients not to use physical violence can decrease the incidents of violence while in counseling. The clients agree not to be violent toward themselves or anyone else and agree to contact a crisis center, a volunteer "buddy," or staff member if they start thinking or feeling that they might become abusive. There is no 100% guarantee that this will prevent an abusive incident; however, just the fact that the client has given his or her word or made a written commitment to the counselors not to be violent is a preventing factor. The clients are also informed that there is always someone available to talk with so they can deal with the anger more effectively rather than become abusive toward their partners. Samples of nonviolence contracts are included at the end of this chapter.

Behavioral Techniques Establishing "Baselines"

Clients are asked to establish "baselines" for almost every behavior presented for change. Baselines are set up for violent behaviors of all kinds, sexual activity, watching television, housework, interactions with children, and numerous other behaviors. Obviously, one must know how much something is occurring before one knows if it is changing or if an intervention works. Clients seem to accept this basic assumption rather quickly and begin to establish baselines with minimal direction from the counselors. Of course, the motivation is occasionally to prove something. For example, one partner may try to show how seldom the other says "I love you" in a week.

Monitoring of Behavior

After a "baseline" has been established, the client is encouraged to monitor the behavior for a period of time, determining the effectiveness of any intervention. Occasionally, we ask a client to monitor a behavior informally, simply by observing and being aware without taking a baseline. The goal is to help the client become more efficient as an observer of behavior or to raise awareness regarding a particular behavior that may have previously gone unnoticed.

Planning an Intervention

After a client has determined that he/she wishes to change a particular behavior and has established a baseline, an intervention is planned. The counselors assist the clients but only as much as needed. It is important that the client see this as their intervention and, one hopes, their success.

Weekly Behavior Inventory and Abusive-Incident Graph

The Weekly Behavior Inventory is to be filled out at the beginning of every session. This will provide immediate information about the current level of violence, if any. It will also initiate discussion about problem areas and provide an opportunity for the counselors to reinforce positive behaviors and deal directly with continued abuse or violence. It serves as a monitoring device and may aid in decreasing violent incidents because they will be noted or dealt with weekly. When working with couples, these must be completed separately and independently in different rooms, and reviewed by the counselors before the sessions. If a woman states that she is afraid, then one counselor talks with her immediately and ensures her safety. She may need to go to the shelter then, or other steps may be necessary.

An instrument used to help clients visualize their progress is the Abusive-Incident Graph. After a number of weeks in counseling, the counselor should chart the information from the Weekly Behavior Inventories on an Abusive-Incident Graph so the client can get visual reinforcement for his or her success from the precounseling level of violence to the current level (see Session 12). It is also acceptable to have the clients chart the information themselves during Session 12. If there have been incidents along the way, these should be discussed with respect to getting the abuse to stop.

Role Play

Role play is an excellent way for the counselors to model certain behaviors and skills. The clients can be encouraged to participate as well. This not only will reinforce the educational information, but can be a way of using demonstration to emphasize situations that need cognitive or behavioral change.

There can be a number of different role-play combinations. In couples treatment, the couple may role play an interaction or practice a communication technique. The counselors may role play with one another. Also the counselors may pair up with clients to role play while the remaining group members observe. These various pairings can contribute greatly to the effectiveness of the role play and the learning of the educational materials as well as development of insight.

Homework

Homework assignments are given to reinforce what is taught during the education segment of the session. It is also intended as a way of encouraging the clients to practice what they have learned. Another goal is that it "forces" the clients to think about and process what has happened in the counseling. This also helps move the information into long-term memory for retrieval at times when problems might arise.

Usually the homework relates directly to the educational material covered during the session. There are times when the information might be needed for the next session. It is then discussed in some way during the next session. The homework may be discussed directly or there may be role play during the session.

If a client is not completing homework assignments, this should be discussed openly. This may be an area of resistance or the client may be acting passive-aggressively. There may be specific reasons for not completing homework or there may be low commitment to the counseling overall. Dealing with this in a nonblaming and nonjudgmental manner can be an excellent way for the counselors to model these types of behaviors. The homework and handouts can be maintained in a binder that is brought to each session.

Personal Stress Management

Stress management is another technique that can be used by the counselors. Specifically, the clients are taught to become aware of their body cues and physiological responses when they are getting upset. If they can identify the cues, then they can respond to situations more appropriately. For example, one man states that his heart starts pounding, he stiffens up, and his face turns red when he gets angry. If he becomes aware of these signals, he can stop at this point and reevaluate the situation so that he can find other means of dealing with the anger instead of hitting his wife or children.

Relaxation training is necessary. Clients are encouraged to be aware of their physical selves at all times. They are encouraged to be aware of heartbeat, rapid speech, a rise in voice pitch, sensations from the stomach, or other physiological cues. These techniques have been helpful in interceding during counseling sessions when the clients become angry. The counselors can point out the observable physical cues and ask him/her about others that may not be visible. This seems to greatly assist the client in developing awareness. The client is also encouraged to comment spontaneously at all times on what he is feeling, to heighten awareness. For example, "I noticed that when you said you would really rather avoid your partner's mother this weekend your stomach seemed to tighten."

Breaking Down Behavior into Specifics

Clients are encouraged to analyze behavior in terms of parts of the whole. For example, a couple reports that they had a "fight." The counselors assist them in breaking down the "fight" into specific behaviors. Perhaps one of the partners reports that the other is "mean" or "stubborn" or whatever. We help the client to describe, in behavioral terms, just what "mean" and "stubborn" is. This not only improves our understanding of what is occurring, but is a necessary process in changing behavior.

Structure

In counseling abusers and couples involved in domestic violence, there is a need for a certain amount of structure. It appears that many abusers and their partners have very little structure in their personal lives. Experiences in working with these clients has taught us that some structure is helpful for the clients in regaining control of their lives and relationships. The use of and the amount of structure required varies with each client and couple according to their needs and situation. It is speculated that the counselors act as an external control for the client who may have little internal control or who feels his/her life is out of control. Over time as the client develops better internal control, structure is reduced.

One benefit of structure assures the counselor that certain education and counseling will take place and lets the clients know their limitations and what is expected of them during the counseling process. One part of the structure is that clients are asked to make commitments to attend the counseling on a regular basis and to avoid all physical violence. This is done by having the clients sign contracts.

The clients are given an outline and verbal description of what each session will consist of. If group counseling is used, the clients and couples are asked to read and abide by the rules of the group. For example, anything that other members say is confidential information and they are not to talk to other family or friends about who else is attending counseling sessions.

Another part of the structure is that meetings are held in a neutral environment and in the presence of the counselors as well as other group members. This adds the element of a "safe environment" in which clients can express themselves. Counselors maintain control of the external environment so that emotions do not get out of control. Initially clients would also be asked to not discuss issues outside of counseling that could lead to a violent incident. After they have learned ways of dealing with emotional situations they will be encouraged to talk about a specific problem area at home at a set time. A part of this is using specific "fair-fighting" rules such as asking for an appointment and taking a time-out if there is a potential for the situation to get out of hand.

In some relationships, it is even necessary to schedule such areas as specific recreation time, times to talk about feelings and problems, or even certain days for sexual intimacy. After there is such a breakdown in communication and in the relationship overall it is necessary for more structure in rebuilding basic foundations of the relationship.

Confronting Minimization

Through education about violence and its effects, clients are given more freedom or permission to talk about the violence in their own relationship. The counselor also uses direct references to battering, hitting, or being abusive instead of minimizing by using such terms as "harming" or "slapped around a little." The violence is discussed openly and in great detail. The counselors analyze a "hit." The clients are asked to describe the hit: open hand, fist, knuckle, side of hand, the way the punch was thrown, and so on. The goal is not to desensitize the client or couple to the severity of the behavior but to encourage an open dialogue about the violence, not only with the counselor but with each other. This helps destroy the "secret" or the conspiracy of silence that exists in most battering relationships. In addition, the counselors need accurate information about the violence in order to determine the effectiveness of the program.

It is important to avoid euphemisms when discussing violent behavior. Terms like "hitting," "assault," "violence," "battering," and so on, are used in describing the behavior and in presenting the educational materials. This is important for changing the unwanted behavior and promoting awareness to the seriousness of the behavior.

Communication Techniques and "Fighting" Analysis

In using the "fighting" analysis technique, counselors can gain insight about the extent of the damage and breakdown in the relationship. They can also learn how the clients or couples are presently interacting. There are two specific methods of "fighting analysis." One is to analyze a prior argument. The counselor can get the client or couple to talk about what some of the major problem areas are in the relationship. They can narrow it down to one specific incident and how each dealt with that incident.

Another method of fighting analysis is for the clients or the counselors to tell of a common problem in a relationship not related specifically to a client in the group. After getting as many details as possible and likely feelings that a client in the situation might be having, the whole group can give input as to what possibilities or options would be helpful in solving this problem. This could open the discussion for clients or couples to share similar incidents and explore possible solutions for their situations.

"Fair-Fighting" Training

After the counselors have obtained insight into the dynamics of the relationship, evaluated the extent of the breakdown in communication, determined what specific problem areas there are and how violent the relationship is, they can use another very effective technique. This technique is "fair-fighting" training. Fair-fighting training consists of teaching the clients or couples how to get their needs met, express themselves, and have a good relationship without resorting to verbal, emotional, or physical violence.

Soon after counseling has started, the clients are taught some specific ways to deal with anger appropriately, and they are taught various fair-fighting rules, communication skills, assertion skills, and many realistic, daily methods of having a more intimate and workable relationship. This is done in Module II (Communicating and Expressing Feelings) for couples, but is sometimes delayed with abusers in gender-specific groups until they obtain more self-management skills as the counselors are not able to directly observe and intervene with the partners in these groups.

Specifically relating to the fair-fighting training, however, are some distinct methods used to promote insight, cognitive rethinking, and immediate behavioral changes. With couples, the training is always done in the office or counseling room where the battered spouse can feel safe. Also, the counselors will have the opportunity to observe and give instant feedback. The counselors may move to a role of referee during some of this training. This may be necessary because the counselor may touch on issues to promote or set up a situation that will stimulate the emotions of the couples. As the emotions build and the old patterns of reacting come out, the counselors can give feedback concerning their observations. Then the couple, the group, and the counselors can discuss other more effective, less harmful ways of handling these or similar situations. Similar techniques are used with gender-specific groups, and role play with the counselors is helpful.

The counselors may take the role of coach in teaching each client how to handle the situation. Counselors might also role play ways of dealing with a similar situation. It is likely they will involve clients in the role play to give them practice with this type of interaction.

The clients are also shown "dirty-fighting techniques" (see Session 7). This is presented in a humorous way to help clients become aware of how they are relating. Often the parties are not aware of the "dirty fighting" that occurs. Also, much of dirty fighting is a repetitive style of communicating guaranteed to destroy a relationship. Sometimes the clients are told ahead of time that this is a satire of inappropriate techniques. As counselors present the "dirty-fighting techniques," clients usually recognize the ways their partners and themselves are fighting dirty. Because the approach is nonblaming and nonthreatening, they usually are open to talking about which apply to their relationship or communication style.

Repetitive Behaviors

Another issue that counselors address is the clients' repetitive behaviors. In talking with them about their specific problem areas and how they deal with them, it is evident that the stimulus and response is similar much of the time. An example might be that one partner knows the other will be angry if she is late for a luncheon date. She does not call to let him know she will be late; she just shows up late. He may know she is probably late because she could not get out of the office when she expected to, but he responds angrily anyway.

The counselors' job is to help clients see the rituals and cues involved and assist with ways to break the pattern of behavior and response. Usually just bringing it to the clients' or couples' attention can make a difference. Then some other cognitive and behavioral techniques might be helpful.

Metaphors, Stories, Tales, and Analogies

The use of metaphors, stories, tales, and analogies can be helpful in counseling because it helps the clients get a different view of situations similar to their own. It also keeps them from being defensive because the counselor is not directly dealing with their specific situation. Of course the story would at some point be brought back to dealing with their relationship.

These methods also help the clients analyze their own situations and problem-solving techniques. These methods are aids for the counselor in the educational segment of the session as they help to relate the educational material to real-life situations in relationships.

For example, in order to clarify what mind reading is, we used a story about one relationship in which the husband expected the wife to know when she was to come after him when he went outside while they were arguing. He believed very strongly that she should know whether to come after him and comfort him or whether she should leave him alone by how hard he slammed the door. Of course whether she went after him or left him alone, he would beat her up because she had not done the right thing, according to him. She, however, could not tell what the slamming of the door meant; therefore, she would lose either way. She could not read his mind, and should not have to anyway.

An example of an analogy that was useful in getting couples to spend more time together was that relationships are like plants; if they are nurtured, they grow and are beautiful, but, if left unattended, they wither and die. Another analogy, labeled "The Lady at the Well," is used to reinforce active listening skills, particularly the need to listen to the words and to the emotional effect of the words. A young man is standing by a well, dropping in small stones. An old woman comes to the well and she asks the young man if he can hear the stones strike the water. The young man replies that of course he can since his hearing is very good. The old woman then asks the young man that because his hearing is so good, can he not hear the stone strike the bottom of the well. If not, he does not really hear everything the well has said.

Humor

At various times the use of humor is an effective technique in counseling. It is not intended to minimize the seriousness of our endeavor, belittle the clients, or suggest that we are not dealing with serious problems. The personalities of the counselors and clients can also play a role in whether humor will be a useful tool. Some clients are very serious because their cultural or family histories, so they may not recognize or be open to humor in the counseling situation. Self-esteem and other factors may also be considerations. The clients may feel that the counselor is not taking their situation seriously, or does not view their concerns as important. Some clients may even feel that the counselor is making fun of them. Therefore, it is important to be somewhat selective in the use of humor. An example of a case in which humor was not a useful technique was with a client who had been abused as a child. He had little education, however, he was very intelligent. He had always, even as a very young child, had to be very responsible in taking care of other people as well as himself. He was very tense in the counseling and the counselors used some humor to try to release some of the tension. He did not even recognize the humor. The counselors were sensitive in seeing that he did not respond to humor and changed their technique.

In most cases, however, humor is a very useful tool. It can be used to help the clients relax. There is more tension at the beginning of the counseling program. The counselors can use humor, directing it at the co-counselor and, as clients respond, they will be more relaxed. Many times the counselors set the mood of the session. If they are relaxed and at ease, the clients are more apt to be at ease.

Humor also serves to lower defenses. Clients, especially men who have battered their partners, come in with very defensive attitudes. They may feel that they are going to be told how awful they are for what has happened in the relationship. When this does not occur and they see the counselors as "real" down-to-earth people too, they will be more open to talking and looking for ways to better their relationship. Counselors can express humor that will lower defenses by talking about some silly blunder that they made or about a situation in their own relationship in which they may have acted like a "dummy," a child, or an adolescent. This can be done without directly telling the client the situation. One counselor can direct the story to the co-counselor. It is sometimes surprising how the clients will join in with their own situations. This can be useful, too, as a way of clients seeing how petty some of their major disagreements are and help them focus on issues that are significant. An example might be that it may be upsetting to the counselor's spouse for her to squeeze the toothpaste from the top of the tube. So knowing this, she squeezed the toothpaste from the top anyway because she wanted to "get back at him" because she felt he had ignored her the night before. The counselor may also say that he wanted to get back at his spouse and he knew she wanted to make love so he said that he had a headache. The counselor may relay this humorously by saying "To get even, I get a headache from the waist down." Most clients catch the humor in this but get the point as well.

Humor can also be used as a means of confronting a client without actually putting them on the spot so they won't end up being embarrassed or defensive. The counselor may know ahead of time that a certain situation has occurred. The wife may have called earlier in the week. The counselors could bring this out by giving an example of a similar situation. For example, the counselor could tell how she had a tough day and when she got home from work, she was in a bad mood, "snorting and snarling at everybody" just daring them to say one word. If they had, she would have jumped down their throats. Then to bring it back to the clients, the counselor could ask if they ever had days like that. Or, the counselor could ask the spouse in a couples group, "Does Joe ever come home in that kind of mood?"

Another use of humor is to aid in lowering resistance. After a certain point during a session, resistance might occur in dealing with a situation, and a counselor "can back off" at this point and lighten things up a bit. A humorous example or two can aid this process, and then the counselor can lead up to being more serious about the situation. It is important to realize that most clients in abusive situations do not have much fun or humor anymore, even though they may have at one time. If they can instill humor and fun in their relationships again, that will help in reducing abusiveness.

The education segment of each session is an excellent time to interject some humor in the examples given. Some of the education is specifically geared toward the use of humor. One example is the "Dirty Fighting Instruction Manual," mentioned previously. To directly tell a client that he or she is fighting dirty may increase defensiveness and resistance; however, introducing the information in a humorous and nonthreatening way seems to be much more effective. The clients seem more open to receiving the information and usually realize when a particular point relates to their relationship. They are also able, at this time, to admit that they use a particular dirty-fighting tactic, without feeling threatened. The spouse is also given more freedom to express the techniques his or her partner uses. Clients have come to later sessions expressing that they had immediately recognized when they or their spouse were using dirty fighting and had been able to stop at that point and deal with the situation by using a fair-fighting technique. Humor helps clients associate and remember information.

Humor can make the sessions less emotionally draining for the clients and the counselors. It also facilitates the learning process. It is, however, a difficult approach for counselors to learn and just as difficult to teach. Probably it is an attribute that the counselors bring to the sessions. The most important considerations involving humor are the assessment of the personalities involved and the timing for interjecting humor.

Thinking Out Loud

Thinking out loud is a technique that the counselor might use to express their hypothesis about a problem. For example, "It sounds like Joe got angry because Mary was late and he was afraid something had happened to her." This technique can be effective in getting feedback about feelings and "facts" from the clients. The hypothesis about the situation would be directed to the co-therapist. This method keeps the client from becoming defensive. The counselors may even discuss possible solutions to the problem without directly involving the clients. The clients would be present listening, of course, and at some point would be asked for their input. If a co-therapist is not present, another client not expressing the concern could be used in a co-therapist role.

Co-therapist Consultation

Co-therapist consultation is a valuable technique that is similar to thinking out loud, but involves much more. It is valuable because it allows the counselors to express ideas, concerns, and problem-solving solutions with the clients present. By consulting with the co-therapist, direct confrontation, defensiveness, and resistance are avoided. The counselor interaction can also be a positive role model for the clients.

There are three ways the counselors can go about using this technique. One method involves the good therapist versus the bad therapist. The counselors could be expressing some concerns about the clients not seeming to be consistent in working on the program, such as not completing homework assignments or not participating in group discussion. One therapist might take the role of expressing, "Well, maybe he doesn't want to be in counseling so he's avoiding dealing with the issues by not participating." The other counselor would come to the defense of the client by saying, "No, I feel that he does want to work on the relationship and that's why he is here." This is not making excuses for client behavior, but a way of getting them to talk without being defensive. The counselors might say, "Well, let's ask Joe. He's the only one who knows for sure what is going on."

Another useful method is called the "set up," which may overlap with the "straight person" approach. In this approach, one counselor may set some groundwork in introducing or dealing with a situation and then the other counselor takes over various points. This is sometimes used to get specific information or responses from the clients. The counselors usually have discussed this before the session and intentionally lead the counseling in a specific direction.

"Stupid" Technique

The "stupid" technique is an indirect method of getting clients to give the counselor more information and a way of helping the client express and think about the situation. The key in this technique is for the counselor to express that he/she doesn't understand what's going on, therefore getting the client to explain in detail what is happening. Sometimes this can be a setup between the therapists. One counselor can tell the other that he or she is not sure what's going on with the client or couple. Of course, this is said in the presence of the clients. The other counselor might verbalize a general assumption about the situation but shift it back to the clients to help this "stupid" counselor understand. Clients tend to enjoy helping the counselor and will go into more detail than they would if a specific question was directed at them. This technique was used quite well by the television character "Columbo," played by Peter Falk.

Promoting Awareness

Promoting awareness is a part of many counseling theories. It is used with abusers and couples to help them understand themselves, their spouse, and the different factors that affect how they relate to each other. This includes giving each client information about him or herself and each other that was obtained through the personality assessments and the social history.

Promoting awareness is also useful when a specific problem situation has occurred that might relate to a personality characteristic or childhood experience. An example might be that the wife is upset because of the financial situation and her spouse is saying, "don't worry about it, it will all work out." She, of course, feels he doesn't care what the finances are. If she's more of a worrier and he's more laid-back and easygoing, this could be a personality difference. The counselor could use this to give each insight by bringing out this difference. The counselor could say, for example, "Well, Mary, do you think Roger doesn't care or could it relate to his general style of not getting upset about anything?"

Another example relating more to social history might arise if Roger says, "Mary seems so cold, distrustful, and doesn't want to be sexual at times." The therapist, knowing that Mary was sexually abused as a child, could remind Roger of this to help him better understand what is going on with Mary. It may even help Mary understand what's going on. This can only be said if Mary has disclosed this to the group if she is involved in couples treatment, or has given permission for the counselor to do this. Just the process of clients learning to better understand what's going on with their partners can decrease the tension in the relationship and often gives them a different perception of events that occur throughout their marriage.

COGNITIVE TECHNIQUES: RATIONAL EMOTIVE BEHAVIOR TECHNIQUES

We have made extensive use of the general principles and techniques of rational emotive behavior therapy (REBT) developed by Albert Ellis. The general REBT approach, with its emphasis on the rational aspects of human behavior, is particularly effective with domestic violence, especially in the early stages of counseling, because REBT approaches have allowed the counselors to make rapid and effective interventions in spite of the very high levels of emotionality often present during the first few counseling sessions. The counselors do not discourage clients or couples from expressing their feelings or from being emotional. In fact, counselors consider this expression to be vital. The unchecked ventilation of emotion through several counseling sessions is generally ineffective for the long-term goal of helping the clients to become more healthy, however. The point is that something must be accomplished. The client must see that change is occurring, skills are being learned, and that the relationship is improving so that he or she can believe that counseling does indeed work. In general, clients seem to be better able to tolerate high levels of emotional expression in the middle- to late-counseling sessions after they have learned certain communication techniques or have begun to experience their perceptions and cognitions in a different way, using REBT and other cognitive perception principles. Finally, REBT approaches seem to fit easily into the psychoeducational approach because it is somewhat didactic in nature. The following is a brief listing and discussion of some of the specific REBT approaches that have been useful.

ABC's

Many abusive men often see their violent behavior as the result of some event. This of course results in excessive blaming of others, an often-cited characteristic of the violent male. A limited presentation of the ABC principles, with frequent reminders and reinforcement, is often effective in helping the clients take responsibility for their own behavior.

Almost all of the clients whom we counsel initially have difficulty accepting this way of looking at their behavior. The counselors must be well versed in this approach as they will most certainly be met with resistance. Often, it is very helpful to have the clients present a specific incident when some event "caused" them to react. It is especially helpful if the event being discussed "caused" them to be angry or lose emotional control.

It may be helpful to discuss the universality of behavior. For example, many male clients may comment that anyone would do what they did in a similar situation. The counselors point out that there is no universal reaction to any incident, that in fact their reaction is a choice, either learned over time or selected spontaneously. As usual, it is critical that the therapist be able to quickly come up with sensible, meaningful examples to illustrate the point: for example, "Not everyone slaps people who call them names. There are other options."

Irrational Belief Systems

Most couples are unaware of the many irrational beliefs that they have concerning themselves, their family, and the world in general. Cognitive restructuring through education and awareness training is a way to change these belief systems. One man, for example, believed in very strict discipline to the point of holding a gun on his teenagers to get them to obey. He was asked what he was going to do when this didn't work. His response was, "I'll shoot them." He was confronted concerning this and his response was that his father had whipped him many times and he turned out okay.

Another case concerned a woman who felt her husband was unaffectionate; the only physical contact they had was when having intercourse. When talking about this his response was, "I've always been this way; guess I'll always be this way." Some clients also have many irrational beliefs about themselves, their spouse, and others. Often their expectation of themselves and others is based on these irrational beliefs. In situations like these, the clients are confronted about these beliefs. Through cognitive restructuring and education, one hopes they will gain a more realistic view of themselves and others. For example, "If he loved me he would spend all of his free time with me instead of wanting to go hunting." Of course the irrational belief here is that the spouse is basing her partner's love on whether he spends all of his free time with her.

Awareness and Control of Self-Talk

Clients can change the way they think, feel, and respond by becoming aware of what they are telling themselves, and when it is negative, learn to change it to positive self-talk. Consider the example, "I'm a failure, I can't do anything right." Of course, this is a negative message. At this point, this person can stop, analyze the negative thinking, and change it to a positive message, such as, "Yes, I blew it this time, but no one is perfect. I don't have to be perfect (rational thinking). I've done a lot of successful things. I'll do the best that I can."

Musterbation

At times, clients think too much about "shoulds," "oughts," "have to's," or "musts," and feel like failures if they fall short of these standards. They also apply this standard to their spouse and children. Either way it causes problems for the family and the relationship. "I ought to just do what he wants so there won't be any trouble." This type of thinking isn't always healthy for the individual or the relationship. Most likely no matter what the partner does there will always be something she hasn't done. This goes along with irrational thinking. Helping the client become aware of this type of thinking and consciously making a change in this is the key to changing behavior and feelings about oneself.

Decatastrophizing

Decatastrophizing is another cognitive behavioral technique. Some clients are very emotional and this, in combination with irrational thinking, causes them personal turmoil as well as relationship problems. This technique is similar to the absurdity technique, which adds a flare of humor. This is used in the counseling sessions to help clients distinguish between what is important to work on and what are petty issues that get blown out of proportion. The issue might be that the husband is upset about the wife being 5 minutes late getting home, so he hits her when she walks in the door. The counselor might, if the timing is right, really exaggerate this issue. For example, the counselor might say "Man, Joe I can see why you're upset. Five minutes late! You're sitting home worrying and she's probably out gallivanting around! She probably even stopped off at the motel on the way home. How could she do this to you after all you do for her?" This could go on. The point is for the client to see how ridiculous his reaction was.

This technique will not be effective unless there is very good rapport between clients and therapists. Also, the client needs to have some sense of humor and insight into his or her thinking and behavior. Another example might be that the wife burned part of an evening meal and this has irritated the spouse. This may be frustrating but it certainly is not a terrible event; children starving to death by the thousands in Ethiopia or being killed in Kosovo are horrible events.

Absurdity Technique

Based on REBT literature, this technique involves the therapist expounding on an irrational or unfounded statement made by the client until the concept becomes fantastic or absurd. For example, a client remarks that his spouse mislaid his car keys so that he would be late for work. The therapist in turn comments that "of course this is true because his spouse does not want him to work, in fact is quite jealous of his work, that she knows that if she hides the keys enough he will be late so often that he will be fired, and that in this way she will be assured that his self-esteem will be weakened, so that she will then be able to control him and dominate him and perhaps even eventually beat him down so much that he kills himself. Yet it all begins with hiding the car keys!" The same approach may be used to attack a thought or cognition such as "Everyone hates me."

USE OF LANGUAGE TO PROMOTE TOLERANCE

With some clients, using stronger language may be helpful in giving them freedom to express themselves. If someone has a tendency to keep feelings inside and only knows how to express those feelings, especially hostility, by being physically abusive, he or she may at first need to be verbal in a more hostile manner. The counselor needs to avoid being offended or shocked when a client uses "foul" language. This may be his or her only way of expressing him or herself verbally. He or she may be trying to get the counselor to react, hoping to upset the counselor, and thereby creating an excuse to drop out of counseling. It could also be his or her way of taking control of the counseling situation. This technique needs to be limited to clients and group members who would not be offended by such language because of moral or religious beliefs. In general, the counselor should "pace" his/her language with the clients to be most effective.

Other Techniques

There are numerous other techniques used throughout the different sessions. The key, however, is to find what is useful for clients. There are many excellent sources available for more information on various counseling techniques, and some are listed at the end of each chapter.

TASKS

Each session lists those key tasks that should be accomplished during that session. The therapists should ensure that all have been appropriately carried out and emphasized. The term "explain" indicates that the therapist should discuss the points in the handouts, give examples, and relate the content to the group members. The term "discuss" indicates the therapist is to state the main points of the exercise and then promote discussion by group members. The therapist should intervene when appropriate to illustrate and promote generalizations. "Describe" indicates that the therapist should point out the main concepts only and refer briefly to the handout, and so on. "Introduce" means to go over briefly the main concepts or the assignments to ensure that the clients understand them. Have the group members relate the concepts to their own lives.

ORDERING OF SESSIONS

It should be noted, as stated previously, that the order of the treatment sessions listed in this manual is the one recommended for couples counseling. It is also used for gender-specific groups. Some clinicians have altered the order of the treatment program with certain gender-specific groups, however, believing that it is better to teach the abusers more self-management skills prior to communication techniques. They have exchanged some of the sessions of Modules II and III. For example, they have exchanged Sessions 13, 14, 15, 16, and 17 with Sessions 7, 8, 9, and 10. The new order, then, for gender-specific groups is Sessions 1–6, 13–17, 11–12, 7–10, and 18–26, as listed in this manual. It should be noted that there are separate workbooks that have the handouts for clients. There is also a version in Spanish that is available.

The treatment program does have the flexibility to be able to allow such changes as the clinicians develop their own preferences. It is important to note, however, that this program does rely on a fixed or closed structure. These are not open-ended, ongoing groups. The assumption is that the clients increase their skills and learn from the previous sessions. Thus, clients must progress through the entire program to benefit; they are not able to begin at Session 10, for example, without having learned and experienced the prior sessions.

Some of the wording in the examples may need to be adjusted depending on the composition of the group, geographical settings, cultural issues, relevance to the clients, and age of the participants. Because there are very few couples programs available, the examples and wording in this manual sometimes focus on these situations. There are many gender-specific programs available with somewhat different models, but our treatment program does enable the techniques to be used in both formats with some modifications. The terms "partner," "spouse," and "wife" are used interchangeably in this manual, but they all refer to a person in a committed relationship who may or may not be married. The terms refer to spouses or cohabiting partners in homosexual or heterosexual relationships. The research is clear, though, that most abusers are male and most victims are female.

MUTUAL ABUSE VERSUS MUTUAL AGGRESSION VERSUS SELF-DEFENSE

There has also been controversy and confusion concerning the notion of "mutual abuse." Some researchers claim that there is a high percentage of mutual abuse in relationships, but their research does not distinguish intent, severity, or psychological factors. It is important to define our terms in this discussion. In our definition, abuse refers to the process of psychologically and/or physically harming and intimidating one's partner. The elements of injury, a pattern of intimidation and control, and fear of harm are present. Someone can be fighting back in self-defense and actually cause some injury, but this may not be abuse if the pattern of intimidation and fear are not present, and the intent is to defend oneself rather than to control the partner. It is important to make these distinctions clear in the treatment as most abusers have numerous excuses for their behavior based on the so-called "abuse" they receive from their partner. It is important to note, however, that many relationships do have mutual aggression. This would not necessarily imply that both partners are abusers, based on the above definitions. Some female partners do indeed hit at times when they feel that they are going to get beaten anyway, during abusive incidents, or to vent frustration and their own anger. The important component is whether the male partner is afraid, is being intimidated, and is being controlled by his partner through the use of power tactics or physical force.

Our treatment program focuses on the actual abuser, according to the above definitions. It is necessary to point out, however, that no one has the right to hit or intimidate another person in a relationship. When we are working with couples, the "no-hitting rule" is emphasized to both partners and both are responsible for their own behaviors, but we are also clear on the process of abuse as distinct from self-defense or mutual aggression.

RESOURCES

Ammerman, R., & Hersen, M. (1991). *Case studies in family violence.* New York: Plenum.

Ammerman, R. T., & Hersen, M. (1990). *Treatment of family violence.* New York: Wiley.

Caesar, P. L., & Hamberger, L. K. (1989). *Treating men who batter.* New York: Springer Publishing Co.

Corsini, R. J. (1993). *Current psychotherapies* (5th ed.). Itasca, IL: F. E. Peacock.

Davies, J. M., Lyon, E., & Monti-Cantania, D. (1998). *Safety planning with battered women: Complex lives/difficult decisions.* Newbury Park, CA: Sage.

Edleson, J. L., & Eisibovits, Z. C. (Eds.). (1996). *Future interventions with battered women and their families.* Thousand Oaks, CA: Sage Press.

Ellis, A., & Harper, R. A. (1975). *A new guide to rational living.* North Hollywood, CA: Wilshire Book Company.

Geller, J. A. (1992). *Breaking destructive patterns: Multiple strategies for treating partner abuse.* New York: The Free Press.

Goldenberg, I., & Goldenberg, H. (1985). *Family therapy: An overview* (2nd ed.). Monterey, CA: Brooks/Cole.

Gurman, A. S. (1985). *Casebook of marital therapy.* New York: Guilford.

Hamberger, L. K., & Renzetti, C. (Eds.) (1996). *Domestic partner abuse.* New York: Springer Publishing Co.

Harway, M. (Ed.). (1995). *Understanding and treating the changing family.* New York: Wiley.

Hoopes, M. H., Fisher, B. L., & Barlow, S. H. (1984). *Structured family facilitation programs: Enrichment, education, and treatment.* Rockville, MD: Aspen Publications.

Ingoldsby, B. B., & Smith, S. (Eds.). (1995). *Families in multicultural perspective.* New York: Guilford.

Jaffe, P. G., Lemon, N. K. D., Sandler, J., & Wolfe, D. (1996). *Working together to end domestic violence.* Tampa, FL: Mancorp Publishing.

Lazarus, A. A. (1976). *Multimodal behavior therapy.* New York: Springer Publishing Co.

Marusund, J. (1985). *The process of counseling and therapy.* Englewood Cliffs, NJ: Prentice Hall.

Meek, C. L. (Ed.) (1990). *Post-traumatic stress disorder: Assessment, differential diagnosis and forensic evaluation.* Sarasota, FL: Professional Resource Exchange.

Mikesell, R. H., Lusterman, D.-D., & McDaniel, S. H. (Eds.). (1995). *Integrating family therapy: Handbook of family psychology and systems theory.* Washington, DC: American Psychological Association.

Napier, R. W., & Gershenfeld, M. K. (1989). *Making groups work: A guide for group leaders.* Boston: Houghton Mifflin.

Pynoos, R. S. (Ed.). (1994). *Post-traumatic stress disorder: A clinical review.* Washington, DC: Sidran Press.

Satir, V. (1967). *Conjoint family therapy* (rev. ed.). Palo Alto, CA: Science and Behavior Books.

Sipe, B., & Hall, E. (1996). *I am not your victim: Anatomy of domestic violence.* Newbury Park, CA: Sage.

Shelton, J. L., & Ackerman, J. M. (1982). *Homework in counseling and psychotherapy.* Springfield, IL: Charles C. Thomas.

Sonkin, D. J., & Durphy, M. (1997). *Learning to live without violence: A handbook for men (revised).* Volcano, CA: Volcano Press.

Van Hasselt, V. B., Morrison, R. L., Bellack, A. S., & Hersen, M. (1988). *Handbook of family violence.* New York: Plenum.

Walker, L. E. (1984). *The battered woman syndrome.* New York: Springer Publishing Co.

Zaro, J. S., Brack, R., Neddleman, D. J., & Dreiblatt, E. S. (1980). *A guide for beginning psychotherapists.* New York: Cambridge University Press.

Basic Assumptions for Therapists

BASIC ASSUMPTIONS

Clients have the ability to **control** their own behavior; **not** society, and **not** the therapist.

Batterers have the ability to **stop** their violent behavior.

Clients have inherent and/or potential **resources** to change their relationship and achieve other goals.

Clients need **motivation** to achieve their goals.

THE THERAPIST'S JOB

The therapist's job is to help the client **stop** the **violence** by helping him **access** these **resources** in a manner that uniquely fits the present situation and thus allows for maximum **motivation** to find a solution to the violence and other difficulties.

TREATMENT ASSUMPTIONS RELATED TO VIOLENCE IN RELATIONSHIPS

1. A systemic approach to treatment is empowering to both partners and assists most effectively in the acceptance of responsibility and change of behaviors.
2. Couples who have experienced violence also may have, or at one time had positive, healthy, and functional aspects in their relationships.
3. It is more important for the clients to learn how violence can be prevented, how to resolve disagreements, and keep arguments from escalating than to understand why fights start.
4. Some degree of ambivalence about the relationship is normal and is to be expected.
5. Violence may be relationship specific in that it usually occurs within the relationship. It is important to follow the clients' lead in order to discover how to help them stop it.
6. Clients are most likely to engage in treatment and stick with it when they are affirmed and feel hopeful.

Adapted from: *Solution Focused Treatment of Domestic Violence* by Eve Lipchik and Kate Kowalski (1989).

Characteristics of an Abusive Family of Origin

The following characteristics are present in abusive families of origin:

1. Lack of respect for one or both genders and for the role related-behaviors of one or both genders; rigidity in the role expectations of both genders.
2. Poor body/self-image and a general shame-based, negative view of sex and the body.
3. Insensitivity to the needs of children at various stages of psychosexual development; inconsistency in approaches to sexual behavior.
4. Exploitation of the touch and body-contact needs of family members, ignoring developmental readiness.
5. Lack of respect for personal privacy, both physical and emotional.
6. Lack of an effective communication system, paucity of feelings expressed, and attitude distortion.
7. Lack of balance in power, control, and influence between partners in the marital dyad.
8. Lack of a satisfactory and mutually meaningful relationship in the marital dyad, including loss of expressiveness, reduced affection exchange, and little capacity for negotiation of sexual interest.
9. Lack of an appropriate parental-role structure through which to guide, protect, and nurture the unfolding of children in age-appropriate ways.
10. Lack of knowledge about sex; rather, an emphasis on stereotypes, myths, and distortions.
11. Lack of an overall value system to transmit from one generation to the next; inability to support autonomous decision making by family members.
12. Overall rigid social boundaries that prevent appropriate information exchange with and consensual validation by the family's social environment regarding sex-related beliefs, attitudes, and values.

Nonsuicide and No-Harm Contract

Name: _____ DOB: _____ Date: _____

I, _____, agree not to do anything that might hurt

myself or anyone else before my next appointment on _____ with

my therapist(s) _____.

In addition, I agree that I will contact and talk to my therapist or the counselor on call by

telephoning the office/agency number, _____ , if I feel like hurting

myself or others. In case I cannot reach my therapist, I will call the emergency hotline of the

local crisis center at _____ for help.

Client: _____ Date: _____
Signature

Witness: _____
Signature

Nonviolence Contract

SELF-VIOLENCE

1. Have you ever thought about attempting suicide?   Yes   No

2. Have you ever attempted suicide?   Yes   No

3. If yes, how many times and when (approximately)?

    _____

4. What method did you use?

    _____

5. Have you thought of harming yourself recently?   Yes   No

SPOUSE/PARTNER VIOLENCE

1. Have you ever thought about being physically abusive toward your spouse/partner?
                                                        Yes   No

2. Have you been abusive to your spouse/partner?   Yes   No

3. If yes, how many times and when (approximately)?

    _____

4. What form of abuse have you used? _____

5. Have you recently thought of harming your spouse/partner?   Yes   No

I will not attempt to harm myself or anyone else in any way.

Also, I will inform a member of the staff immediately if I think about or feel that I am about to harm myself or anyone else.

Client _____   Staff _____

Date _____

Assessment and Screening

The overall goal of assessment and screening is to understand the attitudes, behaviors, history, and psychological makeup of the clients in order to determine the best treatment modality to use, or whether the clients are even candidates for treatment. This view is termed an etiological approach to assessment and screening. The idea is that if the clinicians have information concerning the functioning and background of the clients, they may be more likely to determine the type of treatment that would be most successful. The problem, though, is that we do not have sufficient research data to be confident of these decisions, or to know which treatment works best with which clients. Thus, we are left with decisions based on clinical judgments, which rely on the experience and training of the staff, and whatever information they can obtain before making the decision. Therefore, our treatment program incorporates substantial assessment and screening to obtain as much information as possible in a short time period to aid in the decision-making process.

At a minimum, clinicians should conduct an interview with relevant clients first, and obtain a psychosocial history. This can be structured or more informal (we recommend the former, and have included sample forms in this chapter). We also recommend psychological testing and the completion of various surveys, inventories, and scales whenever possible. This is best accomplished with the cooperation of an interdisciplinary team. Psychological testing is not required as part of our program, but it is recommended. The goal is to attempt to determine levels of dangerousness, whether antisocial personality disorder is present, and possible factors involved in the use of abusiveness in the relationship (i.e., the abuser was exposed to his father abusing his mother in his family of origin, he has never had any consequences for using such control tactics, he had a head injury that has reduced impulse control, he is using alcohol excessively, he is a violent person in general, he has very low self-esteem and high depression, he suffers from post-traumatic stress disorder [PTSD], he was abused as a child, and so on). These are not excuses for the abuse, but they are important for the clinician in determining the areas in need of treatment. It is also helpful to know whether the partner has PTSD (either from the current abuse, from past abuse in relationships, or from childhood abuse), has very low self-esteem and high depression, is using alcohol as an escape from the emotional and/or physical trauma, and so forth. A variety of measures and inventories can be used to help in this assessment process, and these are described in this chapter.

PSYCHOLOGICAL ASSESSMENT

Psychological assessments can give immediate information about a person's self-esteem, personality, temperament, assertiveness level, and specific problem areas in general and in the relationship. Assessment can also indicate possible areas of personality or temperament that could be contributing to conflict in the relationship. It also provides information about possible major mental health problems and helps in the screening process. If the assessments are administered before and again after the counseling, they can also be used as a measure of change in abusiveness, communication, assertiveness, self-esteem, attitudes, personality, and other areas. Psychological assessments should only be administered and interpreted by trained professionals or under strict supervision of trained professionals.

SOCIAL HISTORY

Social histories can give the counselor immediate information about the clients' backgrounds. Any major traumas in childhood, adolescence, or adulthood could be contributing factors to what is a problem area for a client or for the relationship at the present time. Sometimes these issues have to be dealt with before couples counseling, or in conjunction with it, even if both partners desire this approach.

The counselors can go over the social histories with the clients. Many clients and couples know very little about their partner's background. Sometimes this information can give them a better understanding of the partner, and why they may be having certain relationship difficulties. Information gathered in the social histories can be very valuable in later sessions when problems that come up in the group or in the relationship deal directly with the effects of a childhood or previous trauma in the person's life.

PRECOUNSELING AND POSTCOUNSELING QUESTIONNAIRES

A precounseling questionnaire is used to assess the level of violence when counseling is begun and to determine specific needs and expectations of the clients. After the counseling program is completed, a postcounseling questionnaire is administered. This is an excellent tool to use to obtain feedback from the clients. They have the opportunity to express what was helpful and what was not. The postcounseling questionnaire also provides information about any relapse of abuse and violence. This can be used to compare with the precounseling questionnaire. These could be used in conjunction with the Weekly Behavior Inventories to determine if there has been a decrease or elimination of the violence. This information could also indicate the effectiveness of the counseling and education.

INTAKE AND SCREENING

The overall objective of the intake and screening session is to obtain basic client information about the presenting problem, explain confidentiality, receive consent for counseling, determine counseling fees (if relevant) and receive consent for follow-up. Also, the client would be given information about scheduling with a counselor. The client is also informed about the programs that are available, and various releases of information are completed so that information can be obtained from partners and released to partners when necessary, information and progress can be sent to relevant legal or external authorities if required, and information can be obtained or sent to other clinicians. Some sample forms are included in this chapter.

PROCEDURE

Each individual is screened by intake personnel. A client file is then initiated for each individual. A confidentiality statement and release, client consent form, and a consent for follow-up must be signed by the clients and the intake personnel. All forms must show the date that the intake was completed. The intake person would also explain the confidentiality policy and its exceptions. Because there is a threat of violence, the intake person would get each client to sign a written agreement not to harm themselves or anyone else. A nonviolence contract would be used for this purpose. Intake personnel also fill out a progress report on each client. This report states the presenting problem and disposition of the case. In some states or jurisdictions, programs are required to fill out Department of Human Services or other forms as well.

After all paperwork has been completed, the client is then instructed to schedule a second session. The client may ask about the type of counseling that is offered. The intake person then explains that the client will be seen individually for a few sessions. If couples counseling is an option, the clients will be informed that they will be seen in a couples session after the assessment and screening are completed. The assessment and screening process is always conducted separately with couples, even if one or both clients want it to be done together. The general goals of the program are then explained to each client. Additional information concerning the program and treatment will be given to them during the next session. During the present session, the clients are told that they will be given several questionnaires to complete. This assessment helps determine specific individual characteristics and also may provide information about specific problems or issues in their relationship.

During the screening or assessment sessions, it may become evident that a client has some extreme emotional difficulties, a personality disorder, or a problem with drug or alcohol abuse. The clients with emotional difficulties or mental disorders who cannot function in a group-counseling situation will receive a referral that will better meet their needs. If it is determined by the intake person and a counselor that the clients with drug or alcohol abuse problems can function in a couples group if they receive concurrent counseling for the substance-abuse problem, they will be admitted to the program under those conditions; otherwise a referral will be made.

Possible referral sources for clients who are inappropriate for group counseling are an outpatient mental health facility, therapy with a specific private mental health professional, or a support group such as Alcoholics Anonymous, Narcotics Anonymous, and so on.

ASSESSMENT

The objectives of these sessions are to explain the counseling program to the client, build rapport, gather further information, determine the past and current level of abusiveness and violence, administer the assessment measures, and gain a commitment from the clients to complete the entire program. The latter is done even if they are required to be there by another authority.

The questionnaires recommended are the Pre-Counseling Questionnaire (Mantooth, Geffner, Franks, & Patrick, 1987); Client Social History; and Aggressive Behavior Inventory (Geffner, Mantooth, Franks, & Patrick, 1992), a modified version of the Conflict Tactics Scales (originally developed by Straus, 1979). Two checklists that clients can complete to provide general background information as well as to list current or past problems are the Personal Problems Checklist for Adults (Schinka, 1985) and the Personal History Checklist for Adults (Schinka, 1989).

In addition, a number of inventories and scales are available from test publishers. These include the Interpersonal Behavior Scale (IBS) (Mauger, Adkinson, Zost, Firestone, & Hook, 1980), Symptom Checklist—90 Revised (SCL-90-R) (Derogatis, 1975), Beck Depression Inventory (Beck, 1978), Suicide Probability Scale (SPS) (Cull & Gill, 1982), Trauma Symptom Inventory (TSI) (Briere, 1995), and an alcohol screening scale (such as the Michigan Alcohol Screening Test [MAST; Selzer, 1971]). These generally take about 5–10 minutes each to complete, with the exception of the IBS, which takes about 30–40 minutes, and the TSI, which takes about 20 minutes.

In order to obtain information about the relationship, especially for couples counseling, two measures have been helpful: the Marital Satisfaction Inventory (MSI) (Snyder, 1981), and the Family Adaptability and Cohesion Evaluation Scales (FACES III) (Olson, Portner, & Lavee, 1985). Measures have also been developed to focus on wife/partner abuse. Three of these are the Inventory of Beliefs about Wife Beating (Saunders, Lynch, Grayson, & Linz, 1987), the Psychological Maltreatment of Women Inventory (PMWI) (Tolman, 1989), and the Index of Spouse Abuse (ISA) (Hudson & McIntosh, 1981). The MSI takes about 40 minutes and is completed by both partners independently, and the others take 10–25 minutes each.

For psychological testing (i.e., a psychologist may be required to conduct these tests), we recommend the Minnesota Multiphasic Personality Inventory (MMPI-2) (Hathaway & McKinley, 1982, 1989), the Millon Clinical Multiaxial Inventory II (MCMI) (Millon, 1987), and the Coolidge Axis Two Inventory—Revised (CATI) (Coolidge, 1994). The latter two are helpful to focus on personality disorders, whereas the MMPI is a good measure of overall personality. These tests take between 40 minutes and 1¼ hours each.

In general, measures are selected from those just listed (i.e., not all are used with each client). Our testing usually takes about 2–3 hours for each client. The counselor also meets with the clients to explain the counseling program. A major part of this consists of letting them know what will take place during the counseling sessions. As stated in the previous chapter, each counseling group session will be about 1½ to 2 hours in length. There are 26 sessions altogether, and then monthly follow-ups thereafter for 6 months. This does not include the sessions for intake and screening, assessment, psychological testing, and interpretation.

PROGRAM EXPLANATION

The clients are given information during one of the preliminary sessions concerning some basic philosophical approaches of the program and techniques that may be used periodically during the counseling. The clients are told about the use of a male–female counseling team. The clients are also told about some specific techniques used in the counseling process. For example, one of these techniques includes the use of humor, and the rationale behind its use is explained to the clients.

Another philosophical issue is that the counselors use a no-blame approach. This means that they don't point a finger at either of the partners and say, "How awful that you did that." Also, what is discussed in the counseling sessions is kept confidential; if it is a group session, all group members are asked to honor other members' confidentiality. There are some exceptions and these are explained to the clients. The fees for counseling, if relevant, and the clients' responsibility to attend all counseling sessions are also discussed. The counselor obtains a commitment from the client after they receive complete information about the program. This is a big step for many clients in accepting responsibility for their behavior, and their responsibility in making changes to have a better relationship. For some abusers, they may not have been given a choice to attend because they may have been ordered to do so.

This session is also a time of rapport building and information gathering. The clients may be asked to talk specifically about their individual and their relationship situations. At this point, the immediate threat of violence is openly discussed. The counselors explain that sometimes at the beginning of counseling the clients may feel especially tense and defensive, and the tendency to become violent might increase. Because there is a possibility of violence, the client is asked to make a written contract not to be violent. Clients are asked to call the counselors or the counseling center if they start feeling that there might be a violent episode, or if a violent episode should occur.

After explaining about the counseling and the education process, the client is asked to sign a written contract to attend all sessions. Clients are told to call ahead of time if they are unable to attend a session. They are also told that the combined information from all of the assessments and scales yields a comprehensive picture of each client and his or her relationship, and that the results will be discussed.

RISK ASSESSMENT AND PRECONDITIONS FOR COUPLES COUNSELING

It is important to assess, formally or informally, the level of risk and dangerousness for abusive clients and clients who have been abused. This area is in need of much more research, because our ability to predict future dangerousness is not very good for particular individuals. Some of the best work in this area has been conducted by Campbell (1995). Her Danger Assessment questionnaire is brief and would be worthwhile to administer to clients and their partners. Another brief checklist was developed by Geffner and Pagelow (1989), the Spouse Abuse Identification Questionnaire, and has been revised recently (cited in Jaffe & Geffner, 1998). It can be administered to clients in just 5–10 minutes. It is important in the intake interviews to obtain clinical information about the risk of danger for the partners, and to take steps to ensure safety. Sometimes follow-up sessions or telephone calls to monitor this may be needed.

Another area of concern is the decision as to whether particular clients are appropriate for couples counseling. The first requirement is that the wife/partner who has been abused wants such a treatment program. It is important to ascertain whether she is merely repeating what the abuser has indicated or actually desires such a program. If she is not intending to remain in the relationship, this approach would not be appropriate. Even if the wife/partner states that she wants this type of counseling, the clinicians must determine whether she is too intimidated by the abuser to be safe in such an environment with him. The assessment also helps in providing information about her emotional condition, self-esteem, and assertiveness, as well as his personality, level of violence, obsessiveness, and impulsivity. If these preconditions are met and suggest low probability of danger, then the possibility of couples counseling can be considered. The partner must have a safety plan and be informed of the potential dangers in any case. The abuser must also not be consuming alcohol or using other substances during the treatment. If substance abuse has been a problem, then concurrent treatment for alcohol or other substance abuse is required to remain in our treatment program. Neither partner should be exhibiting psychotic behaviors. Finally, the clinicians must be trained in both marital/family therapy as well as in domestic-violence dynamics. The clients must be informed about the consequences of further abusive or violent incidents, and the steps that will be taken should a relapse occur. The clients are informed at the beginning of treatment that if a serious incident occurs, then the abused partner is to report it to the legal authorities; if she does not then we will do this. Thus, the abuser must face the consequences of his violent and criminal acts. We do not necessarily or automatically terminate a client for a relapse, but we reevaluate the situation with staff and the victim of the abuse to make a determination as to the continuation of the treatment. We let the criminal-justice system follow through with their mandates, and we independently decide about the appropriate steps to take. These may include changing the counseling (i.e., from couples to gender specific for the clients), having the abuser begin the program or certain modules again, or terminating the individual from treatment.

EVALUATION OF PROGRESS AND TERMINATION FROM THE TREATMENT

It is also important to evaluate the clients at regular intervals during the treatment program to ensure progress. A structured form has been adapted from Gondolf et al. (1995); it is used to evaluate the progress of the clients at about 6-week intervals. This form is included at the end of this chapter. The clinicians should independently evaluate each client according to the criteria listed on the form. By the end of the first 6-week period, the client should be starting to accept responsibility for the abusiveness, denial and minimization should be decreasing, and he or she should be participating in the sessions. Homework should be completed weekly, and clients should be attending sessions regularly. Clients should be in the early stages of making some changes in their thinking and acting. Near the half-way point, the client should be acting in nonabusive ways, accepting responsibility for his or her own behaviors, participating in a more active manner in the sessions, and beginning to develop some empathy for those they abused. By the third evaluation, the preceding behaviors should be well established, and clients should be gaining more empathy and insight about their behaviors, attitudes, beliefs, and feelings, and those of their partners. By the final evaluation, at 24 weeks or so, clients should be ready for graduation from the program with a good understanding of the dynamics, have techniques to use to avoid relapse, and be able to maintain an egalitarian relationship without the use of power-and-control tactics.

If the clients are not progressing as they should be, then direct feedback should be given to them as to the areas in need of improvement in order to remain in the program. The counselors may need to have some clients repeat a module or actually start the program over again. It should be noted that clients progress at different rates. At the 6-week evaluation, we have had some abusers who did not appear to be able to complete the program. They did gradually begin to "get it," however, and did show improvement over time after a warning. As long as clients are progressing and participating, the counselors should continue to monitor their behaviors and attitudes. If they have not progressed sufficiently by the second or third evaluation, some change in the treatment should occur (i.e., repeating some modules, starting over again, or being terminated from treatment with proper notification to the authorities and/or partners). It is important for liability issues, credibility, and safety concerns, that no one be able to complete and graduate from a treatment program without having significantly changed his attitudes, beliefs, and behaviors such that he can interact with a partner in a nonabusive manner.

ASSESSMENT INTERPRETATION

It is helpful to use a session to go over the results of the assessment with the clients to aid them in better understanding themselves and their partners. This session may continue the rapport building and information gathering that was begun earlier. The profiles of the various measures can even be shown to the clients. If couples counseling is to occur, then this may be the first session that both partners attend together. The desire and commitment needed to participate in this type of treatment must already have been obtained from the partners independently before they are brought together. In addition, the interviews and testing must indicate that the abuser does not have an antisocial personality disorder (commonly referred to as a sociopathic personality), and that the partner will not be intimidated in a conjoint session. A *Weekly Behavior Inventory* should be completed by the clients independently (see Session 1 in the Treatment program).

A discussion of the social histories of the client should then occur. It is important to gently bring out key areas or issues. The clinician should watch for verbal and nonverbal reactions and, if the time is right, check them out to see what the reaction was about. If this session includes a couple, then the clinician should take time to point out similarities and differences in backgrounds and the possible effects of such backgrounds. Information about each person's background and his or her relationship problems should be taken into consideration while interpreting the assessments.

Each person's assessment should be interpreted by a trained and qualified clinician, pointing out both the strengths and weaknesses of the clients. The assessment interpretation is done only with individuals or couples, never in a group setting. The similarities and differences in the personality characteristics, attitudes, and behaviors of each person can be mentioned. Possible conflict areas can be pointed out, along with any relationship problems that may also be present. If a couple is involved in the treatment, then their results on the Marital Satisfaction Inventory or other measures can be shown and discussed. The counselor can suggest that the clients not discuss any problem that might lead to a violent incident during the next week. The therapist can suggest that they only deal with those potentially dangerous issues in counseling until they learn how to deal with them effectively. The clients should be informed that they will be meeting in a group next time, if that is what is planned. They may want to talk about their fears or concerns about group or couples counseling. Emphasize the benefits and confidentiality of group counseling. Go over the rules and assumptions of groups (see Session 1 of the Treatment program). The therapist can suggest that the clients or couples do something that is mutually enjoyable. Examples might be to go out to eat, to go dancing, or some other "dating" activity if they are still in an intact relationship.

RESOURCES

American Psychological Association. (1996). *Violence and the family.* Washington, DC: author.

Ammerman, R. T., & Hersen, M. (Eds.). (1992). *Assessment of family violence: A clinical and legal sourcebook.* New York: Wiley.

Bowker, L. (Ed.). (1998). *Masculinities and violence: Research about men.* Newbury Park, CA: Sage.

Campbell, J. C. (Ed.). (1995). *Assessing dangerousness: Violence by sex offenders, batterers, and child molesters.* Newbury Park, CA: Sage.

Chalk, R., & King, P. A. (Eds.). (1998). *Violence in families: Assessing prevention and treatment programs.* Washington, DC: National Research Council, National Academy Press.

Dutton, D. G. (1998). *The abusive personality.* New York: Guilford Press.

Geffner, R., Mantooth, C., Franks, E. D., & Patrick, T. (1992). *Aggressive behavior inventory.* Unpublished Form.

Gondolf, E. (1997). *Assessing women battering in mental health services: A clinical response to a social problem.* Newbury Park, CA: Sage.

Harway, M., & Hansen, M. (1994). *Spouse abuse: Assessing and treating battered women, batterers, and their children.* Sarasota, FL: Professional Resource Press.

Hilton, Z. (Ed.). (1993). *Legal response to wife assault: Current trends and evaluation.* Newbury Park, CA: Sage.

Mantooth, C., Geffner, R., Franks, E. D., & Patrick, T. (1987). *Family preservation: A treatment program for reducing couple violence.* Tyler, TX: University of Texas at Tyler Press.

Milliken, M., Geffner, R., & Lloyd, C. (1998). *Spouse/partner physical/psychological maltreatment: A categorized bibliography list update for 1991–1997.* Tyler, TX: Family Violence and Sexual Assault Institute.

Demographic Data Sheet

Name of Client (Last, First, Middle)   Home phone   Work phone

Address (Street & No., City, Zip)

M S D W Sep

Marital status   Referred by

M F

Sex   Birthdate   Age   Education (Highest Completed)

Employed? Yes   No   By whom:_____ SS# _____

Where: _____ In what capacity:_____

Previous treatment? Yes   No   When: _____

  By whom: _____

HOUSEHOLD COMPOSITION

Number in household _____

Name   Age   Relationship

_____

_____

_____

_____

Relative/Contact person: _____
Relationship: _____
Address: _____
Home Phone: _____ Business Phone:_____

Family income per year:
_____ None   _____ $15,001 to $20,000
_____ $5,000 or less   _____ $20,000 to $25,000
_____ $5,001 to $10,000   _____ $25,001 or more
_____ $10,001 to $15,000   _____ Don't know

Presenting problem: _____

_____

_____

Confidentiality Statement

We place a high value on the confidentiality of the information that our clients share with us. This sheet was prepared to clarify our legal and ethical responsibilities regarding this important issue.

Personal information that you share with us may be entered into your records in written form. However, an effort is generally made to avoid entry of information that may be especially sensitive or embarrassing. The only individuals with access to our files are staff members who are either directly involved in providing services to you or those performing related clerical tasks. All of these persons are aware of the strict confidential nature of the information in the records. Persons from outside our office are not allowed access to our files without a court order or your written permission.

RELEASE OF INFORMATION TO OTHERS

If for some reason there is a need to share information in your record with someone not employed here (for example, your physician or another therapist), you will first be consulted and asked to sign a form authorizing transfer of the information. Because of the sensitive nature of the information contained in some records, you may wish to discuss the release of this material and related implications very carefully before you sign. The form will specify the information that you give us permission to release to the other party and will specify the time period during which the information may be released. You can revoke your permission at any time by simply giving us written notice.

EXCEPTIONS TO CONFIDENTIALITY

There are several important instances when confidential information may be released to others. First, if you have been referred to this agency by the court ("court ordered"), you can assume the court will wish to receive some type of report or evaluation. You should discuss with us exactly what information we would include in such a report to the court *before* you disclose any confidential material. In such instances, you have a right to tell us only what you want us to know.

Second, if you threaten to harm either yourself or someone else and we believe your threat to be serious, we are obligated under the law to take whatever actions seem necessary to protect you or others from harm. This may include divulging confidential information to others, and would only be done under unusual circumstances, when someone's life appears to be in danger.

Finally, if we have reason to believe that you are abusing or neglecting your children, we are obligated by law to report this to the appropriate state agency. The law is designed to protect children from harm and the obligations to report suspected abuse or neglect are clear in this regard.

In summary, we make every reasonable effort to safeguard the personal information that you may share with us. There are, however, certain instances when we may be obligated under the law to release such information to others. If you have any questions about confidentiality, please discuss them with us.

Confidentiality Release

(For staff) Explain the following areas of the Confidentiality Statement to each client. Give each client a copy of the Confidentiality Statement. Have each client sign this form.

   I. Confidentiality Statement

  II. Release of information to others

 III. Exceptions to confidentiality
       A. Court referrals
       B. Threats to harm yourself or others
       C. Abusing or neglecting your children
       D. Records subpoenaed

The Confidentiality Statement has been explained to me and I have received a copy. I have read and understand the Confidentiality Statement and agree to it.

_____   _____
                 Client   Witness

              _____
                             Date

Client Consent Form

I, the undersigned, authorize _____ to:

    Yes   No—Counsel me and enter me into treatment

    Yes   No—Test and conduct assessment

    Yes   No—Audio/Videotape (for staff supervision or to show to me at a later date)

    Yes   No—Use basic information for research purposes

    Yes   No—Other—Specify (and initial):_____

and release the above agency and staff thereof from liability.

_____
Client Signature

_____
Staff Signature

_____
Date

Consent for Follow-Up

Name_____ Client number _____

Address_____ Termination date _____

_____ Counselor _____

Home phone _____ Business phone _____

Date for follow-up after treatment concludes   Date follow-up completed

   1 month: _____   1 month: _____

   3 month: _____   3 month: _____

   6 month: _____   6 month: _____

   1 year: _____   1 year: _____

   2 years: _____   2 years: _____

May we contact you by mail? Yes   No
May we contact you by phone? Yes   No

How could we contact you if you are no longer at this address or telephone number?

_____

_____

Please contact us if your address or telephone number should change.

_____   _____
            Client   Staff

_____
            Date

Precounseling Questionnaire

Name _____   Client number_____

Classification_____   Date _____

1. How long has the violence been occurring before entering counseling? _____

2. What types of violence have occurred?

    Pushing/Shoving _____   Hair pulling _____
    Physical restraint _____   Cuts _____
    Slapping _____   Use of weapon or object _____
    Hitting _____   Threats to use a weapon _____
    Choking _____   Involuntary sex _____
    Punching _____   Verbal abuse _____
    Kicking_____   Burns _____
    Other: _____

3. How often has the violence occurred?

    Once _____   Once a week _____
    Once a month _____   2–3 times a week _____
    2–3 times a month _____   Daily _____
    Other: _____

4. Have you ever left home after a violent incident?   Yes   No

5. If yes, where did you go?

    To friend _____   For a walk _____
    To family _____   For a drive _____
    To shelter_____   To a club _____
    To motel _____   Other: _____

6. When was the last violent incident? _____

7. What do you think started the last abusive incident?

    Alcohol use _____   Conflicts about children_____
    Drug use _____   Conflicts about/with in-laws
    Unemployment _____   or other family members _____
    Job pressures _____   Jealousy _____
    Sexual demands _____   Financial/money pressures _____

    Physical aggression by partner (Describe): _____

    Other: _____

Precounseling Questionnaire *(Continued)*

8. What happened after the incident?

   Arguments _____   Police were called _____
   Calm discussion _____   Charges were filed _____
   I called other family member _____ Called agency for advice _____
   Spouse called other family member _____ I left the house/apt _____
   Spouse left the house/apt _____ Other (Specify): _____

9. Was there violence or abuse directed toward your children?   Yes   No

10. Was this violence or abuse: Physical _____   Verbal _____   Sexual _____

11. Under what conditions did you enter counseling?

    Voluntary, through self-referral_____
    Voluntary, through other agency _____
    Through court diversion, preplea_____
    Through court diversion, postplea _____
    Joint agreement between partner and self _____
    Other: _____

12. What issues would you like to see addressed in counseling sessions?

    Anger management _____   Exploration of gender roles _____
    Assertiveness training _____   Communication skill training _____
    Stress management _____   Self-esteem enhancement _____
    Parenting skills _____   Relationship enhancement _____
    Money management _____   Personality assessment_____
    Building social support   Drug/alcohol intervention
       systems _____   or treatment _____
    Emotional expression training _____ Emotional awareness training _____
    Support outside sessions (e.g.,   Problem-solving skill training _____
       hotline, access to program   Other: _____
       personnel, etc.)

Client Social History

Date _____   Client number_____

Client name _____

GENERAL INFORMATION

Name _____   SS# _____

Address _____

Home phone _____   Business phone _____

Age _____ Date of birth _____ Sex _____ Ethnic origin _____

Employed? Yes   No   Where _____

Marital status _____   Years married _____

Spouse's name _____   Age _____

Spouse employed?   Yes   No   Where _____

Number of children _____   Sex and age _____

Number of marriages _____   Duration of each _____

Education _____   Religious preference _____

Spouse's education _____   Spouse's religion _____

Military _____   Spouse's military _____

HOUSEHOLD COMPOSITION

Number in household _____

Name   Age   Relationship

_____

_____

_____

_____

_____

Relative/Contact person: _____

Relationship: _____

Address: _____

Home Phone: _____   Business Phone: _____

Referred by:

What are your specific needs?

Client Social History *(Continued)*

Client name: _____

CHILDHOOD: BIRTH TO AGE 12

Date of birth: _____ Place of birth: _____

Mother's condition during pregnancy: _____

Complications during delivery: _____

Developmental problems:_____

Check all of the following that applied during your childhood:

_____ Night terrors	_____ Bedwetting	_____ Sleepwalking
_____ Thumbsucking	_____ Nailbiting	_____ Stammering
_____ Fears	_____ Happy childhood	_____ Unhappy childhood
_____ Other		

Illnesses during childhood (age):_____

Surgery during childhood (age): _____

Accidents during childhood (age): _____

Fears during childhood: _____

Relationships with teachers:_____

Relationships with peers: _____

Relationships with parents: _____

Relationships with siblings: _____

Parent's religious preference: _____

Was your mother physically abused by your father? _____

Were you physically abused (by whom)? _____

Were you sexually abused (by whom)? _____

Feelings about school, problems, grades: _____

Problems with legal authorities (reason): _____

Counseling during childhood (by whom, what reason, how long?):

_____

_____

Were you treated in a mental hospital during childhood (where, age, what reason, how long)?

_____

_____

Client Social History *(Continued)*

Client name: _____

Problems during childhood with drugs/alcohol (to what extent):
_____

_____

Did you attempt suicide during childhood (when, what method did you use, for what reason)?
_____

Describe yourself as a child:

Check all of the following that you feel applied to you sometime as a child:

_____ Loss of self-esteem	_____ Personal guilt or shame
_____ Nervous symptoms (such as nailbiting)	_____ Feeling of maturity/responsibility
_____ Sleep problems (including nightmares)	inappropriate for age
_____ Self-damaging, self-destructive behavior	_____ Withdrawal from normal childhood
_____ Truancy and/or delinquency	activities
_____ Depression	_____ Eating disorders (overeating, fear of
_____ Sudden change in school performance	being overweight, overweight,
_____ Difficulty with social relationships	underweight)
_____ Running away from home	_____ Homicidal ideas (wanting to kill
_____ Preoccupation with sexual matters	someone)
_____ Sexual involvement before age 13	_____ Pregnancy
_____ Desire to have sexual involvement	_____ Sexual abuse of younger children
with same-sex partner	_____ The favored child in the family
_____ Isolated from friends	_____ Bedwetting
_____ Drug/alcohol use	

ADOLESCENCE: AGE 12–18

Where did you live as an teenager? _____

Illnesses during teenage years (age): _____

Surgery during teenage years (age): _____

Accidents during teenage years (age): _____

Fears during adolescence:_____

Relationships with teachers:_____

Relationships with peers: _____

Relationships with parents: _____

Relationships with siblings: _____

Client Social History *(Continued)*

Client name: _____

Was your mother physically abused by your father? _____

Were you physically abused (by whom)? _____

Were you sexually abused (by whom)? _____

Feelings about school, problems, grades: _____

Problems with legal authorities (for what reason): _____

Problems with drugs or alcohol (to what extent): _____

Counseling during teenage years (by whom, what reason, how long)?

_____

Were you treated in a mental hospital during teenage years (where, what age, what reason, how long)? _____

Did you attempt suicide during teenage years (when, what method, what reason)?

_____

At what age did you start dating? _____

Were you sexually active during teenage years (what age)? _____

At what age did you leave home? _____

Describe yourself as an adolescent:

ADULTHOOD: AGE 18 AND OVER

Number of brothers and sisters and their ages: _____

What is your birth order? _____

Are parents living?_____

Parents' education:_____

Parents' occupations: _____

Relationship with parents during adult years: _____

Relationship with children: _____

Relationship with spouse:_____

Age at each marriage: _____

Have you been sexually abused during your adulthood (by whom)?

_____

Have you been physically abused during your adulthood (by whom)?

_____

Client Social History *(Continued)*

Client name: _____

Problems with drugs/alcohol: _____

Problems with legal authorities (for what reason): _____

Counseling during adult years (by whom, what reason, how long?):

_____

Have you been treated in a mental hospital during the adult years (when, where, for what reason, how long)? _____

Have you attempted suicide during your adult years (when, what method, what reason)?

_____

Illnesses during adult years (age): _____

Accidents during adult years (age): _____

Surgery during adult years (age): _____

Describe the present problem and anything that relates to it. Please give details: _____

_____

_____

Describe your present job situation, number of jobs held in the past year, reasons for change:

_____

_____

Describe your present social involvement, and membership in any organizations: _____

_____

_____

Describe your present relationship with your family: _____

_____

_____

Describe how you spend your leisure time; what type activities do you find pleasurable:

_____

_____

Describe your present health, illnesses, medications: _____

_____

Describe how you handle stress: _____

_____

Client Social History *(Continued)*

Client name: _____

PRESENT

Please check any of the following that apply to you:

_____ Low self-esteem
_____ Sense of helplessness (feeling there is no solution)
_____ Prolonged physical symptoms/problems
_____ Eating disturbances (overeating, overweight, underweight, fear of being overweight)
_____ Frequent depression
_____ Hurting or desire to hurt yourself
_____ Lack of self-identity (difficulty describing who you are)
_____ Thoughts of suicide
_____ Passivity (not saying how you feel or what you want)
_____ Anger
_____ Aggression
_____ Guilt
_____ Clinically diagnosed psychological problems
_____ Conflict with partner
_____ Fear of partner
_____ Conflict with parents or in-laws
_____ Difficulty establishing and/or maintaining close friends
_____ Avoiding sexual involvement
_____ Unsatisfactory sexual relationship
_____ Sexual problems
_____ Thoughts of harming your own or other's children
_____ Other:

Aggressive Behavior Inventory

Client name: _____   Date: _____

Please list the approximate number of times you have been involved in the events listed below for each period of time indicated.

Happened to Me	Past week	One month	Two months	Three months	Past year
Pinching	_____	_____	_____	_____	_____
Slapping	_____	_____	_____	_____	_____
Grabbing	_____	_____	_____	_____	_____
Kicking	_____	_____	_____	_____	_____
Punching	_____	_____	_____	_____	_____
Hair pulling	_____	_____	_____	_____	_____
Throwing things	_____	_____	_____	_____	_____
Throwing partner or shoving	_____	_____	_____	_____	_____
Hitting with physical object	_____	_____	_____	_____	_____
Choking	_____	_____	_____	_____	_____
Threat of or use of weapon	_____	_____	_____	_____	_____
Burning	_____	_____	_____	_____	_____
Sexual abuse	_____	_____	_____	_____	_____
Destruction of property	_____	_____	_____	_____	_____
Verbal abuse	_____	_____	_____	_____	_____
Emotional abuse	_____	_____	_____	_____	_____

I Did to Partner	Past week	One month	Two months	Three months	Past year
Pinching	_____	_____	_____	_____	_____
Slapping	_____	_____	_____	_____	_____
Grabbing	_____	_____	_____	_____	_____
Kicking	_____	_____	_____	_____	_____
Punching	_____	_____	_____	_____	_____
Hair pulling	_____	_____	_____	_____	_____
Throwing things	_____	_____	_____	_____	_____
Throwing partner or shoving	_____	_____	_____	_____	_____
Hitting with physical object	_____	_____	_____	_____	_____
Choking	_____	_____	_____	_____	_____
Threat of or use of weapon	_____	_____	_____	_____	_____
Burning	_____	_____	_____	_____	_____
Sexual abuse	_____	_____	_____	_____	_____
Destruction of property	_____	_____	_____	_____	_____
Verbal abuse	_____	_____	_____	_____	_____
Emotional abuse	_____	_____	_____	_____	_____

Progress Evaluation Form

Client's name: _____

Group leader (Initials):_____ Date:_____ Session #: (circle one) 6 12 18 24

INSTRUCTIONS

Please rate the group member named above on each of the listed criteria. Use the 0 to 5 rating scale listed below, based on your impressions and observations. Obtain ratings from the client's partner, if possible, and also list below.

**5 = occurs very often; 4 = often; 3 = occurs sometimes; 2 = not often;
1 = occurs rarely; 0 = unknown**

_____ **Attendance:** Arrives at group session on time; attends regularly; contacts program in advance about absence; has legitimate excuse for absences.

_____ **Nonviolence:** Has not recently physically abused partner, children, or others; no apparent threats, intimidation, or manipulation.

_____ **Sobriety:** Attends meeting sober; no apparent abuse of alcohol or drugs during week; complying to ordered or referred drug and alcohol treatment.

_____ **Acceptance of responsibility:** Admits that violence and/or abuse occurred; not minimizing, blaming, or excusing problems; accepts responsibility for abuse, and contribution to problems.

_____ **Using techniques:** Takes steps to avoid abusiveness; refers to time-outs, self-talk, conflict-resolution skills, etc.; does homework assignments and follows recommendations.

_____ **Help-seeking:** Seeks information about alternatives; discusses options with others in the group; calls other participants for help; open to referrals and future support.

_____ **Actively engaged:** Attentive body language and nonverbal response; maintains eye contact; speaks with feeling; follows topic of discussion in comments; lets others speak; asks questions of others without interrogating; acknowledges others' contributions; participates.

_____ **Self-disclosure:** Reveals struggles, feelings, fears, and self-doubts; not withholding or evading issues; not sarcastic or defensive.

_____ **Sensitive language:** Respectful of partner and women in general; nonsexist language and no pejorative slang; checks others who use sexist language.

_____ **Empathy and insight:** Has insight concerning the abusiveness, its effects on the partner, and its dangerousness; understands the fears and trauma the abuse causes; realizes the negative impact of using power and controlling behaviors in relationships.

COMMENTS

_____

Adapted from E. Gondolf, R. Foster, P. Burchfield, & D. Novosel (1995).

THE TREATMENT PROGRAM

I

Foundations and
Brief Interventions

Session 1

Ground Rules and Assumptions; House of Abuse

OBJECTIVES

To introduce group members to the ground rules for the group sessions, the assumptions of the program, the basic definitions of abuse, and the various types of intimidating behaviors.

MATERIALS

Weekly Behavior Inventory
Group Orientation handout
Counseling and Support Group Assumptions and Rules handout
The Nine Basic Rules handout
House of Abuse handout
Emotional/Psychological Abuse handout
Sexual Abuse and Violence handout

TASKS

1. Explain ground rules, including homework and notebooks.
2. Explain assumptions.
3. Explain *House of Abuse.*
4. Describe different "rooms" of the house.
5. Encourage group discussion about the "rooms."
6. Discuss responses of the participants.
7. Discuss handouts and assigned homework.
8. Explain *Weekly Behavior Inventory (WBI).*

PROCEDURE

COUNSELING AND EDUCATION

Begin the session by having each member introduce him/herself, and then introduce yourself. This will be the first session in which the individuals/couples will possibly be in a group setting. Give them a chance to get acquainted. They can do this by supplying information about themselves and their relationship. Let the participants know that they do not have to share anything now that makes them uncomfortable. Many participants will just give general information about themselves, but others may go into specific details of the problems in their relationship or with their jobs. At this point, do not try to probe for additional information or counsel them concerning problem areas. This is strictly a time for them to give information to each other. Comment and briefly acknowledge differences in ethnic and cultural backgrounds.

Explain the overall goals of the treatment program, and then go over the *Counseling and Support Group Assumptions and Ground Rules, Group Orientation,* and *The Nine Basic Rules* handouts for the program and for the group sessions. It is important to provide reinforcement, encouragement, and confidence that the current abusiveness and other personal or relationship problems can change with persistent work and effort in this program. For this to occur, the learning during the group sessions must also be applied at home between sessions. Therefore, assignments to do at home must be completed and brought to the next session. Inform the group members that each of them will independently complete the *Weekly Behavior Inventory* prior to each session. Pass one out for them to see. If they are in treatment with their partner, these will be completed in separate rooms prior to the session.

Begin explaining the basic concept of the *House of Abuse* (developed by Michael F. McGrane, Wilder Foundation, 1983) by passing out the diagrams of the House of Abuse. By the end of this program, the following categories will be listed in the different rooms:

Physical Abuse	Social Isolation
Verbal Abuse	Male Privilege
Intimidation	Religion
Sexual Abuse	Child Abuse
Emotional/Psychological Abuse	

The Roof is added at the end. This is the symbol of power and control. The theme to emphasize, eventually, is that this roof is supported by all the different rooms of the house. They all support power and control that is most often used by the man in abusive relationships.

As you go through this program, these questions should be asked repeatedly:

Is this a house that you would like to live in?

What do you think it feels like to be on the receiving end of this house of abuse?

It is also important to repeatedly emphasize the "100% RULE." This rule states that we are each 100% responsible for our own behavior. Being angry or hurt does not have to lead to abuse or intimidation. We all choose to act in certain ways, and we must accept responsibility for our own actions.

Begin by asking for a definition of the most obvious kinds of abuse; this will usually involve physical abuse and probably yelling and screaming. Ask the question: "If someone were going to abuse a wife or partner, how would he do it?" "How can somebody abuse another person?" As the group identifies different themes, label the different rooms and fill in some of the examples in the room where they best fit. Here are some basic descriptions of what belongs in each room:

1. **Physical Abuse.** This is the easiest to identify. This includes any kind of physical aggressive contact, including hitting, choking, pushing, and so on. The group members usually describe this first.

2. **Verbal Abuse.** This is also easy to identify. This includes any kind of name-calling, verbal put-downs, criticism, and so on.

3. **Intimidation.** This includes threats to kill or hurt the other person, threats against the kids, or threats of kidnapping the kids. It may involve telling a partner that a judge will never give her custody because she's crazy, she doesn't work, or she has used drugs in the past. Threatening suicide is another example of intimidation: This can be a very powerful way of controlling someone, because it can produce terrible guilt and pain. The goal of these gambits is to produce FEAR, which is used to maintain power and control.

4. **Sexual Abuse.** The most blatant form of sexual abuse is rape, which has only recently been recognized as a crime in a marriage. This is not the only form of sexual abuse in a relationship, however. Demanding that the partner watch or read pornography can be abusive. Insisting on certain sex acts that your partner finds humiliating or degrading can be abusive, as is pressure for sex when your partner does not desire this.

5. **Emotional/Psychological Abuse.** This involves the use of "mind games." When someone "teases" a partner about her weight or her body, psychological abuse occurs. When he humiliates her in public, he is doing the same thing. Often, men drill home the message "you could never make it without me." When a woman hears this enough times, she may begin to believe it. Humiliating a partner for not being successful or competent at something is also psychological abuse. Another form of abuse in this category is ignoring the partner—giving him or her the silent treatment. This can be one of the most powerful mind games of all, it wears the partner down until she tries desperately to "be good."

6. **Social Isolation.** This category is often overlooked. Because many people feel threatened, they may become determined to prevent their wife or partner from becoming independent or successful. This may involve sabotaging the partner's attempts to work, go to school, or to have friends or activities of her own. A man may fear that the woman will not need him anymore if she develops her own network. This is the ultimate indication of insecurity: The man has to keep her down so he can feel more confident and dominant.

7. **Male Privilege.** This form of abuse includes the entitlement that men claim, which leads them to dominate the relationship. The man who insists on using the fact that he is the breadwinner to demand that he make decisions for the marriage and family is an example of male privilege. This same attitude can be used to demand sex, get out of the household chores, or to demand more control over his free time than his wife is allowed. A man may tell his wife that he "needs" to go away with his buddies for a week; what would it be like if she told him the same thing, and if she just assumed that he would watch the kids and take care of the business at home?

8. **Religion.** Using religion as a form of abuse involves invoking the Bible as a rationalization for male domination. It should be pointed out that, like statistics, the Bible can be interpreted as an explanation for just about anything. Be careful here because making remarks that might seem disrespectful about the Bible or religion can be very damaging to initial rapport. It is often helpful to start out by suggesting that one form of abuse can be restricting a partner's right to attend the church she wants or to insist that she participate in religion where or when she does not want to. As the discussion moves on, try asking the question, "How could someone use the Bible as a form of abuse?"

9. **Child Abuse.** Any physical, sexual, verbal, or emotional form of child abuse is likewise an abuse to the marriage. This can often lead to a discussion about the ways in which abused children may be affected, may become abusers, or may become victims themselves in the next generation.

10. **The Roof.** This is the final step. All of the rooms support this roof of power and control.*

Give the group members the *Emotional/Psychological Abuse* and *Sexual Abuse and Violence* handouts, and go over each one.

---

* Adapted from: Michael F. McGrane (1983). Wilder Foundation Community Assistance Program.

HOMEWORK

The homework for this week is to avoid all arguments. The clients should also put together the notebooks in which they will maintain handouts and assignments. Have them review the handouts given today, and think about the House of Abuse discussion at least twice during the week. Warn the clients that it will be rough for the next few weeks, so it is important to avoid any arguments or other tension. Let them know that things usually get worse before they get better because they will be making important changes in their life, they will be dealing with strong feelings, and they will have to talk about their attitudes. If they keep at it, though, things do get better and easier, and they will notice important, positive changes within several weeks.

Weekly Behavior Inventory

Handout

Client name: _____ Date: _____

Please list the approximate number of times you have been involved in the events listed below during the last week. If you were the one slapped, etc., put the number of times. If you did the slapping, etc., put the number of times.

HAPPENED TO ME

Pinching _____
Slapping _____
Grabbing _____
Kicking _____
Punching _____
Hair pulling _____
Throwing things _____
Throwing mate or shoving _____
Hitting with physical object _____
Choking _____
Threat of or use of weapon _____
Burning _____
Sexual abuse _____
Destruction of property _____
Verbal abuse _____
Emotional abuse _____

HAPPENED TO CHILDREN

Pinching _____
Slapping _____
Grabbing _____
Hair pulling _____
Kicking _____
Punching _____
Throwing child _____
Hitting with physical object _____
Scarring child _____
Use of weapon _____
Threat of use of weapon _____
Burning _____
Sexual abuse _____
Verbal abuse _____
Emotional abuse _____

I DID TO PARTNER

Pinching _____
Slapping _____
Grabbing _____
Kicking _____
Punching _____
Hair pulling _____
Throwing things _____
Throwing mate or shoving _____
Hitting with physical object _____
Choking _____
Threat of or use of weapon _____
Burning _____
Sexual abuse _____
Destruction of property _____
Verbal abuse _____
Emotional abuse _____
Acted assertively _____
Communicated effectively _____
Used time-out _____
Controlled angry behavior _____

I DID HOMEWORK _____

I DID TO CHILDREN

Pinching _____
Slapping _____
Grabbing _____
Hair pulling _____
Kicking _____
Punching _____
Throwing child _____
Hitting with physical object _____
Scarring child _____
Use of weapon _____
Threat of use of weapon _____
Burning _____
Sexual abuse _____
Verbal abuse _____
Emotional abuse _____
Acted assertively _____
Communicated effectively _____
Used time-out _____
Controlled angry behavior _____
Spent quality time _____

I DON'T FEEL SAFE
TALKING IN GROUP _____

Group Orientation

Welcome to group therapy. The following is a list of answers to frequently asked questions about the groups. Please read this information carefully.

1. Why were you referred?

   You were referred to this program because of a report that indicated that you were involved in an incident of family violence. The fact that you have been referred to one of our groups indicates that your problem is treatable. If your partner is also in treatment with you, it usually means she made the decision to stay in the relationship and to take part in the program.

2. How often do the groups meet?

   Each group meets for 1½–2 hours, once a week for 26 weeks, followed by 6 monthly meetings.

3. What happens in the group?

   Treatment is divided into four modules. Each module is designed to focus on a particular aspect of ending family violence and on improving important skills. Groups provide an atmosphere in which members can discuss the problems they have encountered, the feelings that have led to the abusive behavior, and the impact abuse has had on the relationship. New ways of communicating, handling stress, and resolving conflicts are strongly emphasized.

4. Is this a class or group therapy?

   Although many of the group sessions may involve teaching of specific skills, such as stress management and improved communication, the groups are considered to be group therapy. This means that there is a strong emphasis placed on self-examination, discussion of feelings, and support for other group members. Most people benefit from the group process based on how committed they are to engage in these tasks.

5. Do I have to come every week?

   Group members have agreed or have been required to attend. The attendance of wives/partners is voluntary. It is not the responsibility of male members to persuade their partners to come to group. Nor is it acceptable for male members to discourage their partners from attending group. Interference of this kind is grounds for dismissal from treatment with associated consequences. In order for you to benefit from the program, attendance must become a priority. As you become more involved in the group, you will probably find that you are motivated to attend, not only for your own benefit, but also to support your fellow group members. You should attend each session even if your spouse/partner is unable to attend.

6. What about absences?

   The staff recognizes that commitments may require you to miss a group meeting. If you are unable to attend a group session for such a reason, contact the program staff ahead of time at the phone number given. Documentation of all excused absences is required, and the homework or other assignments must be completed before the next session. Undocumented absences and those that occur without notification will be considered unexcused.

   You will be required to attend weekly meetings for 6 months. No more than two excused absences can be allowed in any module. If more absences occur, then you will be required to begin the module again; if absences become a pattern, then you will be subject to possible probation/termination from the program.

Group Orientation *(Continued)*

Handout

Unexcused absences, that is, those that occur not as a result of documented prior commitments that cannot be changed and/or illness, indicate a lack of interest or commitment to the decision to change your situation. One unexcused absence will result in the authorities (if relevant) being notified of your failure to attend group. Two unexcused absences will result in your being placed on probation with notification to relevant authorities. Any additional unexcused absences may result in termination from the program. Late arrivals to the start of group will be considered an unexcused absence.

You will also be required to attend six monthly meetings after the 6 months of weekly meetings have been completed. These are large-group meetings that provide follow-up, networking with others, and the opportunity to address issues on how to use the skills you have learned. Your case will be reviewed for closure after the completion of six monthly meetings. Wives/partners are encouraged to attend even when their partners are absent.

7. Who leads the groups?

   All of the group leaders are mental health professionals who have had extensive training in the particular treatment you will receive. Groups may be co-led by both a female and male therapist.

8. Are there additional expectations for successful participation other than group attendance?

   Most sessions have homework assignments that you will be expected to complete and bring to the next group meeting. The therapists will review the homework assignment with you at the end of each group meeting so you will know what is expected for the next session. Therapists will discuss the completed homework at the beginning of each group meeting. Failure to complete homework on three occasions will be considered the equivalent of one unexcused absence.

   You will be given a three-ring binder at the first group meeting. You are expected to bring your binder to each group meeting.

9. What about confidentiality? Can what I say in the group be used against me?

   Because this treatment uses a "team" approach among therapists you can assume that what you say in the group may be discussed with staff members. In order to effectively prepare progress notes regarding your treatment, a case manager may review your progress with the group leaders. Only information that is directly related to your treatment goals is included in these reports. Most of the personal issues and feelings discussed in the group sessions remain confidential.

   In certain situations, the group leaders are obligated to report information that is revealed in the group. These reportable situations include serious threats of hurting or killing someone else, serious threats of hurting or killing yourself, reports of child abuse, or current use of illegal drugs.

10. What about new incidents of abuse?

    a. If the new incident is of a formal nature (i.e., comes from the Court, the police, the military, a medical treatment facility, etc.), the case will be referred to relevant staff for review and disposition. If the incident is substantiated, the following options exist:

    • Terminate services and return the case to relevant authorities, if appropriate.

Group Orientation *(Continued)*

- Place the group member on probation with the provision that a new incident of violence will be cause for the termination of treatment. Services will continue.
- Amend the treatment plan.

    b. If information regarding an incident of violence surfaces as a result of treatment (i.e., the regular surveys used in treatment, interaction with therapists and case managers), case managers and therapists will make clinical judgments regarding the continuation of services and/or referral of your case to relevant authorities for disposition. All incidents of serious abuse will be reported, but continuation of the treatment program will be made on a case-by-case basis.

ADDITIONAL INFORMATION AND OTHER GROUP RULES

1. Groups begin at the designated time. Group members are required to be at the center 10 minutes before the group's start time in order to fill out a questionnaire entitled "Weekly Behavior Inventory." Groups will not begin until everyone completes the questionnaire. Failure to complete the questionnaire will result in an unexcused absence for the group member.

2. Alcohol must not be used the day of group.

3. Group members will not threaten nor intimidate any group members or therapists at any time. Therapists and clients will ensure the safety of all group members.

4. When the treatment includes couples, each individual will return home separately after the group whenever possible or when directed by the group therapists. Carpooling for members of the same gender is encouraged.

5. If couples separate or divorce after group treatment has started, they can still decide to continue treatment, either in the same group or in different groups. Those group members who are required to remain in treatment will do so, either in the same group or in another one until completion of the program.

6. Group sessions may be audio or videotaped to ensure that group therapists are delivering treatment services in the appropriate order and manner. The focus is on the therapists, not the participants. The tapes will be used for *no other purpose*. The only people with access to the audiotapes are those who oversee the work of the therapists.

7. The leaders of the groups will evaluate your progress every 6–8 weeks. These evaluations will be used to assess your progress.

8. You will be asked to evaluate your progress every 6–8 weeks. These evaluations will also be used to assess your progress.

9. You will be asked to evaluate your group leaders every 6–8 weeks. These evaluations will be used to evaluate the work the group leaders are doing.

I have read the above information and agree to the conditions of treatment.

_____   _____
        Group Member's Signature   Witness Signature

                   _____
                          Date

_____

Counseling and Support Group Assumptions and Rules

Handout

Some assumptions have been made in putting this group together.

THESE ASSUMPTIONS ARE

1. Each of us is in this group because we have had a similar experience.
2. Each person can best define how he or she feels about his or her situation or experiences. No assumptions will be made about how anyone "should" or "should not" feel.
3. Each person can best decide what, if anything, he or she wants to do about his or her experiences and decide what changes he or she may want to make in his or her life. No assumptions will be made about how anyone "should" or "should not" act. It is made clear, however, that violent and abusive acts are to be eliminated, and that is one of the main reasons we are here.
4. Each person's experiences are valid and important. They cannot be judged as better or worse than anyone else's experiences.
5. Each of us has inner strengths.
6. This group is meant to be a sharing experience. It is not intended for us as facilitators just to talk to you, but for you to talk to each other. We can support each other and learn from each other.

RULES

1. Once a person decides to enter the group, it should be viewed as a commitment. It is expected that you will come every week except for emergencies. Your presence is needed for continuity. You are truly missed when you are absent. Call if you cannot attend a meeting. The group members need you even when you do not need them.
2. Membership in the group will be limited. When that limit is reached, other people will be put on a waiting list. They will enter the next group formed.
3. Groups will run for a period of 26 sessions, with 6 monthly follow-up sessions.
4. Everything said in the group is confidential. Nothing said by anyone should be used in conversations outside the group. No information heard in group about other members will be discussed with or mentioned to anyone who is not a group member.
5. Each person is his or her own best judge of what he or she feels is okay to talk about in the group meetings. Each is responsible for setting his or her own limits.

The Nine Basic Rules

Handout

1. We are all 100% responsible for our behavior.

2. Violence is not an acceptable solution to problems.

3. We do not have control over any other person, but we can control ourselves.

4. When communicating with someone else, we need to express our feelings directly rather than blaming or threatening the other person.

5. Increased awareness of self-talk, physical cues, and emotions is essential for progress and improvement.

6. We can always take a *"time-out"* before reacting.

7. We can't do anything about the past, but we can change the future.

8. Although there are differences between men and women, our needs and rights are fundamentally alike.

9. Counselors and case managers cannot make people change—they can only set the stage for change to occur.

House of Abuse

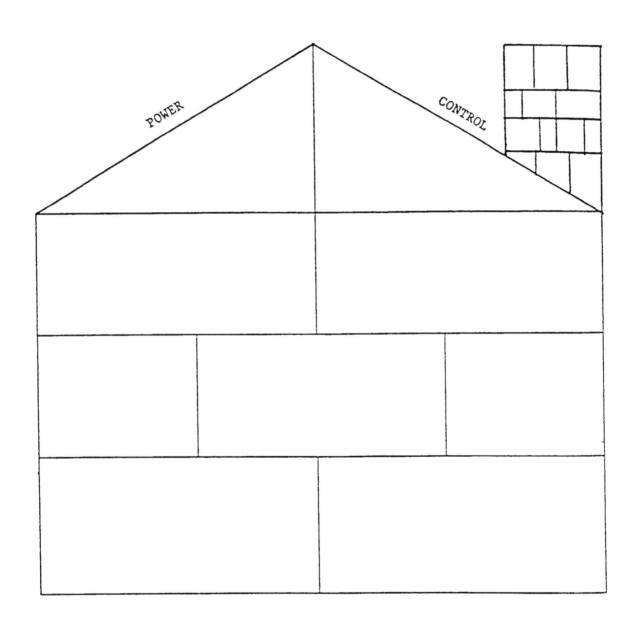

Developed by: Michael F. McGrane, Wilder Foundation, Community Assistance Program, 650 Marshall Avenue, St. Paul, MN 55104.

Emotional/Psychological Abuse

Handout

Psychological/emotional abuse always accompanies and, in many cases, precedes physical battering. Like hitting, targeted and repeated emotional abuse can have severe effects on the victim's sense of self and reality. Use of this list may help answer the perennial question, "Why do battered women stay?"

BRAINWASHING

- Jokes about habits/faults
- Insults
- Ignoring feelings
- Withholding approval as punishment
- Yelling
- Name calling
- Repeated insults/targeted insults
- Repeated humiliation (public)
- Repeated humiliation (private)
- Labeling as "crazy," "bitch," whore," "animal,"and so on
- Threatens violence/retaliation
- Puts down abilities as parent, worker, and lover
- Demands all of the attention (resents children)
- Tells about affairs
- Threatens with abusing children or getting custody
- Offers to stay because he/she "needs" the partner and can't make it alone

POSSIBLE CONSEQUENCES TO VICTIM

- Powerlessness/learned helplessness
- Unpredictable consequences of actions
- Questions sense of reality
- Nervous breakdown, depression
- Dependency
- Emotional instability
- Suicide or attempts

Adapted from Wexler (1990).

Sexual Abuse and Violence

Handout

This is the most difficult aspect of family abuse to identify and discuss, whether in a group or individually. Sexual abuse in the home is, however, more common than many would like to believe. Raising awareness of the possibility of child sexual abuse and giving you permission to articulate your own sexual victimization as a child or in the adult relationship, if these occurred, are expected outcomes of this exercise.

INCEST:
Many women and men were sexually abused in childhood, mostly by family members.

RAPE:
This occurs in and outside of marriage.

Sexual abuse includes the following:

- Jokes about women said in their presence.
- Sexual "put-down" jokes.
- Women/men seen as a sex object (leering).
- Minimizing feelings and needs regarding sex.
- Criticizing sexual "performance."
- Sexual labels: "whore" may alternate with "frigid."
- Unwanted touch.
- Uncomfortable touch (or forced to touch/made to watch others).
- Withholding sex and affection.
- Always wanting sex.
- Demanding sex with threats.
- Forced to strip—humiliation (maybe in front of kids).
- Promiscuity with others.
- Forced to watch.
- Jealousy—may be extreme.
- Forced sex with him or others.
- Forced uncomfortable sex.
- Forced sex after beatings.
- Sex for the purpose of hurting (use of objects/weapons).
- Sexual torture.
- Murder.

Adapted from Wexler (1990).

© 1999 Springer Publishing Company.

Session 2

Safety-and-Control Plans

OBJECTIVES

To develop a specific plan for dealing with stressful situations so that aggressiveness is avoided and to help the couples learn how to take a "time-out" when angry.

MATERIALS

Weekly Behavior Inventory (WBI)
The Safety-and-Control Plan handout

TASKS

1. Check *WBI* and have group check in.
2. Explain need for *Safety Plan* for the women and *Control Plan* for the men to deal with anger.
3. Describe early warning signs of anger.
4. Explain Time-Out and role play.
5. Have same-gender groups work out *Safety-and-Control Plans*.
6. Give handouts and assign homework.

PROCEDURE

COUNSELING

Before the session begins, hand out the *Weekly Behavior Inventory* to each member to complete privately and independently. The therapist should review the inventories to see whether any serious problems occurred during the week. If any did occur, the therapist should briefly confer privately with the person to ensure safety and the ability to participate in the session.

Begin the session by asking clients to identify any significant events that occurred during the week (positive or negative). Follow up on the discussion of last session's *House of Abuse*, and their thoughts and feelings about this during the week.

Introduce the idea of having a plan for episodes when it feels like behavior is getting out of control. This requires the personal responsibility of each partner to recognize the signals and to act responsibly in those situations. The odds of being successful with this plan are much higher when people have thought about it, planned for it, and rehearsed it in advance. Hand out the *Safety-and-Control Plan*. **The purpose is to ensure safety for battered women and control for batterers.**

Explain the different categories listed on the the *Safety-and-Control Plan*. These categories are explained clearly on the handout. In the group discuss different examples that may fit into each of the categories so that everyone gets the idea.

Ask group members to form dyads and develop their own *Safety-and-Control Plan*. Each person should write it on his or her own form. Each partner should develop his or her own separate plan. Dyads in these groups should never include members of a couple.

Present each *Safety-and-Control Plan* to the group and review. The members should not reveal the phone numbers or names of the people whom they are planning to contact. Set up a same-sex "buddy" system.

EDUCATION

Time-Out: Walking Away to Cool Down

Aggression can be averted if one can recognize the early warning signs of anger, nonaggressively say he or she needs to leave for awhile, and take a "time-out." The technique does not help the couple resolve the issue at hand; thus, it is a "stop-gap" measure. However, it often prevents violence, which is the primary goal. Communication skills can be learned later, after the fear of violence is gone. Present this rationale to the group in simple terms.

Write the major ingredients of the technique on the board:

1. "I'm beginning to feel angry."
2. "I need to take a time-out."
3. "I'll be back in (a half hour or 1 hour, whichever is necessary)."
4. While away don't drink, use drugs, or drive.
5. Do something physical.
6. When you come back, decide together if you want to continue the discussion. Each person has the right to say "no" to further discussion at that time and to suggest a different time for discussion. If anger escalates again, take another time-out. By checking in after an hour, trust can be established to overcome your partner's fears of abandonment.

Demonstrate the use of the skill with the co-therapist or one of the group members. If possible, have each person practice time-out twice with mild conflict situations, with some brief feedback given after each rehearsal. During the rehearsal, have the client actually walk away from the situation and quickly walk around the room.*

HOMEWORK

Give them *Basic Anger Management—What About Anger?* and *Appropriate Alternatives to Violence* handouts. Have them review and bring to next session. Have them rehearse their *Safety-and-Control Plans* twice, independently during the week.

---

* Adapted from: Wexler and Saunders (1991).

Safety-and-Control Plan

TIME-OUT PLAN

(If you need to leave, what will tell you that you need to go; what will you do to leave; or while leaving, where will you go; what will you do?)

"BUDDY'S" NUMBER:

(A good friend from group or otherwise.)

GROUP NUMBERS:

(Alternative phone numbers in case "buddy" is not home.)

PREVIOUS PLANS

(What have you done in the past to help yourself cool down or deal with anger in an appropriate way?)

PHYSICAL-EXERCISE PLAN

(How can you work off energy or anxiety in a nondestructive way, sport, or other activity?)

STRESS-REDUCTION PLAN

(What do you enjoy doing, something that relaxes you and helps you think straight?)

Emergency: _____   Battered Women: _____

Crisis Line: _____   Child Abuse: _____

AA: _____   E. R.: _____

Taken from Wexler (1990).

Session 3

Basic Anger Management

OBJECTIVES

The objective of this session is to teach basic anger education and management skills. The group members are encouraged not to use violence toward each other and that other options might be used in place of aggressive behavior.

MATERIALS

Weekly Behavior Inventory
Basic Anger Management—What About Anger? handout
Appropriate Alternatives to Violence handout

TASKS

1. Review homework assignments and go over *WBI*.
2. Review safety ground rules for the counseling discussions.
3. Ensure that both partners and both therapists participate.
4. Explain *Basic Anger Management* and role play.
5. Introduce *Appropriate Alternatives to Violence*.
6. Give handouts and assign homework.

PROCEDURE

COUNSELING

Before beginning the counseling part of the session, ask the clients to fill out the *Weekly Behavior Inventory*. Take a look to see if there was any violence during the week and of what kind. Do not refer to it at this point unless a serious incident occurred (if so confer with the client). This will be useful information later in the session.

You might begin by asking if the couples did the homework assignment, which consisted of them reviewing handouts. Follow up on the *Safety-and-Control Plans* to see how the rehearsal went and whether they needed to use their plans. Ask how it went. You can probe into whether there were any problems during the week and how they were dealt with. Each person involved should talk about his or her feelings concerning the problem situation. Get some closure by dealing with the specifics and offer some other options to handling the situation if it should come up again. Make certain the individuals are okay emotionally and have gotten the closure they needed. You may even ask directly if this is going to be a problem after the session. If so, it may need to be dealt with further. Get a commitment from the clients to be open and deal with what is going on during the session. Ask them to agree not to attack each other or their partners after the session. Explain that the only way that counseling is going to help is if all concerned feel safe during the counseling to discuss the problems and how they feel about them. At this point, you are giving them permission to be open and the message that it is "safe" to express themselves. You are also setting some ground rules for them to talk about it then and that it is not okay to fight afterward.

EDUCATION

Move directly from the counseling stage into the education part of the session. Start by having each member review the *Basic Anger Management* handout. Go over the handout, asking the clients for their input concerning each part of the handout. You might give some examples concerning how and when they know that their spouse is angry. Refer to yourself and your partner or use your knowledge of other couples' experience, but always maintain confidentiality. The counselor can go into as much detail as necessary for explanation, clarification, or to meet specific couples' needs. Role play ways to effectively deal with anger. Have the couples try a role-playing example. Go over the *Appropriate Alternatives to Violence* handout. [This education section on anger management is intended only to give the clients some basic information as well as to give them an immediate way of dealing with situations that might otherwise lead to physical violence. There will be other sessions dealing with anger management. If other materials or information are needed during this session, however, refer to the suggested readings and resources where other materials and ideas may be obtained.]

HOMEWORK

Have the couples try one or two of the techniques from the *Appropriate Alternatives to Violence* handout this week if they feel themselves getting angry. Ask the couples to choose two of the alternatives that they feel would be effective for them in dealing with anger appropriately. Give them the *Stress-Reduction Techniques* and *Methods of Relaxation* handouts. Have them review these before the next session. Have the partner plan a "date" or enjoyable activity to do together during the week.

RESOURCES

Bach, R. G., & Goldberg, H. (1974). *Creative aggression.* New York: Doubleday.

Dyer, W. W. (1976). *Your erroneous zones.* New York: Funk and Wagnalls.

Ellis, A. (1977). *Anger: How to live with and without it.* Secaucus, NJ: Citadel Press.

McKay, M., Davis, M., & Fanning, P. (1981). *Thoughts and feelings: The art of cognitive stress intervention.* Oakland, CA: New Harbinger Publications.

Weisinger, H. (1985). *Anger work out book.* New York: Quill.

Wexler, D. B. (1990). *Men's group for domestic violence.* Unpublished treatment manual for the Navy Family Advocacy Program. San Diego, CA.

Basic Anger Management— What About Anger?

Handout

WHAT IS ANGER?

- An emotion like love, fear or joy.
- A feeling. It affects the way you experience life.
- A communication. It sends information to others.
- A cause. It produces specific effects and results (Weisinger, 1985).

Anger tells us there is something wrong that needs changing. It is important to growth and adjustment to learn to feel and express a wide range of emotions. Anger is normal. Inappropriate behavior is not "normal," however. Inappropriate behavior is exhibited by physical violence, threats, verbally abusive comments, and sexual abuse.

ANGER TRIGGERS

- Frustration
- Extreme stress
- Feeling put down
- Fear of rejection
- Social learning experience
- Someone hurts you

THREE COMPONENTS OF ANGER

- Physiological—This is exemplified by body changes, such as sweating, increased heart rate, quickened breathing, trembling, brain-wave pattern changes, facial flushing.
- Feeling—Anger shows itself with changes in affect, tense, emotional, depressed thinking, "flight or fight" response.
- Expressive—Anger can be expressed through violent verbal outbursts, physical violence, threats of violence (slamming doors, etc.), or creative expression such as art, music, writing, sports, energized behaviors, and so on.

WHEN IS ANGER DYSFUNCTIONAL?

- When it is excessive, frequent, prolonged, or expressed inappropriately.

WHAT FACTORS INFLUENCE ANGER?

- Degree of arousal, awareness
- Past learning
- Past experience
- Present situation

Basic Anger Management— What About Anger? *(Continued)*

Handout

- Interpretation of the arousal
- Environment
- Temperament, personality
- Self-esteem

WHY DOESN'T EVERYONE EXPERIENCE THE SAME EMOTIONAL REACTIONS IN A SITUATION?

- Different past experiences
- Focus on different cues to explain the arousal
- Label feelings differently
- Different personalities

EFFECTS OF ANGER

- Positive— Can motivate and energize behavior
  Creative expressions, such as art, music, writing
- Negative—Physical problems, illness
  Mental and emotional problems
  Lowered self-esteem
  Work problems
  Relationship problems
  Behavioral problems, violence

HOW CAN YOU TELL WHEN YOUR SPOUSE IS GETTING ANGRY?

- Behavior—Slamming doors, stomping feet
- Verbal—Sarcastic tone, attitude, talking loudly, gruff, saying directly that he is angry
- Bodily cues—Face flushes, ears turn red, tense body posture, fists clinched

HOW DO YOU REACT TO YOUR SPOUSE'S ANGER?

- Get angry
- Ignore it
- Walk away
- Leave the house
- Withdraw in fear
- Other _____

Basic Anger Management—
What About Anger? *(Continued)*

Handout

SOME WAYS TO DEAL WITH ANGER

- Be aware of your body's cues.
- Identify the source of the anger. Why are you angry?
- Deal with the situation or problem causing the anger.
- Talk to someone.
- Accept anger as normal; however, remember inappropriate behavior is not "normal."

There are many other ways of dealing with anger. Refer to the homework handout, other references, or recommended books.

Appropriate Alternatives to Violence

You Cannot Hurt Living Things or Any Property Not Expressly Obtained for That Reason. The Actions Must Not Intimidate Your Partner, Affect Your Partner's Property, or Scare Your Partner.

Alternatives to violence can be decided on jointly or suggested by counselors. The following is a list of ways to direct anger into harmless behavior.

Jogging or Walking Briskly—This is a benefit both for stress reduction and general health. When you feel good physically, you can confront stressful situations better. Also, the physical activity helps divert attention away from the stressful environment. A walk around the block is good if you cannot jog.

Physical Work or Exercise—Physical work and exercise can release energy while at the same time leading to a constructive accomplishment. The exercise can be at home or where you work.

Tearing Cardboard or Magazines—Any available scraps of cardboard or magazines are usable. You merely take the object and continue tearing until physically exhausted. This physical activity works off excessive anger.

Time-Out—This is getting off alone for awhile. You can listen to music, just sit quietly and daydream, or walk alone someplace where it is restful, such as a park, lake, woods, and so on. (Perhaps the couple can set a time limit for this.) You can also have a room at home where you can go to be away from everything for a while.

Deep Breathing—Just stop for a minute when you feel tension and take some deep breaths. This adds oxygen to the body, and helps you think more clearly, calm down, and change the focus from the situation. Also stretching or walking around while taking deep breaths can help.

Talking—Talking about the stressful situation to another person is helpful. Anyone who will take time to listen will be okay; the idea is to just talk about what is bothering you. Awareness of the physical symptoms prior to anger and then talking before "blowing up" will help reduce stress.

Relaxation Procedures—Tense and relax muscle groups. Refer to the relaxation session in the manual in Session 4.

Session 4

Effective Stress Control

OBJECTIVES

The objective of this session is to help the client learn to recognize tension buildup and to express and manage anger through effective stress-reduction techniques.

MATERIALS

Weekly Behavior Inventory
Stress Reduction Techniques handout
Methods of Relaxation handout

TASKS

1. Review *WBI* and weekly events.
2. Review homework assignments; include all partners and model.
3. Explain relation between stress and anger.
4. Demonstrate and have group practice muscle relaxation.
5. Go over handouts.
6. Demonstrate and have group practice Personal Relaxation Program.
7. Assign homework.

PROCEDURE

COUNSELING

The clients should fill out the *Weekly Behavior Inventory*. Permit each person to tell about their week and discuss any specific issues that come up. After dealing with the specifics of the week, lead into whether the clients did their homework assignment. This assignment consisted of them reading the handouts.

Discuss whether they applied one or two of these techniques and whether the techniques were helpful in dealing with their anger. Ask the clients which other techniques listed might be helpful to them. The counselor might even ask the spouses which techniques they feel would be helpful to their partners. Suggest that they consciously continue to use these techniques when situations arise that cause anger. Ask about the mutually agreed upon activity and the outcome.

Check with each group member to make certain he or she is okay emotionally and has received some closure to any issue or area discussed during counseling.

EDUCATION

The counselors can introduce this segment by presenting information about the relation of high stress to inappropriate expressions of anger. Although aggression is not always preceded by anger, it often is. A necessary component of anger is physical arousal. Relaxation training is a way to reverse this arousal. It is also an important stepping stone for learning other skills. Explain that learning to relax is a skill like any other. Stress robs you of energy. The energy can be physical or emotional. If tension builds, the clients are more likely to be irritable and snap at their partners or to feel "down."

Relaxation training can do a number of things. First, clients can become more aware of body tension so they can have a signal when anger or anxiety begins. Second, they can learn to keep some muscles very relaxed and other muscles tense, so they can save energy when they are physically active. This is why relaxation training is sometimes used by athletes. Third, they will probably find that having control over muscle tension will give them more control over thoughts and feelings, including anger. At first the training will take some practice—clients must work at relaxing—later, relaxation will become a habit for them. Practice in the group first to make sure the clients know how to do the techniques. (Saunders, 1990).

Continue the session by giving the *Stress-Reduction Techniques* handout. Some of the clients will know specific techniques that have been helpful to them. Discuss the *Methods of Relaxation* handout. The group should role play the *Personal Relaxation Program* (#8) during the session. The counselors could also choose another method to discuss. There are also numerous relaxation tapes available that can be useful in group settings. The clients could be encouraged to purchase their own for home use. There are also a number of helpful books about different relaxation techniques available at local bookstores.

HOMEWORK

For the clients' homework assignment, have them choose two of the stress-reduction techniques to apply this week and one of the methods of relaxation. They should also be encouraged to continue spending time together. Giving each other a back rub can also be suggested. Give the *Reducing Stress and Anger, Cycle Theory of Violence,* and *Cycle-of-Violence Behaviors* handouts for the group members to review for the next session.

RESOURCES

Benson, H. (1975). *The relaxation response*. New York: Avon.

Bloomfield, H. (1975). *TM: Discovering inner energy and overcoming stress*. New York: Dell.

Brief, A., Schuler, R., & Van Sell, M. (1981). *Managing job stress*. Boston: Little, Brown.

Charlesworth, E. A., & Nathan, R. G. (1982). *Stress management: A comprehensive guide to wellness*. New York: Ballantine Books.

Davis, M., Eshelman, E. R., & McKay, M. (1982). *The relaxation and stress reduction workbook*. Oakland, CA: New Harbinger Publications.

McKay, M., Davis, M., & Fanning, P. (1981). *Thoughts and feelings: The art of cognitive stress intervention*. Richmond, CA: New Harbinger Publications.

Saunders, D. G. (1990). *Alternatives to aggression: A curriculum developed for the Alaskan prison system*. Ann Arbor, MI: University of Michigan School of Social Work.

Selye, H. (1974). *Stress without distress*. New York: Signet.

Stress-Reduction Techniques

Handout

1. Learn to relax and enjoy some pleasant, fun things in life.

2. Get physical exercise on a regular basis.

3. Accept things and situations that cannot be changed.

4. Eat properly.

5. Set priorities in your life.

6. Learn to delegate.

7. Break the routine periodically. Do not get in a rut.

8. Use relaxation methods wherever you are. For example, use them while you are stopped at a red light.

9. Keep a diary for 2 weeks to note what upsets you. See if there is a pattern and what changes can be made.

10. Retreat from everyone for 15–30 minutes a day so you can relax and be alone.

11. Give yourself and others permission to feel their experiences.

12. Reward yourself when you handle a situation effectively and do not use violent methods.

13. Talk to your spouse or someone else about the stress you feel.

14. Learn to recognize your body's physiological response to stress.

15. Do not expect yourself or others to be perfect.

Methods of Relaxation

1. **Deep Breathing**   Take a deep breath and let it out very slowly. Try to take twice as long to exhale as to inhale. Breathe deep, down into your abdomen, not just your chest, then exhale very slowly. Do this for a few minutes several times a day.

2. **Meditation**   This can be used if you are already aware of this technique.

3. **Autogenic Exercise**   While in a relaxed and comfortable position, slowly say to yourself "warm and heavy." Repeat this to yourself over and over.

4. **Environment Awareness Exercise**   Choose a comfortable chair. As you are sitting in the chair, think about the chair and be aware of how it is supporting you. Let the chair be the support instead of your body doing the work.

5. **Deep-Muscle Relaxation**   While breathing deeply, tense and relax each muscle from head to toe. Focus on each muscle as you do this. Practice this at least twice a day.

6. **Mental Imagery**   Think of a very peaceful, soothing, and relaxing scene. You could picture a peaceful blue sky, a lovely green meadow, and so forth. While focusing on this, breathe slowly and naturally.

7. **Do Something for Someone Else**   Sign up for some volunteer work, do something for the family, or do something for a neighbor or elderly person.

8. **Personal Relaxation Program**   Usually, such a program would include three components: Progressive Muscle Relaxation, Breathing Exercises, and/or Mental Imagery. An example of such a program is:

   • Sit in a chair and relax your body (your arms and jaw should be "loose").
   • Close your eyes and erase all thoughts from your mind.
   • Create in your imagination a vivid, soothing mental scene . . . a peaceful sky, a green valley, ocean waves, and so forth.
   • Focus on breathing slowly and deeply . . . let your breath out slowly.
   • For additional relaxation, repeat a phrase or sound that you find soothing (such as the word "flower" or the number "one").
   • Repeat this exercise at least three times each day, whether or not you are tense, for about 30 to 50 seconds.
   • After 2 weeks, your body will be conditioned to relax whenever you do this exercise, and you will feel yourself calming down.

Session 5

Desensitization Techniques for Reducing Anxiety and Anger

OBJECTIVES

The objectives of this session are to teach the clients to manage anger through desensitization, to learn early warning signs of anger, to learn how to take a "time-out" when angry, and to help the group members understand some of the typical stages in family violence. This understanding can help both partners anticipate what is to come and not be fooled into accepting one stage as permanent.

MATERIALS

Weekly Behavior Inventory
Reducing Stress and Anger handout
An Anger Ladder handout
Cycle Theory of Violence handout
Cycle-of-Violence Behaviors handout

TASKS

1. Have clients check in regarding weekly events, and go over *WBI*.
2. Discuss homework assignment and relaxation techniques used.
3. Discuss and role play anger and stress cues.
4. Explain "Desensitization" and review handout.
5. Practice first few steps in group and role play.
6. Explain *Cycle of Abuse* and red-flag triggers.
7. Introduce handouts and assign homework.

PROCEDURE

COUNSELING

The counselor should have the clients fill out the *Weekly Behavior Inventory*. Let each person check in about the week. Talk about the time spent together. Then discuss the different stress-reduction

83

techniques used. If the ones chosen were not helpful, encourage the clients to use some of the others. Discuss methods of relaxation used and their usefulness. Ask if there were preferences and why. Ask if any of the clients gave their partner a back rub. What were the feelings of each when this occurred?

After completing the homework discussion, discuss some specific stressors in the relationship that may at times lead to anger and inappropriate expression of anger. Discuss any cues that the group members are aware of that lead to their anger.

EDUCATION

Desensitization

Because the last session dealt with stress management, specifically relaxation techniques, it would be an opportune time to discuss using relaxation as a way of becoming desensitized to the situations that lead to inappropriate expressions of anger. The counselors can begin by briefly explaining desensitization. Discuss the steps in desensitization. Review the handout, *Reducing Stress and Anger.* Choose one of the methods of relaxation and review it. The counselors should role play a situation and go through each of the steps. Have the clients brainstorm about different situations that they usually get "uptight" about. Apply these to situations to develop a hierarchy as an example to the clients. An audiotape, *Anger Ladder,* can be used here for demonstration.

We can learn the early warning signs of our anger by paying attention to physical cues inside of us, and then we can get away from the storm! Simply being aware of the physical cues can help us to take action to stop the escalation of anger into aggression. Explain that when we feel threatened we have a tendency to respond by fighting or fleeing. There is a powerful physiological response that is triggered. Ask for physical cues that they notice in themselves and list them on the board. Common cues are: raised voice, pacing the floor, hot rush to the head, tightening arm muscles, rapid heartbeat. Practice an *Anger Ladder* (see handout) in the group by having the first few on the list done during the session (Saunders, 1990).

Cycle Theory

Review the *Cycle Theory of Violence* and *Cycle-of-Violence Behaviors* handouts. The handouts focus on the three primary stages in the cycle of family violence: tension building (escalation); violence (explosion); and calm, loving (honeymoon).

First, present an overview of the three stages, and ask the group members if they can recognize some of the signs from each stage. Next, discuss the tension-building stage: What are the cues and triggers that are likely to provoke the escalation? These are RED FLAGS or HOT BUTTONS.

• The physical signs of escalation are muscle tension, increased heartbeat, disorientation, and so on.
• RED FLAG or HOT BUTTON words are those that stir things up. What are the key phrases or words that can make someone "see red" or have "their buttons pushed?" Where do they come from? School? Family? Friends?
• RED FLAG or HOT BUTTON situations: paying bills, hearing certain questions, dealing with kids. Which room sets the stage for more conflict? Bedroom? Kitchen? Which rooms are most dangerous? Maybe the bathroom because of the hard fixtures, or the kitchen because of the potential weapons.
• Trigger thoughts: "She's trying to make a fool of me . . ." or "He doesn't love me anymore . . ." [adapted from D. Wexler & D. G. Saunders (1991); The Wilder Foundation (1983)].

Discuss the Calming phase. This is the phase in which the tables often turn, and the man who has been so dominating becomes very dependent. He recognizes how much he needs his partner and can often cling desperately. This stage can be extremely difficult for the partner to resist, because the vulnerable emotions are so appealing. In keeping with the basic ideas of behavioral psychology, both partners may come to believe, unconsciously, that this state can only be achieved in the aftermath of violence, or when "making up." Discuss these stages with the members. Ask them how this information can be used in their situation and whether it seems to fit.

HOMEWORK

Give the clients the *Anger Ladder* handout. It goes along with the exercise they just completed during the session. Ask them to complete this and be prepared to discuss it during the next session. An "Anger Journal" may help them keep track of their physical cues, time-outs, and their ways of dealing with anger. Such a journal example can be found in Sonkin and Durphy's (1989) *Learning to Live Without Violence* (p. 71). Recommend that an Anger Journal be kept during the next week.

RESOURCES

Ellis, A. (1977). *Anger: How to live with and without it*. Secaucus, NJ: Citadel Press.

Martin, G., & Pear, J. (1983). *Behavior modification: What it is and how to do it* (2nd ed.). Englewood Cliffs, NJ: Prentice-Hall.

McKay, M., Davis, M., & Fanning, P. (1981). *Thoughts and feelings: The art of cognitive stress intervention*. Oakland, CA: New Harbinger Publications.

Sonkin, D. J., & Durphy, M. (1989). *Learning to live without violence*. San Francisco: Volcano Press.

Walker, L. E. (1984). *The battered woman syndrome*. New York: Springer Publishing Co.

Weisinger, H. (1985). *Anger work out book*. New York: Quill.

Wolpe, J. (1982). *The practice of behavior therapy* (3rd ed.). New York: Pergamon Press.

Reducing Stress and Anger

You can reduce stress and anger with a technique called "desensitization." This helps you cope with situations that are threatening or frustrating to you. The key to desensitization is being able to relax while you imagine scenes that progressively become more stressful or anger provoking. As you learn to relax while imagining threatening or frustrating situations, you can transfer the results to life situations.

TWO PRINCIPLES OF SYSTEMATIC DESENSITIZATION

1. One emotion (relaxation) can be used to counteract another (anger).
2. A person can adjust to threatening and upsetting situations and have a minor emotional reaction.

STEPS IN USING AN ANGER LADDER (SYSTEMATIC DESENSITIZATION)

1. Take several days or more to learn to relax. This step is important because you learn that it is impossible to be physically relaxed and emotionally tense at the same time. There is a physiological link between your body and your mind. Choose a specific relaxation technique from Session 4, and practice it several times a day.

2. Make a list on the *Anger Ladder* of situations or experiences in which you have become angry.

3. Group all of the experiences or situations that bother you according to their common themes.

4. Put these situations in order, ranked from the lowest to highest levels in producing anger and anxiety. A high-level example might be that you get very angry if your spouse is late and has not called. This list is like a "ladder" of least disturbing, upsetting scenes that climbs to those that are most upsetting.

5. Start practicing the relaxation techniques in group. Visualize the scenes in your list, with the lowest first. As the anxiety builds, continue practicing the relaxation technique in group. Continue this process with each situation that produces anger. Go up your "ladder" gradually to the more upsetting scenes. Do not go higher until you are able to picture the scene while remaining calm. After you practice this in the group, continue imagining the lower level anxiety scenes on a daily basis. This process will take a few weeks overall.

ROLE PLAY

Example: A person you work with has a tendency to irritate you with his or her behavior. You have talked with this person, but he or she continues to irritate you. Shift into relaxation response so that his or her behavior does not bother you.

An Anger Ladder

Handout

An *Anger Ladder* is used to help you overcome the stress associated with anger. You can list five situations that produce varying levels of anger, and then rank them from least stressful to most stressful and anger provoking. You can also list and describe below, next to number 5, a situation that has made or would make you most angry. Next, list and describe a situation after number 1 below that has made or would make you the least angry. Then fill in situations for numbers 2–4 that produce increasing levels of anger, frustration, and anxiety. Your counselor or group leader will help you use these anger-producing scenes in combination with relaxation to help you overcome stress and better cope with anger.

1. Low Anger: _____
   _____
   _____
   _____
   _____

2. _____
   _____
   _____
   _____
   _____

3. _____
   _____
   _____
   _____
   _____

4. _____
   _____
   _____
   _____
   _____

5. Extreme Anger: _____
   _____
   _____
   _____
   _____

Before beginning to think about these situations, remember to review your relaxation techniques. Think about the first situation or least anger-producing situation in your life. This could consist of specific incidents with your spouse that triggered an angry reaction in yourself. As you are thinking about this situation and starting to feel your body react to the situation, begin applying the relaxation techniques that you have learned. You will notice yourself not reacting so strongly to the situation. Do this several times with each item on your list until you are comfortable thinking about these things, talking about them, and being in the situation face to face. This may take several sessions.

Cycle-of-Violence Behaviors

Handout

TENSION BUILDING

His Behavior

- Moody
- Nitpicks
- Isolates her
- Withdraws affection
- Puts her down
- Yells
- Drinks or takes drugs
- Threatens
- Destroys property
- Criticizes
- Acts sullen
- Crazy-making

Her Behavior

- Attempts to calm him
- Nurtures
- Silent/talkative
- Stays away from family, friends
- Keeps kids quiet
- Agrees
- Withdraws
- Tries to reason
- Cooks his favorite dinner
- Feels like always walking on eggshells

ACUTE EXPLOSION

His Behavior

- Humiliates
- Isolates her
- Abuses verbally
- Hits
- Chokes
- Uses weapons
- Beats
- Rapes
- Other abusive or violent behaviors

Her Behavior

- Protects herself anyway she can
- Police called by her, her kids, neighbors
- Tries to calm him
- Tries to reason
- Leaves
- Fights back

CALMING

His Behavior

- Shows remorse/begs forgiveness
- Promises to get counseling, go to church, AA
- Send flowers, bring presents
- Says, "I'll never do it again."
- Wants to make love
- Declares love
- Enlists family support
- Cries

Her Behavior

- Agrees to stay, returns, or takes him back
- Attempts to stop legal proceedings
- Sets up counseling appointment for him
- Feels happy, hopeful

Cycle-of-Violence Behaviors *(Continued)*

Handout

Denial works in each stage of the cycle to keep the cycle going (only by breaking through this denial can the cycle be broken):

TENSION BUILDING

His Behavior

- He denies by blaming the tension on her, work, the traffic, anything; by getting drunk or taking drugs; denies responsibility for his actions.

Her Behavior

- She denies that it's happening, excuses it to some outside stress (work, etc.); blames herself for his behavior, denies that the abuse will worsen.

EXPLOSION

His Behavior

- He blames it on her, stress, etc. ("She had it coming.")

Her Behavior

- She denies her injuries and minimizes them ("I bruise easily," didn't require police or medical help); blames it on drinking ("He didn't know what he was doing"); does not label it rape because it was her husband.

CALMING

His Behavior

- He believes it won't happen again.

Her Behavior

- She minimizes injuries ("It could have been worse"); believes this is the way it will stay, the man of her dreams, believes his promises.

Adapted from: Wexler and Saunders (1991).

The Cycle Theory of Violence

Handout

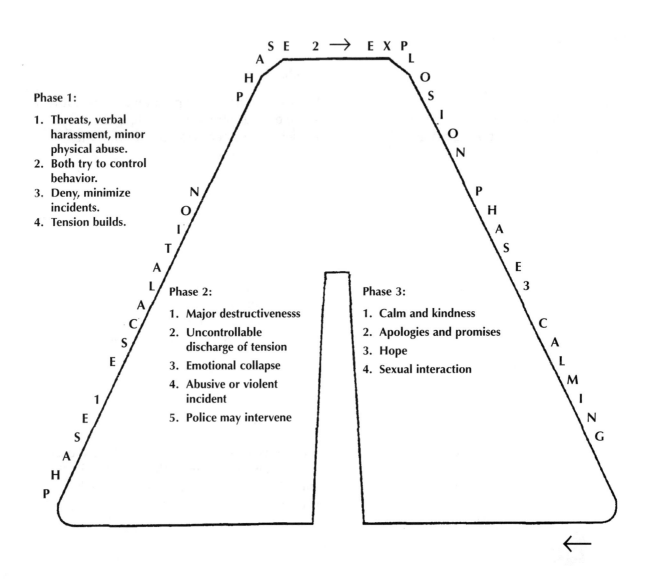

Phase 1:

1. **Threats, verbal harassment, minor physical abuse.**
2. **Both try to control behavior.**
3. **Deny, minimize incidents.**
4. **Tension builds.**

Phase 2:

1. **Major destructivenesss**
2. **Uncontrollable discharge of tension**
3. **Emotional collapse**
4. **Abusive or violent incident**
5. **Police may intervene**

Phase 3:

1. **Calm and kindness**
2. **Apologies and promises**
3. **Hope**
4. **Sexual interaction**

Adapted from: Walker (1984).

© 1999 Springer Publishing Company.

Session 6

Social Roots of Aggression and Alcoholism Issues

OBJECTIVES

To increase awareness of how aggression was taught in childhood through role models, childhood traumas, and social conditions; to understand the link between childhood traumas and aggression; and to understand the relationship of alcohol use and aggressiveness.

MATERIALS

Weekly Behavior Inventory
Alcohol and Abuse: What's the Connection? handout

TASKS

1. Review homework and discuss desensitization.
2. Discuss and role play anger situations; include both partners if couples counseling.
3. Discuss family-of-origin issues and the relationship to aggression.
4. Explain relationship between alcohol, anger, inhibitions, abuse, and escape, and introduce the handouts.
5. Discuss cultural differences.
6. Give handouts and assign homework.

PROCEDURE

COUNSELING

Go over the *Anger Ladder* homework. Did the group members try out these techniques? What were the results? Encourage them to practice before they discard the anger ladder as a possible way of dealing with anger control. Discuss the other options of anger control and get feedback from each client or couple as to which techniques have been most helpful and least helpful to them.

Because the clients listed six situations that sometimes lead to anger, have them choose one to discuss in the group or counseling situation. Always get input from all clients, if possible, about the situations as well as what techniques might be helpful in dealing with that situation. Get as much closure as possible.

Remember to reinforce positive experiences and clients' efforts. Emphasize successful experiences and improvements in behavior. Did the clients take "time-outs" during the week? Was this for practice or did they need to do so to keep from losing control? What was the outcome? Let the group members discuss their experiences, adaptations, and uses of the various techniques discussed thus far in the program. Particular examples of problem areas can be discussed and even used for role play by the group members or counselors.

EDUCATION

[The following has been adapted from D. G. Saunders' (1990) *Alternatives to Aggression*.] Patterns of aggression are often learned early in life. Most of the group members may have observed violence or abuse in their homes. Aggression is also learned when children are subjected to aggression. Even though they may have vowed never to be like the aggressor (father, mother, or sibling), under stress the aggressive patterns come to the surface. Nonviolent traumas can also have a strong impact on later aggressiveness; for example, being the child of an alcoholic parent or being sexually molested can have very negative effects on later behavior.

Have the following questions on the board or written ahead of time or make up a handout and have the clients take turns discussing them in pairs. Warn them not to share more than they are prepared for. Suggest that if they start to recall some upsetting events that they schedule some time for individual counseling.

How was anger expressed in your family when you were a child? How did your parents settle conflicts between them? How were you punished? Did the method of punishment affect your relationship with that parent? Were you mistreated verbally or physically by a brother or sister? Have you found a way to forgive any family member who abused you? Do you sometimes find that you act the same way in which you were abused or observed in your family even though you told yourself you never would? Why do you think we mistreat the one's we love the way we were mistreated?

Ask about other childhood traumas (not necessarily their own) that can occur and list the responses on the board. Do not push anyone to reveal more than he or she is prepared to reveal. Add the following if they are not included:

- Having a mentally ill parent
- Having an alcoholic parent
- Being sexually abused by a family or nonfamily member
- Being emotionally rejected by a parent or sibling
- Severe verbal abuse between parents
- Severe ridicule by siblings or classmates

Explain the connection between these types of trauma and aggression in adult life. Suggest that the following may occur:

Confusion, Anger, and Hurt → Desire for Self-Protection
→   Aggression as a way to protect one's self
→   Aggression is sometimes used beyond the point in time it is needed for protection.
→   Aggression is often seen as a "normal" way of behaving if that is what occurred in families of origin.
→   Those experiencing or acting out aggression may sometimes believe it is deserved.

Aggression in society reinforces the patterns of aggression in the family. A society that solves conflict through aggression or violently oppresses certain subgroups teaches us that aggression is acceptable. Ask clients, "How were you encouraged to be competitive, tough, and aggressive? Have clients thought about or actually acted out a violent scene that they read about or saw in a film? Have they been influenced by violent pornography?"

ALCOHOL AND ABUSE: WHAT'S THE CONNECTION?

Most people who hurt the ones they love have problems with alcohol. Some also have problems with other drugs, like pot, crack, and cocaine. Ours is a culture that often encourages the abuse of alcohol, and the display of aggression under this influence. Consequently, people under the influence sometimes do things impulsively they may not ordinarily do, and their judgment and control are further impaired.

Explain that people use chemicals for many different reasons. Ask the reasons they or others use chemicals and list them on the board. Ask if they feel alcohol causes aggression, or contributes to aggression through impairing control. Ask why people drink or take drugs when it impairs their judgment. List their responses on the board. Try to guide their responses into the following major themes:

1. **Social Drinking**—Peer and cultural pressure to use/abuse alcohol. Currently commercials even emphasize "Why Ask Why? . . . Have another beer."
2. **Habit**—Many people equate socializing with alcohol use. Others believe the only way to unwind is through drinking. Drinking becomes a routine.
3. **Psychological Dependency**—This occurs at a point when alcohol use is so established, it is hard to imagine doing without it. Perhaps by this stage temporary attempts have been made to abstain.
4. **Physical Dependency**—In its later stages, withdrawal can have severe effects. Medical, legal, vocational, and family problems attributed to alcohol abuse likely have already indicated a problem with alcohol.

Explain that no one ever establishes a goal of developing an alcohol/drug problem. Indicate that alcohol use may precede abuse, and that abuse is often progressive. Ask if participants ever conducted themselves under the influence in ways they later regretted. If so, ask them to consider how healthy it is to continue to use chemicals that impair their judgment. Ask if any members have ever experienced memory lapses or "black outs." Ask if any have ever been told that they have an alcohol problem.

Indicate that *any* "yes" answers indicate that their alcohol use has impaired their ability to be fully in control of their lives. Reemphasize the 100% responsibility rule. Point out that alcohol problems are progressive—without help, they get worse. Ask if they are really committed to being 100% in control, if they continue to use alcohol or drugs. Ask if someone wants to share a personal story of what he or she has learned about the alcohol–aggression connection. Point out that help is available through recovery programs. Explain that referrals can be made to assist personnel in getting the help they need.

(We are grateful to Ken Marlow, LCSW, in San Diego for helping to write this section.)

HOMEWORK

Ask the clients to monitor their drinking of alcoholic beverages and any effects on behaviors, even subtle changes. In couples counseling, have the partners also monitor their spouse's behaviors when drinking, if this occurs during the week. Have the group members observe how often alcohol use is shown on TV and how often violence also occurs. Have them note their observations. Give them the following handouts to review: *"Fair Fighting" Rules* and *"I" Messages*.

Alcohol and Abuse: What's the Connection?

Handout

Some people who hurt the ones they love have problems with alcohol. Some also have problems with other drugs, like pot, crack, and cocaine. Ours is a culture that often encourages the abuse of alcohol, as well as the display of aggression under its influence. For example, this type of situation is often portrayed in movies. Consequently, people under the influence sometimes do things impulsively they may not ordinarily do, while their judgment and control are further impaired.

People use chemicals for many different reasons. You need to list for yourself the reasons you use chemicals. Then, you need to identify whether alcohol causes you personally to become aggressive, or to impair your judgment. Major themes that are often revealed during this thought-and-listing process are:

1. **Social Drinking**—There may be friend and/or cultural pressure to use/abuse alcohol. Currently commercials even emphasize "Why Ask Why? . . . Have another beer."
2. **Habit**—Many people equate socializing with alcohol use. For others, they believe the only way to unwind is through drinking. Drinking then becomes routine.
3. **Psychological Dependency**—A psychological dependency occurs at a point when alcohol use is so established, it's hard to imagine doing without it. Perhaps by this stage, temporary attempts have been made to abstain.
4. **Physical Dependency**—In the later stages of dependency, withdrawal can have severe effects. Medical, legal, vocational, and family problems attributed to alcohol abuse likely have already indicated a problem with alcohol.

No one ever established a goal of developing an alcohol/drug problem. Alcohol use may precede abuse, and the abuse is often progressive. You need to ask yourself if you have ever conducted yourself under the influence in ways you have later regretted. If the answer is "yes," the next question must be how healthy it is to continue to use chemicals that impair your judgment? You need to think about whether you have ever experienced memory lapses or "black outs," or to consider if you have ever been told that you have an alcohol problem.

Any "yes" answers to these questions indicate that alcohol use has impaired your ability to be fully in control of your life. Remember the 100% rule regarding responsibility. Alcohol problems are progressive—without help, they get worse. Can you really be 100% committed to being in control, and continue to use alcohol or drugs?

Help is available through recovery programs. Referrals can be made to assist you in getting the help you need.

This handout was developed by Ken Marlow, LCSW, in San Diego, CA.

II

Communicating and Expressing Feelings

Session 7

Communication: "Fair Fighting, Dirty Fighting"

OBJECTIVES

The objective of this session is to introduce a cognitive structure for couple communication. It also sets up a nonthreatening atmosphere in which the couples can reveal their specific relationship and communication difficulties.

MATERIALS

Weekly Behavior Inventory
"Fair-Fighting" Rules handout
"Dirty Fighter's" Instruction Manual

TASKS

1. Have group check in and discuss weekly activities; go over *WBI*.
2. Begin to discuss more marital issues, and include both partners if couples counseling.
3. Explain *"Fair-Fighting" Rules*.
4. Role play *"Dirty Fighter's"* techniques in serious and exaggerated manner.
5. Discuss the importance of communication and use of humor.
6. Give handouts and assign homework.

PROCEDURE

COUNSELING

Have the client fill out the *Weekly Behavior Inventory*. Note any violent or abusive incidents. Ask the clients to discuss any violent incidents or situations that could have led to violence or emotional upset. Help the clients discover what the underlying factors were, such as what they were doing and feeling at the time. Discuss whether there was any resolution. Also, discuss whether this issue has come up before, when, and how it was dealt with. By doing this the counselor can get a picture of what some specific problem areas are and determine the patterns used by the clients to deal with them. Go over the homework assignments. Briefly discuss clients' observations concerning alcohol, TV programs, and violence. Did they monitor their own drinking? What was observed?

Another area to deal with during the counseling segment of the session is to ask the clients what they feel are the major problems in the relationship. Always get feedback from each partner, if possible. Also give the clients the opportunity to express their feelings about what their spouse has said. Watch for nonverbal cues from the person talking as well as his or her spouse in couples counseling. These could be tone of voice, facial expression, body posture, and so on. Check these out to clarify what is being said or how the spouse is reacting. After finding out what each feels the problem areas are, ask them what they feel needs to happen to resolve these problems. Get feedback from each partner. If there are numerous problem areas, the counselor could deal with one or two that seem to be most pressing. Other stated areas could be dealt with in future sessions. Compare to see if there are areas of compromise and work toward getting a commitment from both partners to use the agreed on way to resolve their specific problems. The counselor can help clients come up with other options, but let them decide which to use. It is better if they come up with an option of their own. Check with each of the clients to make sure they are okay emotionally and have received some closure to any issue or reactions discussed during the counseling. The education segment of the session is then presented.

EDUCATION

One way to lead into the education part of the session is to state that there are problems in all relationships and that there are going to be times when issues need to be discussed that might get emotional and could get out of hand. Therefore, it is good for a couple to have agreed on specific rules for the discussion before the difficult issues are probed. A guide, called the *Fair-Fighting Rules,* is used to help clients keep the conversation or situation from getting out of hand. These are a brief set of communication guidelines designed to promote the restoration of productive communication and reduce the likelihood of hostile interaction. Go over each of these techniques in the handout, step by step, using examples and applying them to each couple's situation. Promote discussion and client feedback as much as possible without letting the discussion stray too far from the main topic. The counselor could, if time allows, role play some of the techniques.

After completing the *Fair-Fighting Rules* and getting a commitment from the clients to try these techniques when there is an emotionally charged situation or topic, begin teaching the clients the "Dirty-Fighting" techniques. Role play these techniques in a serious but exaggerated manner. This educational tool is not literally meant to promote or teach dirty fighting. It is, however, a tongue-in-cheek, humorous way to help clients become aware of unhealthy and damaging ways in which they communicate. The counselor should present each technique in an exaggerated yet serious tone. During the presentation, let the clients believe that you really want them to try some of these and decide which they are best at. The counselor can state which techniques they are best at, which the spouses are best at, or which the co-counselor is best at. Examples using prior clients might be helpful, but always maintain confidentiality.

It will soon become obvious to the clients, one hopes, that you are not serious about them using these techniques. At the end clarify that this was an exercise to promote awareness of the dirty-fighting and negative techniques that take place in relationships. Give the clients a copy of the *Dirty Fighter's Instruction Manual.* Emphasize that as they become aware they will have more control in handling situations and communicate more effectively. This educational tool has been very useful in getting clients to look at themselves humorously as well as their patterns of interaction. This approach seems to help avoid defensiveness, which usually occurs when approaching how couples communicate inappropriately. Also, because it is a nonthreatening, nonblaming approach, there is less anxiety in talking about such sticky issues. The use of humor is important and healthy. When the clients and their partners can laugh at themselves (keeping in mind that the abuse is not funny), this is a positive step.

HOMEWORK

Ask the clients to read the *Dirty Fighter's Instruction Manual*. As they read it, ask them to identify whether a technique is frequently used by themselves, their spouse, or both. Have them bring this handout back next week for further discussion. Remind the clients to use the fair-fighting rules if a problem comes up or if there is any emotional issue to deal with. When an argument occurs this week, have the clients write down what happened before the argument and during the argument. How was the argument resolved? At the next session have the clients go over the problem, evaluate the outcome, and try to point out what led to the argument. Decide where the problem originated. Did the couple stick to the issues? What Dirty-Fighting techniques did the couple use? What Fair-Fighting techniques were used? Give the clients the *Family Communication Rules* handout. Ask the couple to participate in a mutually agreed on leisure activity again this week, or have the clients set this up with their partners.

RESOURCES

Bach, G. R., & Wyden, P. (1970). *The intimate enemy.* New York: Avon Books.

Bandler, R., Grinder, J., & Satir, V. (1976). *Changing with families.* Palo Alto, CA: Science and Behavior Books.

Buscaglia, L. (1984). *Loving each other.* Thorofare, NJ: Slack.

Goethals, G. R., & Worchel, S. (1981). *Adjustment and human relations.* New York: Alfred A. Knopf.

Goldberg, H. (1983). *The new male–female relationship.* New York: New American Library.

Lazarus, A. A. (1985). *Marital myths.* San Luis Obispo, CA: Impact Publishers.

McKay, M., Davis, M., & Fanning, P. (1983). *Messages: The communication book.* Oakland, CA: New Harbinger Publications.

Napoli, V., Kilbride, J. M., & Tebbs, D. E. (1985). *Adjustment and growth in a changing world.* St Paul, MN: West Publishing.

Satir, V. (1967). *Conjoint family therapy* (rev. ed.). Palo Alto, CA: Science and Behavior Books.

"Fair-Fighting" Rules

1. **Ask for an appointment for the discussion.**
   a. Set a mutually agreed on time.
   b. Set a mutually agreed on place.
   c. Determine the approximate duration.
   d. Advise regarding content.

2. **Do not argue "below the belt."**
   a. Don't call each other names, direct or indirect.
   b. Don't call each other's friends or family names, direct or indirect.
   c. Don't threaten, verbally or nonverbally.
   d. Don't use physical violence.

3. **Use "I" messages.**
   a. Example of "you" messages.
      • Promotes defensiveness.
      • Gives away power.
      • Gives responsibility to the other person.
   b. Example of "I" messages
      • Reduces defensiveness.
      • Retains control.
      • Shows acceptance of responsibility.

4. **Deal with feelings first.**
   a. Express your feelings
      • Become aware of what you are feeling.
      • Label what you are feeling.
      • Verbalize and describe what you feel.
   b. Listen
      • Be aware of what the other person is feeling through verbal and nonverbal cues.
      • Label the feelings so you can proceed accordingly.
      • Accept his or her right to feel what he or she wants to feel.

5. **Check that you are correctly labeling the other's feelings.**
   a. Words
   b. Nonverbal cues
   c. Check for incongruities.
   d. Be aware of thoughts and mind-reading.

6. **Ask for specific action.**
   a. Ask for what you want in detail.
   b. Ask what he or she wants; get details.
   c. Compromise and negotiate.

"Fair-Fighting" Rules *(Continued)*

7. **Take a time-out, if needed.**
   a. Know when to take a time-out.
   b. Know how to take a time-out.
   c. Mutually agree on when and how to take a time-out.
   d. Agree on the next appointment.

8. **Use teamwork.**
   a. Don't use fair fighting as a weapon or as a competition.
   b. Work together to use the rules.

9. **Never give up.**

Adapted from Bach & Wyden (1970).

"Dirty Fighter's" Instruction Manual*

INTRODUCTION

Not only can dirty fighting be a casual interest, a pleasant pastime, and a creative outlet, but many find it a way of life. Besides adding hours of excitement and entertainment to an otherwise drab existence, with dirty fighting one can obtain what people want most but are often least able to get: Their own way.

Although fighting dirty is practiced as a matter of course in homes and offices, at school, and at play, it is often thought that our ability to engage in underhanded warfare is natural and that no particular attention need be paid to developing one's abilities in this endeavor. All people do not come to the arena of human interaction equally equipped to do battle, however. On the contrary, many people find themselves unnecessarily crippled by moral, ethical, and temperamental biases that inhibit self-expression and leave them to face the world with a profound disadvantage. To make matters worse, our educational system has largely ignored this important area. It is for this reason, in an effort to make up for this unfortunate deficit, that this modest work has been created.

SOME GENERAL CONSIDERATIONS

Setting the Proper Tone

Like choosing the right timing, setting the proper tone is crucially important to getting a good argument going. Develop the ability to be hostile, ornery, unpredictable, or to throw temper tantrums and sulk for days when necessary. It is important also to learn the proper use of sarcasm, disapproving looks, exasperated sighs, and so on. Once an argument has started, move to the approach that will be most effective. Shouting and screaming are favorites for many, with occasional threats and intimidating remarks thrown in for emphasis. Although some people find that becoming hysterical usually produces the desired result, others prefer to let the partner be the one to get hysterical. In any case, be sure to follow through with statements such as, "If I had known you'd get so upset, I wouldn't have brought it up in the first place," or "Obviously you can't control yourself, so there's no point in discussing it any further."

Develop the Proper Attitude

There are a number of circumstances that automatically qualify you as being right and/or justified. The following are a few lead-ins that can be used to get you started on the right track:

1. **Family Wage-Earner**—"I'm working to pay for it, so the discussion is over."
2. **Person in Authority**—"That's the way things are. If you don't like it, that's just too bad. As long as you're here, you'll do what I tell you to do."
3. **Friend**—"I wouldn't think of bothering you unless I really needed your help. I'll really be hurt if you refuse."

---

* *Note:* **These are negative techniques that are often used in relationships—they are presented in this manner to exaggerate and point out their inappropriateness.**

"Dirty Fighter's" Instruction
Manual *(Continued)*

4. **Loved One**—"I shouldn't have to ask you to do things for me. You should know how I feel without my having to tell you."
5. **Parent** (with children)—"I'm your father (or mother) and I know what's best for you."

The Importance of Good Timing

Many potentially lethal dirty fighters miss golden opportunities because they are unaware of the value of proper timing. Begin an argument just before your husband leaves for work. Argue with your wife at bedtime after a tiring day or when she has to get up early the next morning. Pester your children with household chores or homework just as they sit down to watch their favorite TV program or before they go out to play. In general, keep in mind that it is best to attack others when their guard is down, when they least expect it, or when they are least able to defend themselves.

Developing a Winning Style

Many people win arguments not because they are right, but because they have a style of arguing that is unbeatable. Choose the style that best suits your personality.

1. **Monopolize the conversation**—Don't let anyone get a word in edgewise. If the other person tries to speak, either ignore him or her completely or accuse him or her of cutting you off before you are finished.
2. **Meander**—Make short stories long, make mountains out of molehills, talk about things that are irrelevant to the issue. Do not, under any circumstances, come to the point.
3. **Don't listen**—While the other person is talking, use the time productively to think about how you are going to answer back. When it is your turn, ignore any and all concerns that may have been mentioned and go right to the points you would like to make.
4. **Be a problem solver**—This style is useful when the main concern is the other person's feelings. The approach here is to ignore the feelings and simply hand down decisions, solutions, or suggestions. Once you have offered a solution, that's all that needs to said, and the issue is closed.

SOME SPECIFIC TECHNIQUES

Collect Injustices

Collect slights, hurts, injustices, inequities, and let your anger build up to the point where you explode over relatively minor issues. Then, when you've had enough, shout, scream, terrorize, even threaten. You will be surprised to learn how good it feels getting things off your chest. An added benefit of collecting injustices is that you then rationalize almost anything you later wish to do, like getting a divorce, quitting your job, or having an affair.

"Dirty Fighter's" Instruction Manual *(Continued)*

Help with a Vengeance

There are countless opportunities to give advice, tell people what they should do, how they should feel, what they should think, all in the interest of being helpful. It doesn't matter whether or not they have asked your opinion; go ahead and give others the benefit of your experience. If someone should object to your unsolicited suggestions, point out to this person that you are only saying these things for his or her own good and that he or she should be able to accept constructive criticism.

Don't Get Mad, Get Even

Anger expressed openly can be uncomfortable for all concerned, so learn to find other ways to channel your feelings. Get revenge by sulking, having an affair, going on shopping sprees, rejecting the other sexually, and so on. In general, it is always a good idea to find ways to undermine the other's confidence or independence, because this tends to increase the effectiveness of your anger.

When the Going Gets Tough, the Tough Get Going

If the other person is saying something you don't like, it is time to get going. Walk out of the room, clam up, refuse to talk about it; when arguing with children, send them to their rooms. No need to hang around an unpleasant situation. No matter how much the other person feels his or her complaint is justified, no issue is so important that it can't be walked away from. Better yet, refuse to acknowledge that the situation even exists.

Play Psychiatrist

This is closely related to the previous technique, but it extends the concept somewhat. Analyze others, point out their shortcomings, their "hang-ups" and, where possible, explain in psychological terms the weaknesses you see in their character. Example: "You have a mother complex," or "The reason you say that is because you are basically insecure." The real secret in playing psychiatrist, however, involves the skillful use of labels. For instance: "You're an egomaniac," or a "dominating bitch." With a little forethought you can find a label for any behavior you don't like. If someone is drinking to relax, he or she is a "potential alcoholic;" if the person doesn't want sex, he or she is "frigid" or "impotent." By the way, if the person objects to your clinical evaluation, it is undoubtedly because he or she has an "inferiority complex" or "can't face the truth."

Devastate with Humor

Keep in mind that the most devastating remarks are often said in jest. Therefore, tease and humor your opponent. Be sarcastic but always smile to show that it's all in good fun. If the other person begins to get defensive, you can accuse him or her of being overly sensitive. This is an excellent tactic to use in public, because it shows that you are a fun-loving person with a sense of humor and that the other person is a spoilsport.

"Dirty Fighter's" Instruction Manual *(Continued)*

Play One Person Against the Other

When out with your partner, always take long wistful looks at passing strangers of the opposite sex. Compare the success of others to those of your partner. A parent should never miss a chance to hold up the accomplishments of one child to another. A child should likewise never miss an opportunity to play one parent against the other.

Play the Martyr

Go out of your way to sacrifice your pleasure for others, even to the point of letting others take advantage of you. Later, when you want to get your way, preface your remarks with statements like: "How could you do this to me after all of the things I've done for you?" or "See how I've suffered because of you." You will be amazed at the power a little guilt gives you. The possibilities here are limitless.

Never Back Down

Backing down can only be considered a sign of weakness by the opposition. Right or wrong, you have to stand up for yourself. If you don't who else will? By the way, when was the last time you were wrong about something anyway?

Never Accept an Apology

Just because someone has said he or she is sorry, right away you are expected to forget about the wrong done to you. Never let the other person think he or she is forgiven. How else will he or she remember the next time? Learn to hold grudges, for years if necessary. A person's misconduct can be thrown up to him or her over and over again, giving you a decided edge in future disagreements.

Put the Other Person in a Double Bind

Criticize your spouse for gaining a little weight, not keeping up his or her appearance, and the like. Then, when he or she dresses up and looks especially good, accuse him or her of trying to impress people or flirting. Hound your children about hanging around the house too much. Then, when they are getting ready to go out to play, remind them of some chore they were supposed to do or tell them it's too close to supper. The idea is damned if you do, damned if you don't. Double binds artfully used can and do literally drive people crazy.

Chinese Water-Torture Technique

This heading is a grab-bag for a number of techniques that are meant to exasperate the opposition. Here are a few possibilities; make up your own variations:

1. **Be a chronic forgetter**—Never keep a promise; forget to do an errand. Act surprised when the other person gets upset as if to imply it didn't matter anyway. Forgetting birthdays and anniversaries also adds a nice touch, as does forgetting to call when you are delayed.

"Dirty Fighter's" Instruction Manual *(Continued)*

2. **Be a procrastinator**—Delay carrying out promises or obligations. The more others are depending on you, of course, the better. If there is a complaint, take the tack: "What are you getting excited about? I said I would do it, didn't I?" or "You're always nagging me about something; no wonder I never have a chance to get anything done." Being a procrastinator makes you look good because it gives the impression that you have so many important things to do that you don't have a chance to get all the trivial things done as well.

Note: "Important" means important to you; "trivial" means important to the other person.

The Kitchen-Sink Technique

Throw everything into the argument but the kitchen sink. No need to stick to the issue at hand; now is the time to bring up all the other incidents that have been bothering you. Talk about his or her past failings or defects in character, past injustices, unsettled issues from the last argument, and so on. Before long, so many irrelevant issues will have been brought up that the other person will begin to feel that winning an argument with you is next to impossible.

Ambush—-The Art of Getting the Other Person Into a Corner

Be on the lookout for situations you can capitalize on later. Go through your spouse's wallet, listen in on the telephone extension, quiz your children's friends to find out what your kids have been up to. You will be amazed to find how much ammunition you can gather for your next fight. Once you have become proficient in this tactic, others will think twice about bringing up even the most legitimate grievance.

Note: Excerpts from *The "Dirty Fighter's" Instruction Manual* are reprinted with permission by Alan L. Summers, Transactional Dynamics Institute, Glenside, PA.

Session 8

Communication: Rules and Barriers

OBJECTIVES

The objective of this session is to teach the clients some general communications rules and their application. A second goal is to help clients become aware of the different barriers to effective communication.

MATERIALS

Weekly Behavior Inventory
Family Communication Rules handout

TASKS

1. Discuss mutually agreed on activities for the clients.
2. Review homework and weekly events.
3. Allow and encourage more role playing among clients and couples concerning problem areas.
4. Explain handout of *Family Communication Rules;* have clients role play.
5. Facilitate awareness by pointing out communication styles.
6. Give handouts and assign homework.

PROCEDURE

COUNSELING

Begin the session by asking the clients to fill out the *Weekly Behavior Inventory*. Before discussing any potential or violent incidents, talk about whether the clients participated in a mutually agreed on activity. In relation to this, the counselors might get information about what the clients enjoyed doing before they were married and while dating. Another good source of information and a way of rekindling some good feelings and memories is to get the couple to talk about how they met and what were the main characteristics they liked about their mate. Counselors at this point should consider whether the things that each liked about the other might be a source of discontent today. For example, if she thought he was so good-looking and strong at the beginning, she may now see him as thinking he is "God's gift to women" and domineering. Promote as much discussion as possible. The clients could then describe when they felt the first major problems in the relationship occurred and what the situation was at the time.

Now move back to what has been happening in the past week and any specific problems that occurred. Inquire as to how these were dealt with and if prior educational techniques had been used, such as the fair-fighting rules. Also, see if each did his or her homework assignment of labeling the dirty-fighting techniques each client uses. Let each tell about one or two techniques that he or she uses often and one or two the spouses use. Get feedback from the spouses in couples counseling as to their perceptions of their partners' choices. Watch for verbal and nonverbal cues of discontent. Check these out before proceeding to the next education section.

EDUCATION

To begin this educational session the counselor should talk generally about the importance of good communication in a relationship and the consequences that result when good communication doesn't exist. This would be a good place to lead into the *Family Communication Rules* handout. There are several opportunities for discussion and role play, so encourage client participation.

Ask for clients to express what they feel is the main drawback in their communication. Always bring discussion back to the positive. In this case, let them express what they feel could increase communication in their relationships. Check with the spouses in couples counseling to see if they feel this will be helpful. Make sure closure has occurred before giving the homework assignment and dismissing the group.

HOMEWORK

Suggest that clients read the handouts again and become aware of times when they were not communicating effectively and replace those techniques with some that are effective. Again, encourage the couples to spend time together doing a mutually pleasurable activity. Encourage them to spend time talking with each other about positive things they have learned in counseling. Suggest that each decide on one specific thing that has helped him or her thus far during the counseling and educational sessions. Give them *"I" Messages, Effective Expression and Listening*, and *Six Blocks to Listening* handouts to review for the next session.

RESOURCES

Bach, G. R., & Wyden, P. (1970). *The intimate enemy.* New York: Avon Books.
Martin, R. J. (1983). *A skills and strategies handbook for working with people.* Englewood Cliffs, NJ: Prentice-Hall.
McKay, M., Davis, M., & Fanning, P. (1983). *Messages: The communication book.* Oakland, CA: New Harbinger Publications.
Satir, V. (1967). *Conjoint family therapy* (rev. ed.). Palo Alto, CA: Science and Behavior Books.

Family Communication Rules

Handout

Counselors may explain all the following rules to clients, or use only those that are appropriate for a particular couple.

Rule 1:	Actions speak louder than words, or nonverbal communication is more powerful than verbal communication.

People always send two messages when they communicate. They send a verbal message and a nonverbal message. The verbal is what you say with words. The nonverbal is what your body, voice, and physical mannerisms indicate. This includes facial expressions, gestures, tone of voice, and so on. Because there are so many nonverbal ways to communicate, it is very difficult, if impossible, not to communicate.

Example   A contradictory, inconsistent, or double message—A husband comes in the door after work and his wife is sitting on the sofa with a sad look on her face and she does not speak. He says hello, gives her a kiss, and asks if everything is okay. She responds by saying everything is fine, but she turns her face away and starts to cry.

When a family member sees or hears a contradictory or inconsistent message, the contradiction should be pointed out, discussed, and resolved.
(Think of examples and role play both inconsistent and contradictory messages.)

Example   If a wife feels that her husband is giving one message verbally but another with his body posture or facial expression, she should question this. A way of doing this might be to say, "Honey, you're saying that you feel okay, but your face looks flushed. You look really tense and you seem very quiet. Is there anything you want to talk about?"

Sometimes it is helpful to practice communication rules before a mirror, paying particular attention to nonverbal messages and contradictions.

Rule 2:	Define what is important and emphasize it; define what is unimportant and ignore it.

One of the main problems with this rule is that few couples can find a topic that can be labeled unimportant. This rule covers faultfinding. When criticism is always used, it is called faultfinding and leads to destructive consequences in a family relationship. What is important would be constructive criticism from some concerned and loving partners who can express this in a nondestructive manner. Criticism is a necessary and important part of helping another person grow as a human being. Destructive criticism is just what the term implies, and one needs to decide the type of criticism he or she is going to give *before* giving it. Timing is an important factor because any criticism, at certain periods of stress, will not be accepted.

Couples who have trouble determining the differences between important and unimportant issues can have counselors examine the issues one by one to help agree on the classification. They must then stick to the agreed-on important topics and not refer to the unimportant matters. Problem-solving techniques will work in this area.

Family Communication Rules *(Continued)*

Example   "I'm so angry because you never talk to me, you don't help around the house, you
            always squeeze the toothpaste from the bottom of the tube, and you never smile at
            my mother."

It is important to decide what the major problem areas are and separate them from the picky
areas of faultfinding.

> **Rule 3:   Be clear and specific in communication.**

Being clear and specific in communication is especially important in problem solving. Some people tend to be very vague in their statements. A problem that is stated vaguely is less likely to be
solved than a problem that is stated clearly. The following are suggestions to help ensure clear,
specific communications:

1. **Discuss one problem at a time.**

   Some people tend to bring up a number of problems at one time. The more problems that
   are talked about at one time, the less likely it is that any of them will be solved.

Example   If the main issue that you want to solve is getting the rest of the family to help with
            household chores, then don't bring up other issues. "You and the children never
            help around the house. I know you don't like my mother, and you are never affec-
            tionate to me anymore."

2. **Avoid vagueness or generalities.**

   Define and clarify the terms and expression you use, and ask your partner to define and
   clarify his or her terms and expressions.

Example   "I don't like your **attitude.**" (Clarify attitude.)
            "You're never **nice** to my mother." (Clarify nice.)
            "I want you to be more **romantic.**" (Clarify what being more romantic would involve.)

3. **Do not accept the use of vague words by your partner.**

   Again, ask for feedback and clarity from your partner. Even one vague word in a confrontation with someone can lead to an argument, as meanings become lost through personal perception and interpretation. This perception of the other person's intent may or
   may not be accurate so probing is needed.

Example   "I'm feeling real **bummed out.**" (Check this out by asking the person what they mean
            by "bummed out.")
            "You **hurt** me." (How did I hurt you? What did I do that hurt you?)
            "You're acting **hostile.**" (What am I doing that makes you think I'm acting hostile?)

Family Communication Rules *(Continued)*

Handout

> **Rule 4:** Test all your assumptions verbally. Get your partner's okay before you make a decision that involves them.

Testing your assumptions is critical in relationships. Some people consider the failure to test an assumption or failure to consult with them regarding a decision as rude and insulting.

Example   A wife is told by her husband that he has invited another couple for dinner. He has "assumed" his wife would not mind. In fact, she may become angry, because she was not consulted. A woman decides to rearrange the bedroom furniture. The husband feels that he has been ignored and that his opinion does not matter.

Here again, mind-reading comes into play. Find out what mind-reading is, if you do not already know. Play a game called "I know something you don't think I know." Each person guesses what the other is thinking by nonverbal clues only. List at least four feelings or thoughts you believe the other is feeling or thinking. These must be conveyed with nonverbal information. Then check the perception verbally. How accurate were you? Can you afford to be wrong even one time? It is important to ask questions.

> **Rule 5:** Realize that each event can be seen from a different point of view.

One way to begin to discuss this rule is to check which sensory system each partner uses to relate to the environment and other people. These are visual (eye), auditory (ear), and kinesthetic (touch). Counselors can ask questions to help focus on which system is used most by the individuals. Then compare and see if they use the same system. If not, they can still communicate, but they must learn to use the other person's system to relate to him or her.

When a member of a family makes a statement from a perception that he or she believes to be true, another person may not agree because his or her interpretation of the situation presented is contrary to the first person's belief. When this happens, counselors need to draw attention to this discrepancy and have family members explain specifically what they mean.

> **Rule 6:** Learn to disagree without destructive arguments.

A discussion is an exchange of ideas or feelings, in which the objective is to solve a problem or reach more understanding.

An argument is an expression of ideas and feelings, but the intentions are to hurt the partner or raise one's own self-esteem at the expense of the partner. Arguments are often accompanied by intense anger, nagging, or whining.

Some will avoid a disagreement for several reasons. These are fear of losing control, losing the argument, having faults exposed, not wanting to hurt the other, and so on.

Learning the Fair-Fighting Rules can help reduce some of these fears. For contrast, counselors can use the *Dirty Fighter's Manual* for a humorous opposing view. It must be emphasized that this is a tongue-in-cheek approach. Even if discussions do not lead to positive results, they are still better than an argument that leads to hurt feelings, unfair attacks, sarcasm, and humiliation, in which case no one gains.

Family Communication Rules *(Continued)*

Rule 7:   Be open and honest about your feelings.

It is not likely that family members will *always* be open and honest. When discussing this rule, the counselors need to offer explanations. First, not all subjects need to be discussed openly.

Example   "I don't like your hair, your face has too many pimples, your ears are too large, I have gas, and so on."

Second, some issues that are not discussed need to be brought into the open if they are indirectly leading to the problems.

Example   If one member is angry about something but only keeps it inside, he or she may take it out on others by overcriticizing a minor event. This can lead to inappropriate, angry outbursts. This can also result in other members "walking on eggs" for reasons they are not sure of.

Third, an honest expression of feelings will let others know exactly what is going on and even if no answers can be found, at least the others are aware of the problem. A definition of the problem is the first step toward solving it, and this can be pointed out to the clients.

Rule 8:   Let the effect, not the intention, of your communication be your guide.

Often an unintentional hurtful comment can be made, and when the person realizes this, a countercomment such as "I didn't mean it" or "I was only kidding" does not solve the original hurt effect. This behavior will then influence the partner's perception of what is being communicated in future discussions. It is important for the one who is hurting the other to realize what the effect has been and that he or she created the hurt feelings. The intention of a comment must be in harmony with the actual verbal communication. When this problem is witnessed by the counselors, they need to bring attention to it and try to help create a clarification of effect and intent.

Rule 9:   Do not preach or lecture.

With children, lecturing can have its usefulness, but with teenagers and adults the benefits are limited. Little needs to be said about this rule except that lectures and sermons are generally destructive. They result in defensiveness or low self-esteem. If problems arise, the best course for counselors is to teach problem-solving techniques found in the session about problem solving.

Rule 10: Do not use excuses or fall for excuses.

The difference between excuses and reasons is the important aspect of this rule. A legitimate reason for being late is better than a made-up excuse. Excuses are used for repeated inconsiderate acts whether a family member, a boss, a coworker, or a friend is involved. Such statements (i.e.,

Family Communication Rules *(Continued)*

Handout

running out of gas) can be a reason if it happened once. It is an excuse if it happens over and over. Accepting excuses can lead to resentment and unresolved feelings of conflict and hostility.

Parents use excuses when communicating with their children, thereby teaching them to use excuses themselves. Parents will make excuses to the child when they are reluctant to give the real reason for saying "no" to a certain request.

Excuses are often rationalized and designed to fool the user him/herself. At the other end of the spectrum are excuses to protect him/herself from some unpleasant consequence. Many times both partners are aware of the invalidity of the excuse, but they say nothing. This allows some resentment or anger to develop that will one day surface in an argument or it may even be the reason for the argument.

> **Rule 11:** Learn when to use humor and when to be serious. Do not subject your partner to destructive teasing.

Humor when appropriately used is an important emotional resource. Humor clears the air and bring relief from pent-up tensions. Humor is pleasant, and people enjoy laughing with the one who elicits the humor. Humor can be destructive, however. This can occur when it is directed toward another for the purpose of making fun of the other person. Using humor to avoid an uncomfortable situation, when in reality the situation needs to be dealt with, is another time when humor is inappropriate.

There is an expression called "kid serious," which means that someone makes a hurting comment directed at another person and then follows that comment with "I was only kidding." The humor is lost and the hurt is all that is left. Kid serious is a game many play and it leads to hurt, anger, and resentment. Counselors need to point this out whenever it is observed and give other examples to clients. Role play can be used here. Kid serious robs communication of clarity and honesty, and it results in lowered self-esteem.

Teasing is another form of humor that can be destructive, depending on the intent and the person to whom it is directed. Children can tease each other and have fun; but when one teases another into doing something that will get the child in trouble, then the teasing becomes a problem. In general, teasing another about things over which he or she has no control (such as the shape of a nose, length of legs, etc.) and teasing for the purpose of making another do something he or she does not want to do should be avoided.

Session 9

Communication: Expression and Listening

OBJECTIVES

The objective of this session is to further develop communication skills through knowledge of expression and effective listening.

MATERIALS

Weekly Behavior Inventory
"I" Messages handout
Effective Expression and Listening handout
Six Blocks to Listening handout

TASKS

1. Review the *WBI* and group members' feelings about interactions.
2. Review homework and allow clients to share their own experiences.
3. Explain *"I" Messages* and role play examples.
4. Practice active listening and expression of clear messages.
5. Introduce *Blocks to Listening* and have clients discuss.
6. Give handouts and assign homework.

PROCEDURE

COUNSELING

Begin counseling by getting the clients to fill out the *Weekly Behavior Inventory*. As the clients talk about the happenings of the week and how the relationship is doing, investigate whether there were any problems or violence during the week and how they were dealt with. Discuss this as well as other issues brought up concerning the clients' feelings about the weekly activities. Make sure to get input on each person's feelings about what's being said. There have now been enough sessions to begin being more confrontive. There should be sufficient rapport as well as trust

114

between the clients and the counselors. Briefly and gently suggest that each person is responsible for his or her own behavior and reactions. This will set the groundwork to deal with this more strongly later. As part of last week's homework, the couple was to think of one specific thing in the counseling so far that has been helpful to them and their relationship. Give each couple in couples counseling an opportunity to share this and get each person's feelings about what the other says.

If time allows during the counseling segment, discuss another specific problem area of the relationship and help the clients or couples come up with options to deal with it. If possible, apply some of the techniques and education learned thus far in the program.

EDUCATION

Lead into the educational segment of this session by talking about the two major ways that we communicate. There is no real communication if it stays one-sided. Not only do we need to be able to express ourselves, but for true communication to take place, we need to be good listeners. Review the handouts about communicating effectively. Cover some role playing in Effective Expression and Listening. Do some role playing at various times to give the clients practice in applying these techniques. If time allows, briefly go over the *Six Blocks to Listening* handout. Ask the clients which block they use periodically.

HOMEWORK

Ask the clients, or partners in couples counseling, to spend a half hour twice during the week taking turns expressing themselves as well as actively listening to their partner. Encourage them to be aware of the times that the blocks to listening come up. Suggest they make written or mental notes so they can share this experience the following week. Give them the *Handling Criticism and How to Offer Criticism* handouts to review for the next session.

RESOURCES

Butler, P. E. (1981). *Self-assertion for women*. San Francisco: Harper & Row.

Gabor, D. (1983). *How to start a conversation and make friends*. New York: Fireside Books.

Garner, A. (1981) *Conversationally speaking*. New York: McGraw-Hill.

Martin, R. J. (1983). *A skills and strategies handbook for working with people*. Englewood Cliffs, NJ: Prentice-Hall.

McKay, M., Davis, M., & Fanning, P. (1983). *Messages: The communication book*. Oakland, CA: New Harbinger Publications.

Satir, V. (1967). *Conjoint family therapy* (rev. ed.). Palo Alto, CA: Science and Behavior Books.

"I" Messages

"I" messages are specific, nonjudgmental, and focus on the speaker. In contrast, "you" messages are hostile, blaming, and focus on the other person and cause him or her to feel attacked. Reframing "you" messages into "I" messages can help you communicate because the other person will not feel attacked. Being attacked and blamed makes most of us put up our defenses and get ready to fight.

To construct an "I" message:

1. Describe the **behavior** that is affecting you.
   (Just describe, don't blame.)
2. State your **feelings** about the consequence the behavior produces in you.
3. State the **consequence.**

An easy formula to construct "I" messages uses these phrases:

1. When you (state the behavior), _____ ,
2. I feel (state the feeling),_____ ,
3. Because (state the consequences), _____ .

Note: Stressing the word "because" can help by more strongly connecting the feeling and consequence elements of the message. This minimizes blame and keeps the focus on you.

The parts of an "I" message do not have to be delivered in order, and sometimes the inclusion of the feeling statement is not necessary. The important thing to remember is to keep the focus on you and avoid placing blame.

EXAMPLES

1. When you take long phone calls during dinner, I get angry because I begin to think you don't want to talk to me.
2. When you don't come home or call, I get scared because I'm afraid something has happened to you.
3. When you yell at me when things are hectic, I get so rattled that I end up making more mistakes.

Effective Expression and Listening

Handout

EFFECTIVE EXPRESSION

1. **Messages should be direct.**
   A. Know when something needs to be said. Don't assume that people know what you want or think.
   B. Don't be afraid to say how you feel or to ask for what you want. Avoid hinting.

   Example   During commercials a husband keeps asking if the movie is almost over, hoping his wife will get the hint that he wants her to spend time with him.

2. **Messages should be immediate.**
   A. Anger has a way of smoldering and building up; it may then come out in aggressive ways.
   B. There are two main advantages of immediate communications:

   • People are more apt to learn what you want and to make efforts to meet those needs or wants.
   • Intimacy increases because you are sharing your responses.

3. **Messages should be clear.**
   A. Don't ask questions when you need to make a statement.

   Example   "Do we really need to go to that party?" What may be meant is that the person doesn't really want to go.

   B. Make sure what you say verbally matches the nonverbal messages you might be giving. Avoid double messages.

   Example   You tell your spouse he needs to get out of the house more instead of sitting around watching TV. When he does get out of the house, however, you accuse him of always running off and leaving you to do everything at home.

Role Play

Practice saying "Right now I feel _____." and "Right now I want _____." Do this several times. Also, give feedback about what your partner has said and what you saw in your partner's nonverbal cues, such as tone of voice, eye contact, or how he or she holds his or her body while speaking.

   C. Distinguish between observations and thoughts. Determine what is happening (the facts) as opposed to your judgments, theories, beliefs, or opinions.
   D. Focus on one thing at a time. Stick with a topic. Don't jump around. It may be confusing as to why you are upset or what you want.

4. **Messages should be supportive.**
   A. Supportive messages are a way of honestly saying how you feel and what you want without intentionally devastating the other person.
   B. Ways of hurting someone:

   • Using labels such as you're stupid, lazy, evil, cruel, and so on
   • Using sarcasm
   • Dragging up the past
   • Using negative comparisons

Effective Expression and Listening *(Continued)*

- Using judgmental "you" messages: you never help me anymore
- Using threats: you threaten to leave or get a divorce

ACTIVE LISTENING

1. **Mirroring**
   A. Active listening or mirroring involves paraphrasing. Paraphrasing is stating in your own words what you think the other person has said.
   B. Active listening is a communication technique that enables you to be certain you understand what the other person is saying. It can also be used to make sure the other person understands what you are trying to say.
   C. Some lead-ins used in mirroring are:

      - What I hear you saying is . . .
      - In other words . . .
      - What happened was . . .
      - Do you mean . . .

2. **Clarifying**
   A. Clarifying is basically asking questions to get more information.
   B. Clarifying also lets the other person know you are interested in what he or she is saying.

3. **Feedback**
   A. Feedback is letting your spouse know about your perceptions, reactions, and what is happening inside you concerning the situation or discussion at hand.
   B. Feedback helps the other person know the effect of his or her communication. This allows the opportunity to clarify any error or misunderstanding in the communication.
   C. Feedback should be immediate, honest, and supportive.

Role Play

Talk to your partner and use the types of phrases that follow. Give time for your partner to respond.

"I notice (body gesture or expression) and I wonder what that means."

Example   "I noticed that you slammed the door and kicked the cat when you came in and I wonder what that means."

"I notice (body gesture or expression) and I am afraid it means _____."

Example   "I notice that your body posture is stiff, your legs and arms are crossed and you refuse to make eye contact with me, and I am afraid it means that you are angry with me."

Clear up any ambiguity and talk about what you meant to communicate.

Effective Expression
and Listening *(Continued)*

4. **Empathy**
    A. Empathy means trying to understand what the person is feeling. This does not mean that you agree.
    B. Try to understand what danger the person might be experiencing, what he or she is asking for, and what need is producing the emotion (i.e., anger).

5. **Openness**
    A. Listen without judging or finding fault.
    B. Try to see the other person's point of view. This does not mean you have to agree.
    C. Listen to the whole statement; don't make premature evaluations.

6. **Awareness**
    A. How does the information being communicated fit with known facts?
    B. Listen and look for agreement between what is being said and the nonverbal expressions that are present.

Note: **Some keys to being a good listener:** Have good eye contact, lean slightly forward, reinforce by nodding or paraphrasing, clarify by asking questions, avoid distractions, try to understand empathetically what was said.

Six Blocks to Listening

1. **Comparing**—How someone measures up.
   Example   Direct—"You've been on your job just as long as Bill has, but he's a supervisor."
   Less Direct—"Don't those tall men look so lean and handsome." (Your partner is short and broad.)

2. **Mind-Reading**—Assume you know what the person is thinking or feeling.
   Example   "I know what you're thinking. You're afraid if I go do anything that I'm going to flirt with women."

3. **Filtering**—Selective listening. Does not hear all that is said.
   Example   After an evening out, the wife says to the husband, "Really fun evening, the restaurant was nice, but the drive was too long." All the husband heard was the last comment about the drive, he took it as a negative put-down, and says, "You never want to have a good time with me; you are never happy."

4. **Identifying**—This means referring everything to your own experience.
   Example   Someone is trying to tell you about a problem with his or her boss and you start telling him or her about your problems.

5. **Advising**—Problem solving without permission.
   Example   A woman comes in and tells husband about a problem at work. He immediately gives her a laid out plan of action. All she wanted was for him to listen.

6. **Being Right**—Wanting to win.
   Example   Seeing every discussion as an opportunity to win instead of trying to compromise; making excuses if you can't win.

Talk about which of these blocks to listening you use. You can role play some of these in Group.

Session 10

Communication: Handling Criticism

OBJECTIVES

The objectives of this session are to teach the clients and have them experience some specific ways to give and handle criticism effectively.

MATERIALS

Weekly Behavior Inventory
Handling Criticism handout
How to Offer Criticism handout

TASKS

1. Review homework and have clients discuss events.
2. Point out nonverbal messages and cues.
3. Encourage interaction and discussion among couples.
4. Explain *Handling Criticism* and typical negative responses.
5. Model positive techniques and have group members role play.
6. Introduce *How to Offer Criticism*.
7. Give handouts and assign homework.

PROCEDURE

COUNSELING

Have the clients fill out the *Weekly Behavior Inventory*. Check to see how each person is doing and if there are any specific problems the group needs to talk about. There are usually several problem areas that the clients and couples have experienced during the week. Having enough time to deal with them and getting closure usually presents difficulty. It is seldom that everything has been "hunky dory" all week for the couples. Sometimes they say "no problem," but if you watch for the nonverbal cues such as tone of voice, body posture, attitude, or general tension, you will know there is something going on. If a couple refuses to look at each other or continually glares at each other, there is definitely a problem. Other cues are usually easily observed. In this case, investigate further and in most situations the clients will begin to open up.

It seems that when one person begins to talk, others feel more freedom to do so. If you are conducting groups, they should have bonded well enough by now to take risks and open up. Counselors can aid this process by sharing something personal about their own relationships whether it is work related or with a spouse.

After dealing with some of the specifics of the week and how the couple dealt with them, check for the homework assignments. The assignment for this week was for the partners to spend a half hour twice during the week taking turns expressing themselves as well as listening to their partners. They were also to be aware of communication blocks that might come up during the communication process. Have each partner share his or her experiences and feelings about the mutual activity for the past week. The counselor could explore whether the time together is beneficial to the couple and to the relationship. Explore positive and negative aspects of responses.

EDUCATION

Usually spouses are critical of each other whether in a constructive or destructive way. It is difficult for most people to deal with criticism and in most cases they get defensive. Of course, at that point good communication has stopped. A major part of communicating effectively is learning to give constructive criticism as well as to receive criticism. Therefore, the objective of this session is to teach the clients skills and tips in giving and taking criticism. Review the *Handling Criticism* handout. The nonconstructive ways of dealing with criticism can be portrayed in a humorous way, similar to the tongue-in-cheek way the dirty-fighting techniques were presented. Again, the counselor can use examples to clarify each one or role play exercises. Examples and role play should also be used when teaching constructive ways of handling criticism.

After practicing handling criticism, talk about the *How to Offer Criticism* handout. These are some specific guidelines for giving criticism to others.

HOMEWORK

For a homework assignment, ask the clients to write down two examples of when they felt their partner was being critical. Have them write their feelings, whether the criticism was constructive or destructive. Have them consider whether the other person could have handled the situation differently and how they would have preferred the other person to handle it. The client should also practice giving and receiving criticism with his partner. Ask members to be prepared to discuss this briefly next time.

Also, have couples continue a mutually pleasurable activity. It doesn't have to be the same thing. It might even be better for them to try a variety of activities to see which ones they might prefer. Sometimes if couples do the same thing all the time it gets boring and isn't as much fun. At this point they could do something that the spouse really likes but that they don't totally object to. It may a good idea to have one spouse plan the activity this week and then the other do so next week.

The couple can continue to alternate the planning of their weekly "dates." Have the members review the *How Do You Feel Today?* and *Jealousy: Taming the Green-Eyed Monster* handouts.

RESOURCES

Bach, G. R., & Wyden, P. (1970). *The intimate enemy.* New York: Avon Books.

Butler, P. E. (1981). *Self-assertion for women.* San Francisco: Harper & Row.

Garner, A. (1981). *Conversationally speaking.* New York: McGraw-Hill.

McKay, M, Davis, M., & Fanning, P. (1983). *Messages: The communication book.* Oakland, CA: New Harbinger Publications.

Handling Criticism

Everyone is occasionally criticized by someone. No one is perfect. How you handle criticism is especially important in intimate relationships. It is not uncommon to react (respond) defensively to critical observations.

Typical responses to criticism are:

NEGATIVE

1. **Avoid the criticism or critic.** Ignore, change the subject, make jokes (be funny), refuse to talk about it, be too busy, withdraw, or even walk away.

   Examples   When someone says something critical to you, don't respond verbally, just give the person a "go to hell" look, and walk out of the room.

   When the other person is talking to you, look at the floor, stare into space, or just look through the person. Avoid making direct eye contact.

   Make statements indicating that you are just "too busy" to deal with the person right now. "Okay, get with me later, I'm late for an important meeting."

   "I don't want to talk about this: Subject closed!"

   Your boss is upset because you were drunk at the party last night and really acted crazy. Make light of what he is saying by saying, "Yeah, did you see me dancing on that table with a bucket on my head?"

   Suppose you are late for work and your boss confronts you. You could change the subject by talking about how you're going to have to get your car fixed so it will be more reliable.

2. **Deny the critical comment.** Deny facts, argue, present evidence, do not entertain the idea of accepting anything.

   Examples   Argue about what the facts are. Fight about all the minor details.

   "No, I wasn't late on Monday, I think it was Tuesday."

   "No, I didn't call your mother a toad, I said she was always croaking about something."

   Deny that it happened: "I wasn't drunk at the party."

3. **Make excuses.** Explain your behavior in detail, be very sorry, have an alibi or excuse, or argue the importance of your behavior.

   Examples   You were late to pick your spouse up, so you go into detail about how the keys got lost, you had to search for them, and the baby is always losing everything. Your spouse will soon just want to forget he or she ever said anything.

   Again, you are late and your spouse is upset: "Well, it was just a movie, look at all the important things I have to take care of everyday."

   "So I had my tongue in her ear at the party, that doesn't mean I care about her. You know you're the only one for me."

Handling Criticism *(Continued)*

Handout

4. **Fight Back.** Attack, get even, the best defense is the best offense, fight fire with fire.

   Examples   Suppose a family member says something about you gaining weight. Attack this person's weight, housekeeping, handwriting, parenting skills, and so on. or you can get even by burning the meal or being late when he or she really wanted to be somewhere on time.

POSITIVE

1. **Ask for details.** Criticisms are often vague or given in generalities. "You're lazy" or "I don't like the way you're acting." When you ask for details you find out exactly what the other person is talking about. When you ask for details try to find out who, what, where, when, and how.

   Examples   **Who** do I pick on?

   Exactly **what** did I do that hurt your feelings?

   When was I late?

   Where did this take place?

   Why do you think I don't consider your feelings?

   How do I act when you say I bore you?

2. **Agree with the accurate part of the criticism.** A second step to handling criticism effectively is to agree with the part of the criticism that is true. Even if you feel the other person is completely wrong, you can use two types of agreement statements.

   A. Agree with the truth. Agree with the accurate part of what is being said.

      - Do not put yourself down.
      - You do not have to agree to change.
      - Do not defend yourself.
      - Use self-disclosure instead of self-defense.
      - Watch for generalities in the criticism.
      - Listen, attend, and monitor.

   Example   Your spouse says, "You were rude to my mother." Respond, "Yes, I was rude to her that one time when I said her red dress looked like a gunny sack."

   B. Agree with the critic's right to an opinion. This doesn't mean you have to agree with his or her opinion.

      - Avoid issues of right/wrong, good/bad, okay/not okay.
      - Use self-disclosure.
      - You do not have to defend your opinion, but you may wish to explain if possible.
      - Listen, attend, and monitor.

Handling Criticism *(Continued)*

Example   Suppose you go to a movie and you like the movie but the other person did not enjoy it. "I enjoyed the movie, I guess we have different tastes in movies." These agreement statements will decrease the chances of the person being defensive.

General guidelines for handling criticism

- Learn to see criticism as an opportunity to learn and grow.
- Try to avoid being defensive.
- Listen actively.
- Use attending behavior.
- Watch nonverbal language.
- Monitor physical and emotional cues.
- Act, do not react.

How to Offer Criticism

Handout

1. **Cool down.** Try to avoid offering criticism when you are too emotional. Wait until you have better control of your emotions.

2. **Consider your intent.** Realize the difference between constructive and destructive criticism. Is your intent to create a more positive relationship or zap your partner?

3. **Separate fact from fantasy.** Did your partner really use most of the gas in your car so that you would run out of gas in a bad part of town and be killed? Try to be rational.

4. **Do it now.** Try to offer criticism as soon after the act as possible. This will help you avoid saving up grievances for an emotional explosion in the future. Also, it is usually much easier to deal with something that just happened, rather than trusting a faulty memory.

5. **Make an appointment.** If you can't do it now, make an appointment to discuss it later. Both should agree on time, length of discussion, place, and content.

6. **Offer ideas, suggestions, and options.** It is helpful if you can offer possible solutions, constructive alternatives, or any ideas to solve the problem. Think of it as a team effort.

7. **Know when to be emotional, and when to be logical.** It is acceptable and healthy to talk about how you feel about a particular behavior; but when it comes to problem solving, it is generally best to be more logical.

8. **Do not play psychologist.** Try to limit comments regarding the causes, motives, or unconscious meaning of another person's behavior. Focus on the behavior and possible solutions to the problem.

9. **Be specific.** Avoid generalizations in criticism. No one can change unless he or she knows exactly what you want. Consider who, what, when, where, why, and how when you offer criticism.

10. **Praise in public, criticize in private.** No one likes to have his or her faults pointed out in front of an audience. On the other hand, most people won't object to a little public stroking.

11. **Praise more than you criticize.** It is okay to criticize, even necessary and productive if done correctly; but remember that people are more likely to respond favorably to criticism if they receive praise on a regular basis.

Session 11

Identification of Feelings

OBJECTIVES

To become aware of a full range of emotions; to learn to express emotions more directly, disclose feelings, and accurately listen to the feelings of others.

MATERIALS

Weekly Behavior Inventory
How Do You Feel Today? handout
Jealousy: Taming the Green-Eyed Monster handout

TASKS

1. Have group check in and review homework.
2. Have clients discuss weekly interactions and problem areas, and role play alternative techniques.
3. Describe types of feelings and review handout.
4. Introduce concept of jealousy and review handout.
5. Role play examples of jealousy and encourage group participation.
6. Give handouts and assign homework.

PROCEDURE

COUNSELING

Have the members fill out the *Weekly Behavior Inventory.* Let the clients check in and share accomplishments or problems that occurred during the week. Discuss the homework assignments from the last session. Point out different techniques that the group members have learned and are applying. During this session, briefly review the *Handling Criticism* handout and the homework assignments. Let the clients share what they wrote down when their spouse was critical. Have them share their feelings at the time and whether they thought the criticism was constructive or destructive. It is also very important to inquire what their response (behaviors) were to the criticism. Ask each how he or she have wanted his or her spouse to have presented the criticism. Get feedback from each partner in couples counseling, as well as other group members.

Briefly have the clients talk about their mutually pleasurable activities. Have each partner in couples counseling share his or her feelings about this activity. Determine if both are enjoying this or if one is just going along to please the other. Discuss this in more detail if needed. Especially at this time emphasize being open about feelings. How have these activities affected the relationship?

Now proceed to dealing with a specific problem area for each client. Try to come to some resolution or compromise for the clients or couples. Use as many of the techniques learned during counseling as possible. Have the clients describe recent examples of good and poor communication. Role play possible ways that communication could have been improved.

EDUCATION

Men have feelings, but they usually do not acknowledge or express them. Men often cut themselves off from a full range of feelings because of their socialization into a "macho" role. In general, though, it is difficult for men and women to know themselves, much less be able to express themselves to others. It is not the case, as many assume, that men do not have feelings. What happens is that the softer feelings of hurt and fear become quickly converted into anger and then into aggression. Men feel, but it often isn't very obvious to themselves or to others. Many women are able to express certain feelings but not others.

Explain that women and men cheat themselves by not knowing themselves fully. The tendency for men to hold in the "soft" emotions or to act out the "tough" ones helps to explain why men die 7 years earlier than women on the average. A common fear is that if men express hurt or fear the other person will use this against them. In a close relationship, just the opposite will happen. The tendency for women to be nonassertive can prevent them from getting their needs met. Continuing passivity and caretaking can lead to a negative self-image and subsequently to anger and hostility. Not expressing these feelings can foster resentment.

Explain that feelings are emotional states. There are four primary feelings: sadness, joy, fear, and anger. Just as the primary colors have many shades and hues, so there are many shades to feelings.

List the four primary feelings across the top of the board. Ask the clients to name similar feelings under the primary ones. Point out the range of intensity in the examples given. Emphasize the importance of expressing feelings when they first arise—at the low intensities. Use the *How Do You Feel Today?* handout for examples of feelings. Briefly discuss jealousy as one of the strongest emotions, and that it is often based on fantasy stemming from insecurity and fear. This feeling is often based on cultural norms and ideas that can lead to aggression and anger, stifling a relationship. Explain the points made in the first part of the handout *Jealousy: Taming the Green-Eyed Monster.* Give them the handout and read or paraphrase one or more stories. Discuss similar feelings that they may have experienced (adapted from D. G. Saunders, 1990).

DISCUSSION QUESTIONS

What feelings were you punished for having as a child? What positive things can you tell yourself when you show hurt or fear? The key to intimacy and closeness is the exchange of feelings. We think that "intimacy" means sexual contact, but it is something quite different. If irritation, frustration, anger, and rage are expressed verbally, there is also a good chance that they will decrease in strength.

Explain that the group members will find the greatest closeness with their partners when they exchange feelings with them.

Explain that expressing feelings lets the other person know what is going on with you. If done correctly, expressing feelings avoids the common pattern of blaming others or defending oneself. Expressing feelings when they first occur keeps them from building up.

- Take a moment to look inside yourself and ask, "What am I feeling? Do I have more than one feeling right now?"
- State your feelings without blaming the other. A good way of doing this is to include the phrase "I feel . . ." in the statement.

  Example   "I'm feeling sad right now because I'm thinking about my mother's death."

  "When you ask if I've been job-hunting, I feel hurt and annoyed because I think you are being critical."

  "I feel lots of satisfaction from coaching Little League."

- Avoid disguising thought or opinions as feelings. For example, "I feel you are on my back a lot" is not a feeling statement even though the phrase "I feel" is used. Ask the clients to practice the skill in pairs or with partners, or in the group. Provide some situations on the board for them to use and some guides for giving feedback to each other. What did the other person do well? What else could have been done to make it better? (Adapted from D. G. Saunders, 1990.)

HOMEWORK

Give the clients the *Emotional Awareness and Expression* handout to complete and bring to the next session. Couples should also continue sharing a mutually enjoyable activity. It is also recommended that clients and their partners devote time during the week to openly expressing feelings.

How Do You Feel Today?

Handout

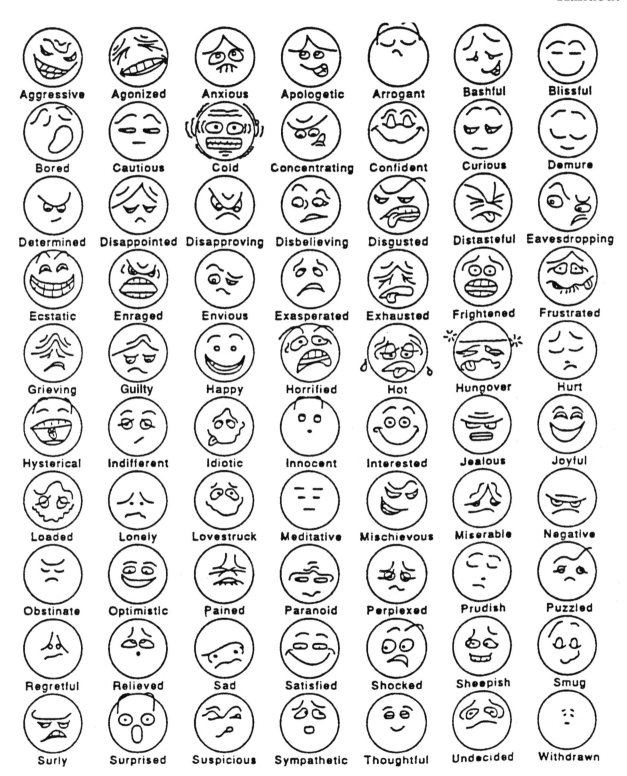

Jealousy: Taming the Green-Eyed Monster

Handout

Jealousy is one of those emotions that can tie our stomach in knots in a hurry. A little bit of jealousy is natural, especially when we fear losing someone close to us. Jealousy becomes a problem when we spend too much energy worrying about losing a loved one, when we let jealousy build and we try to control another through aggression, or when we stifle a relationship by placing extreme restrictions on our partners.

Pete got himself really worked up whenever he went to a party with his wife, Sue. It seemed that she was attracted to some of the other men, and apparently they were attracted to her. Deep inside he was afraid that she would find another man more attractive and exciting than he was. He feared losing her love. But what usually happened after a party was a fight, a fight not about jealousy but about some other matter.

One day after one of these fights, Pete was thinking about how upset he made himself with jealousy. He tried to look at the situation in a more objective way—the way an outside observer would. After a while he was able to say to himself: "There are many aspects of my wife I find attractive. It is only natural that other men will sometimes find her attractive too. If that happens, it does not mean I will lose her. My fears and anger come from doubting my worth, not from other people's behavior and thoughts. If other men like my partner, then they agree with my opinion of her, and that's positive."

Joe's jealousy was even stronger than Pete's. He would question his wife at length when she came home, asking where she had been, who she had been with, and the details of her activities. He sometimes tore himself up wondering if she was having an affair. He would get urges to follow her everywhere or demand that she stay home. It seemed that the more he questioned her the more he disbelieved her.

It was after hearing his friend, Steve, talk about wanting to have an affair that he realized what was happening. The times when he was most suspicious of his wife were the times when he had sexual fantasies or romantic fantasies about other women. Now when he noticed jealousy, he asked himself, "Am I projecting my fantasies onto my partner because I'm feeling guilty about them?"

For many men, mentioning jealous feelings is not a cool thing to do—to admit jealousy is to admit a weakness. If, however, you view some jealousy as natural and as another "okay" emotion to share with your partner, both you and your partner can have the privilege of getting to know each other better.

Sally found the best way for her to "tame the monster" was to let her husband know she felt jealous. She felt very relieved being able to talk about the subject. Instead of responding with ridicule, her husband seemed to respect her more. Both of them went on to tell each other which of their partner's behaviors they could not tolerate—affairs, flirting, and so on. They were able to work out some contracts that specified the limits of the relationship.

What Pete, Joe, and Sally learned about taming jealousy was the following:

- Some jealousy is normal, and it's best to talk about it rather than hide it.
- I can choose to see my partner's attractiveness and behavior as either negative or positive—if I see it negatively, I am likely to upset myself and waste energy.
- It will help me to ask: "Is my jealousy coming from a projection of my own fantasies or behavior?"
- I have a right to request and contract for some **specific** limits on my partner's behavior (not thoughts), and my partner has the same right.

Adapted from *Alternatives to Aggression* by Daniel G. Saunders (1990).

Session 12

Emotional Awareness and Expressing Feelings

OBJECTIVES

The objective of this session is to increase the participants' awareness and expression of their own emotional and physical arousal states and to increase their ability to properly identify the nature of their anger. By accomplishing these objectives, there will be a greater chance of decreasing the potential for violent reactions that result from emotional arousal.

MATERIALS

Weekly Behavior Inventory
Emotional Awareness and Expression handout
Anger Styles handout
Abusive-Incidents Graph handout

TASKS

1. Review *WBI* and levels of violence/intimidation since treatment began; obtain feedback from group members.
2. Reinforce clients' progress and discuss changes.
3. Discuss homework assignment.
4. Model appropriate communication styles and have clients practice and role play.
5. Introduce the *Anger Styles* handout.
6. Use humor to explain examples; complete *Abusive-Incidents Graph*.
7. Give handouts and assign homework.

PROCEDURE

COUNSELING

The counselor should ask the clients to fill out the *Weekly Behavior Inventory*. While finding out about the week, evaluate the level of violence and abuse that has occurred since the beginning of the counseling. Get feedback from the clients about the level of violence, the changes in the relationship, and what they attribute the changes to. We hope at this point there has been a noticeable decrease in the level of violence and an increase in the well-being of the relationship.

After this has been completed, discuss the homework assignments. Ask if each client was able to talk about some "I feel" statements and give feedback to his partner. Also, give the clients an opportunity to talk about some of the feelings they could not express and the possible reasons for this. If they did not do this at home, let each couple practice during this time or have group members pair up to do this.

Next, go over the *Emotional Awareness and Expression* homework assignment. Talk about each situation listed and go through the five steps of awareness and expression. It is likely that other situations that are more relevant to the clients will come up. Discuss these and apply the steps in teaching the clients how to be aware of their feelings and express them in "I feel" statements. The counselors may need to do some role playing for this. Get feedback from the clients about the usefulness of this exercise.

This session would be a good time to find out the clients' views of the quantity and quality of time in their relationship. Get a consensus of opinion from each client or couple and a decision for change where it is necessary.

EDUCATION

Active Listening

Active listening takes work, especially when there is conflict in a close relationship. Active listening is a skill like other communication skills and with practice it can become a habit.

Explain that to be close to others and to resolve conflict, we all need to improve our ability to listen accurately. To grasp the meaning of what is said, some activity is needed on the part of the listener. The goal is to show the other person through your words that you really understood what was said. Once that is accomplished, the other person is likely to have the good feeling of being understood. As clients might guess, the skill is most difficult to apply in the heat of an argument. Remind the group to review the handouts in Session 9.

Summarize the following guidelines on the board:

1. Before responding with your own thoughts or feelings, say back to the other person in you own words what you just heard them say—*paraphrase.*
2. Focus in particular on the person's stated feelings or ones you imagine the other person has—*tune into feelings.*
3. Ask if you are "on target"—*don't assume, ask questions.*
4. If necessary, *make corrections* in what you said to improve the accuracy.
5. Once you have captured the meaning of the other person's statements, *express your own feelings.*

Example:

Woman:	Sometimes I wonder if you care at all about the kids. You spend hardly any time with them.
Man:	Are you angry that I've been gone a lot this last month?
Woman:	Yes, and hurt too! Do you really care?
Man:	You're hurt and angry I've been away from all of you?
Woman:	Yes, I wish you didn't have to travel so much.
Man:	Me too. I missed all of you a lot, and it feels good to know that you want me around more.

A defensive response to the partner's first statement might have sounded like this:

Man: Are you crazy? Of course I care about the kids! I just brought them back lots of gifts didn't I?! Don't say stupid things like that!

Note that when stating back what was just heard, it is often best to put it in question form unless you are very sure what the other person is feeling. For example, "Are you angry?" or "You sound really angry," rather than "I know you're angry" or "I really know why you're angry." The latter is a form of mind-reading that will escalate arguments. (Example adapted from D. G. Saunders, 1990.)

DISCUSSION

Have the clients think of a statement they can recall their partner saying that seemed to trigger defensiveness. How could they have responded with active listening? Have the clients practice the skill in pairs, with their partners, or before the entire group. Give constructive feedback after each rehearsal and have the person repeat the rehearsal. Finish with more feedback.

The counselor should review the basic anger-management information used in Session 3. Encourage the clients to give examples for each of the three components of emotion, and especially in relationship to anger. Emphasize the importance of these components in managing anger effectively. Have the client talk about the specifics of increasing awareness and let them role play using "I feel" emotion statements.

The counselor could take all of the *Weekly Behavior Inventories* to give to each client so he can see the changes in the number of abusive incidents. Have the clients, during the session, use the *Abusive-Incidents Graph* to plot the results. If there are time constraints, the counselors can either plot the results themselves or have an assistant do so, so they will be ready to give to the clients in Group. The counselors should give lots of reinforcement to the clients or couples for their effort in accomplishing these positive changes. If there have not been positive results thus far, the counselors should openly discuss and get feedback from the clients as to why there have not been changes and what it will take to produce some. This might be a good time for each client to review his or her commitment to work on the relationship and to implement the techniques they have learned thus far.

HOMEWORK

Give the clients the *Self-Esteem Dynamics* handout and assign the *Self-Concept Life Graph* as homework. Couples should also continue having some specific amount of time together doing something mutually enjoyable and expressing their feelings openly with "I" messages.

RESOURCES

Deschner, J. P. (1984). *The hitting habit: Anger control for battering couples.* New York: Free Press.

Ellis, A. (1977). *Anger: How to live with and without it.* Secaucus, NJ: Citadel Press.

Ellis, A., & Harper, R. A. (1975). *A new guide to rational living.* North Hollywood, CA: Wilshire Book Company.

Madow, L. (1972). *Anger: How to recognize and cope with it.* New York: Charles Scribner & Sons.

McKay, M., Davis, M., & Fanning, P. (1981). *Thoughts and feelings: The art of cognitive stress intervention.* Oakland, CA: New Harbinger Publications.

Weisinger, H. (1985). *Anger work out book.* New York: Quill.

Emotional Awareness and Expression

For each situation that follows:

- **Acknowledge your feelings.**
- **Identify the specific emotions felt.**
- **Describe the physical sensations are you having.**
- **Express how you feel by using "I feel" statements.**

Your spouse was going to meet you downtown for lunch, and you have been waiting over an hour. She finally arrives and says she had a few errands to run before she came.

You are visiting your mother-in-law and she says, "You've gained some weight, haven't you?" You are sensitive about your weight.

You are well qualified for a promotion, but your boss promotes his best friend who is not as qualified and has been there only a short time.

You are late getting home and your spouse demands an explanation, but as soon as you begin he/she interrupts and starts yelling and saying how inconsiderate you are.

Anger Styles

People have different ways of expressing anger. Understanding each other's anger style may make it easier for us to live with one another.

FIVE ANGER STYLES

1. **The Terrible-Tempered Mr. Bangs**   Anger is part of these people's daily lives. They have a tendency to take everything very personally and do not trust anyone. This type will run you off the road or swear at you if your driving displeases him.

2. **The Quiet Ones**   When these people get angry they tend to withdraw. They may not speak for days or might just mope around letting you guess what is going on. Even when asked, he or she may say very politely and coldly, "Nothing's wrong." This person's battle plan is to simulate "The Cold War."

3. **The Martyr**   These people may be very upset inside but not show any outward anger at all. They have a tendency to be indirect in their attack plan. They may be continually late or burn your favorite meal.

4. **The Hipshooter**   These people are quick to become angry, but get over it just as quickly. They may be impulsive, volatile, and wonder why the other person is still upset after they have already forgotten what they were upset about.

5. **The Counterattackers**   These people hide anger by being critical of others. They may give the message: "If you don't like me, I don't like you."

Decide what your anger styles are, and if any of the preceding types describes you. What about your partner?

Abusive-Incidents Graph
Physical—Verbal—Sexual

**Number of
Incidents
Per Week**

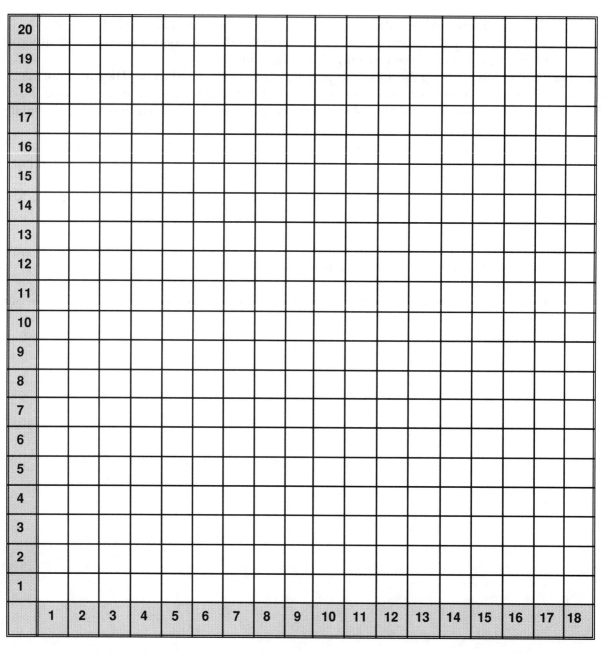

Week

III

Self-Management and Assertiveness

Session 13

Dynamics of Self-Esteem

OBJECTIVES

The objective of this session is to improve clients' self-esteem and educate them about the dynamics and importance of a person's self-concept.

MATERIALS

Weekly Behavior Inventory
Self-Esteem Dynamics handout
Self-Concept Homework handout
Inventory of Strengths and Weaknesses handout
Self-Concept Life Graph handout

TASKS

1. Check in with group members.
2. Review weekly events and have clients share their experiences.
3. Role play situations with clients or couples.
4. Discuss *Self-Esteem Dynamics,* and have partners or other group members give positive statements about each other.
5. Discuss the *Self-Concept Life Graph.*
6. Have couples or clients continue "fun" activity during week.
7. Give handouts, explain and assign homework.
8. Do evaluations of clients and have them evaluate therapists.

PROCEDURE

COUNSELING

Begin the session by having the clients fill out the *Weekly Behavior Inventory.* Let the clients check in and share the accomplishments or problems of the week. Encourage them to share situations that they handled effectively. Give lots of positive reinforcement anytime they handled a situation well. Discuss their experiences and feelings concerning the guidelines for communicating and expressing feelings that have been emphasized in the recent sessions. Go over the specifics of particular examples reported by the clients or couples, both those that were positive and those that were not resolved. Role play better ways to improve the communication; have the couples, or group members, do most of the role playing, with the counselors providing appropriate interventions and comments as needed. Try to use positive examples during the counseling segment of the sessions.

EDUCATION

For the educational segment of the session, review the *Self-Esteem Dynamics* handout. Go over the handout, giving examples and applications to each client where possible. Discuss the *Self-Concept Life Graph*, and have group members relate their graph to current situations.

Get input from the partners, if possible, about their own self-concepts and what they view as their positive or negative traits. Generally discuss the characteristics of men who are violent toward their partners and women who are in abusive relationships. Note that most research indicates that both the abuser and the abused woman usually have equally low self-esteem. Have each person think about his or her own esteem level and whether they feel that self-esteem can be changed. To aid the partners in understanding and becoming aware of their self-esteem, have them do the homework assignments.

HOMEWORK

For the homework assignment, give the clients the *Self-Concept Homework* and the *Inventory of Strengths and Weaknesses* handouts. This assignment will help them become aware of how they feel about themselves. It will also help them see which life situations have contributed to these feelings and what their present strengths and weaknesses are. The clients are to fill out the homework sheets and bring them to the next session. Have them also complete the *Inventory of Strengths and Weaknesses* for their partners as well.

Also, have the clients continue doing some activity together. The counselor could suggest that the couple begin to increase their time together. This time could be used in a "fun" activity or to talk about something specific in the relationship.

RESOURCES

Coopersmith, S. (1967). *The antecedents of self-esteem.* San Francisco: W. H. Freeman.
Hamachek, D. E. (1971). *Encounters with the self.* New York: Pocket Books.
Harris, T. A. (1973). *I'm OK—You're OK.* New York: Avon Books.
Lair, J. (1972). *I ain't much, baby, but I'm all I got.* New York: Fawcett Crest.

Self-Esteem Dynamics

Handout

Self-esteem is the value we choose to place on ourselves. It is how we view ourselves, not how others view or value us. We tend to perceive, judge, and act in ways consistent with our self-esteem.

TYPES OF SELF-ESTEEM

1. **Positive Self-Esteem**—This is viewing yourself as worthwhile.
2. **Negative Self-Esteem**—This is viewing yourself as worthless or only worthwhile if you accomplish what you think you should. Sometimes people with negative or low self-esteem have an **inferiority complex.** They may have strong and persistent doubts about their competence. They may feel less important, inadequate, or worthless in comparison to others.

SYMPTOMS OF AN INFERIORITY COMPLEX

- Sensitivity to criticism
- Inappropriate response to flattery
- Tendency toward blaming
- Hypercritical attitude
- Feeling of persecution
- Inappropriate feelings about competition
- Tendency toward remoteness, shyness, and timidity

DIFFERENT AREAS OF SELF-CONCEPTS

1. **Identity**—A person's identity involves having direction for his or her life. It involves answering such questions as "Who am I?" and "What's my purpose in life?"
2. **Self-Acceptance**—Self-acceptance involves knowing and accepting the strengths and weaknesses you have and feeling that you are okay.
3. **Self-Satisfaction**—Self-satisfaction involves being satisfied with who you are and where you are on the road of life. Some dissatisfaction is healthy, because it motivates people to strengthen their weaknesses or change their situations.
4. **Moral, Ethical Self**—The moral, ethical self relates to how you feel about yourself in relation to being ethical in dealing with others and in doing what you feel is right or wrong. It could relate to how you feel about your relationship to a superior being such as God.
5. **Physical Self**—The physical self involves how you feel about your physical appearance, your body, and about your health.
6. **Personal Self**—The personal self relates to how you feel you present yourself to others. It could involve the use of gestures, facial expression, and nonverbal expression.
7. **Family Self**—The family self relates to how you feel about yourself in relation to your family, husband, wife, children, or parents. It could involve whether there are problems in the relationship, or whether you feel the "family" likes you or thinks you are okay.
8. **Peer Self**—The peer self relates to how you feel about yourself in relation to those outside your family. This could include friends, fellow employees, or employers.

Self-Esteem Dynamics *(Continued)*

Handout

WHY IS SELF-ESTEEM SO IMPORTANT

1. It determines how we let others treat us.
2. It affects the decisions and choices we make, such as the spouse we choose, the friends we choose, employment, and so on.
3. It affects our academic and career achievement.
4. It affects how motivated we are or how hard we try.

WHICH SIGNIFICANT FACTORS INFLUENCE OUR SELF-ESTEEM?

1. Parents, family
2. Social class, money
3. Intellectual ability
4. Physical appearance, face, body type
5. Job, role
6. Education
7. Physical strength, stamina
8. Sexual prowess

Some of these are areas that are difficult or impossible to make major changes in and often need to be accepted. One's self-esteem need never become entirely dependent on any of these areas, however. Anytime we put ourselves in a situation in which we compare ourselves with others, we may come out feeling inferior. There are always going to be others who are better looking, have more money, own a better car, have a nicer house, have a higher IQ, and so on.

Self-Concept Homework

Handout

Make a list of 5 words you would use to describe yourself, and what they mean to you:

Example: Friendly—Because I say hello and smile when I meet new people.

Descriptive word	What it means to me

1. _____

2. _____

3. _____

4. _____

5. _____

1. What do you think and feel about yourself?

2. Do you like yourself as you are?

Inventory of Strengths and Weaknesses

Handout

List what you consider to be five of your strengths and five of your weaknesses:

Strengths	Weaknesses
1. _____	1. _____
2. _____	2. _____
3. _____	3. _____
4. _____	4. _____
5. _____	5. _____

Which weaknesses can you change and how?

_____

_____

_____

Which weaknesses do you need to accept and why?

_____

_____

_____

Self-Concept Life Graph

Handout

On the graph below plot important events, both positive and negative, in your life. Place these events above or below the neutral line and label your age at the time.

Positive Events +	Positive Events +

Birth _____ Today

– Negative Events	– Negative Events

How do you feel about the above picture of your life?

Where is the graph going to go from here? Are you in charge of it?

Session 14

Self-Esteem Enhancement

OBJECTIVES

The objective of this session is to give the clients ways of changing self-esteem through self-awareness, cognitive restructuring, or modification of lifestyle.

MATERIALS

Weekly Behavior Inventory
Techniques for Changing Self-Esteem handout

TASKS

1. Have group members check in; reinforce positive experience.
2. Review homework; point out strengths, improvements, and changes for the clients.
3. If couples counseling, then have couples describe feelings concerning partner's descriptions.
4. Have each group member discuss self-esteem issues and feelings.
5. Discuss *Techniques for Changing Self-Esteem.*
6. Have group members reinforce each other.
7. Give handouts and assign homework.

PROCEDURE

COUNSELING

Have the clients fill out the *Weekly Behavior Inventory.* Give each person a chance to check in and tell how his or her week has been. Ask if there were any problems or violent incidents during the week. Discuss each client's situation and how he or she handled it. Give positive reinforcement and other options to handling the situations. Be sure to point out different techniques that they used or could have used.

The counselor should be aware when clients may be blaming their spouses for their reactions in a situation. Help clients take responsibility for their own feelings and behaviors. This can be done by reminding them that no one can "make" them feel or behave a certain way, but that they choose for themselves. Ask whether there have been other incidents when they felt their spouse was to blame. The counselor should try to determine whether there is a pattern of behavior, and point it out to them.

If time allows in the counseling segment of the session, another problem area could be dealt with. Otherwise, move on to discussing the homework assignment.

Discuss the five description words from the *Self-Concept Homework* and what they meant to the client. In couples counseling, get feedback from the spouses as to how they feel about their partner's description of themselves. Also, discuss the person's strengths and weaknesses. Let each share what weaknesses he or she feels needs to be changed. Help them come up with ways to bring about those changes. Discuss which weaknesses need to be accepted and why. Have the partners share the strengths and weaknesses of their spouses.

Review again the *Self-Concept Life Graph* homework. Discuss some events each member listed and his or her feelings about them. Encourage feedback from other group members, if possible. Give members a chance to talk about plans for the future and how much control they feel they have in making those plans come true. Make sure each person has a chance to express this. Discuss whether the group members think self-esteem has anything to do with goal accomplishment. Point out the strengths and improvements of each group member. Let members know it takes time for important changes to occur.

EDUCATION

Begin the education segment by reinforcing the importance of positive self-esteem and how self-esteem can be changed. Discuss the *Techniques for Changing Self-Esteem* handout. A good group activity at this time would be to have each group member say something positive about each of the other group members. This can aid the bonding process as well as build self-esteem. Discuss any unusual reactions, and be sure to assess the person's feelings about what was said about him or her.

HOMEWORK

Have each client decide on two or three techniques he or she could use to increase self-esteem. Ask clients to use these techniques during the week to build self-esteem. The couple should continue spending time together. Have the group members review *Faulty Self-Talk* and *Unproductive Self-Talk* handouts.

RESOURCES

Burns, D. D. (1980). *Feeling good: The new mood therapy*. New York: New American Library.
Harris, T. A. (1973). *I'm OK—You're OK*. New York: Avon Books.
Lair, J. (1972). *I ain't much, baby, but I'm all I got*. New York: Fawcett Crest.
Satir, V. (1972). *Peoplemaking*. Palo Alto, CA: Science and Behavior Books.

Techniques for Changing Self-Esteem

Handout

1. **Rewrite Internal Monologue—The Way You Talk to Yourself**

   A. **Accept the past: You can't change it.** No matter when, where, or how something happened in the past, you cannot go back and change it. What you can do is change the present.
   B. **Quit putting yourself down.** The purpose of life is to find enjoyment and meaning, not to evaluate yourself. Give up "shoulds," "oughts," and "musts," and replace them with "wants."

   Example   Say to yourself, "I want to be the best person at my job." Do not say, "I must be the best person at my job."

   C. **Think about good experiences you have had in the past.** Be proud of your achievements. Dwell on your successes, not your failures. Use the techniques that helped you be successful in the past.

   Example   If you did well in athletics, then get active in some type of sport again.

   D. **Make positive goals for the future.** With small, realistic goals you will be successful and motivated to reach your end goal.

   Example   If you want to lose weight, make a goal to lose a pound a week. Continue to try to do this every week until you reach your desired weight. This is much more realistic than a goal to lose 25 pounds in 1 month.

   E. **Techniques for thought change.**

   - Record negative thoughts in detail. This will help you be aware of the negative thoughts you are having. Also, it will help you discover their patterns and what triggers them. Awareness helps you change and control negative thoughts.
   - Block negative thoughts. When you have a negative thought tell yourself silently or out loud to **STOP**. Refuse to allow yourself to think negatively.
   - Replace negative thoughts with positive thoughts. After saying **"STOP"** to the negative thought, think of a positive thought immediately. Remember to draw from your successes.

2. **Diagnose Lowered Self-Esteem Cues**

   A. **Decide what situations cue low self-esteem.** Do you feel inferior when you think someone is not interested in what you say? (Rejection) Are you comparing yourself to others: physically, intellectually, financially? Is it the circumstance, event, setting, or interpersonal interaction that are making you feel this way? Is it because of physical or personal isolation?
   B. **Use your knowledge of what cues lower self-esteem to help you overcome it.** It may be necessary to avoid certain things or situations that make you feel this way. Or you may choose to work on improving in a certain area.

   Example   If lowered self-esteem is a result of non-assertiveness, then you could attend assertiveness-training classes to improve this skill.

Techniques for Changing
Self-Esteem *(Continued)*

Handout

3. **Learn to Relax**

   A. **Relaxation.** Lie or sit in a comfortable position. Close your eyes. Breathe deeply, tense and relax each muscle group. Begin with your arm, move on to your abdomen, legs, neck, and facial muscles. Concentrate on feelings of warmth and relaxation. Practice doing this at least once a day. Review Session 4.
   B. **Exercise.** Choose something you like and will continue doing. Join an aerobics class or ride your bike. Pick a time of day that is convenient and exercise at least 2–3 times a week.

4. **Modify Unrealistic Standards**

   A. **Rational thinking.** You are influenced by your view and perception of the world. Often this takes precedence over actual reality. How you see things is often more important than what really happened. Your beliefs about yourself influence how you feel and what you do.

   Example   Your boss tells you that you made a mistake in your last project (event); you tell yourself, "I am worthless" (belief). You become depressed and feel horrible about yourself (emotion).
   The point is that bad things happen. Acknowledge that this is a fact of life. Do not give yourself additional stress by following a belief system that hurts you. Adopt a healthy belief system, and you will be happier and more successful.

   B. **Are your expectations reasonable and obtainable?** Again, set your expectations and goals so that they are obtainable. Do not place obstacles in your way by making goals that demand perfection or that are impossible to reach. Make small goals that lead to your end goal. Reward yourself when you reach each goal.
   C. **Don't expect perfection in yourself or others.** This sets you up for failure. Enjoy your uniqueness and that of others. Learn to appreciate yourself and others. Again, stop rating yourself or others. Give yourself freedom to make mistakes and still like who you are. Extend this freedom to others also.

5. **Create Better Social Support Reinforcement**

   A. **Seek people who give you positive reinforcement.**
   B. **Be pleasant to others.** Talk and act in a positive manner.
   C. **Be nice, even when you do not feel like it.**
   D. **Do not expect everyone to like you.**
   E. **Do not expect everyone to be perfect.**
   F. **Do not talk about your problems all the time.** Others do not like to hear negative things constantly. Think about positive and funny events.
   G. **Be assertive, not aggressive.** Let people know what you want and need in an appropriate way. Do not expect them to know what you need.

Techniques for Changing
Self-Esteem *(Continued)*

6. **Learn to Meet Your Needs**

   A. **Love and be loved.** Giving up unrealistic demands on yourself and others allows you to love and be loved more generously. Having a loving relationship with at least one other person may be crucial to your well-being.
   B. **Feel worthwhile.** Doing something you feel is useful and worthwhile is important for everyone. Give yourself credit for anything you are doing that makes you feel worthwhile.
   C. **Have fun.** Allow yourself to have fun. Do something that you find enjoyable every day. If there is something that is particularly fun to you that you have not done for some time, make it a point to indulge in this activity very soon.

   Example   Have your hair done, have a manicure, go rollerskating, go to a ball game, go bowling, play tennis, or call your best friend from high school.

   D. **Be free.** Keep in mind at all times that you are free to make choices. Forget the past and live in the present. Accept responsibility for making meaningful choices in your life. You are free to choose how to live your life.

Session 15

Self-Talk and Irrational Beliefs

OBJECTIVES

To introduce group members to the basic concept of self-talk and to increase awareness of how interpretations of events can determine feelings and reactions.

MATERIALS

Weekly Behavior Inventory
Faulty Self-Talk handout
Unproductive Self-Talk handout

TASKS

1. Review weekly events and have clients discuss problem areas.
2. Have clients share self-esteem techniques.
3. Review previous anger education from Session 3.
4. Explain self-talk concept and ABCDE REBT model.
5. Discuss *Faulty Self-Talk* and *Unproductive Self-Talk* handouts.
6. Give handouts and assign homework.

PROCEDURE

COUNSELING

As in previous sessions, begin this session by having the clients fill out the *Weekly Behavior Inventory*. Find out about the events of the week. Discuss any specific problem areas. Relate the self-esteem education to the situation if it is relevant. Let each client share which self-esteem techniques he or she has been using and whether these have been effective. Encourage couples to share with each other. The counselors could discuss whether the clients feel there is any relationship between self-esteem and anger control. The counselors can briefly review the basic anger education from Session 3, then lead into the education segment of this session.

153

EDUCATION

Introduce a basic working model of "self-talk." Try the ABCDE model, emphasizing how the way we interpret events can determine the way we feel and act.

A. **Objective Event**—This is the initial *Activating* event that blocks achieving successful goals (e.g., a woman comes home and says, "I hate my job!").

B. **Self-Talk**—This is the *Belief* that the client creates from the preceding event. These could be rational or irrational (the latter is what usually occurs in abusive relationships). Thus, the husband might say, "She's trying to tell me that she doesn't want to work and that I should be making more money so she shouldn't have to!"

C. **Feelings and Behavior**—These are the *Consequences* of the beliefs from the preceding process. Depending on the interpretation, the husband reacts; he might be critical of her, act defensive, sulk, or worry. He may get angry as a result of his interpretation of her comment, and might say to her, "Quit complaining! You think you're the only one who has it tough?"

D. **New Self-Talk**—This would be a *Different* interpretation *Disputing* the irrational belief based on using appropriate self-talk. The goal is to get the client to interpret what was said another way. The husband might think, "Maybe she was just tired and needed some support, like we all do. Maybe it was not intended as a negative message or critical comment about me." The husband might then say to himself, "Sounds like she had a rotten day. What can I do to help?"

E. **New Feelings and Behavior**—This would be the new *Effects* of the positive self-talk with rational beliefs. The husband now might say, "Let's talk about it." He might try to cheer her up, or he might just whisk the kids off into another room and let her be alone for a while. His response would now be based on what he thought she might need, rather than defending himself against a perceived attack.

The counselor should explain the preceding ideas to the clients, and then discuss the categories of faulty self-talk compiled from Ellis and Harper (1975), Beck (1979), and Burns (1980). Teach the names of the categories and go through the different examples. Ask the group members to come up with examples of their own that would be relevant for them . Go over the *Unproductive Self-Talk* handout briefly. As an option, have members give examples of faulty self-talk from their past, and have the other group members try to figure out which faulty self-talk category the example fits into. This can be done in a humorous way to help relax the group while still teaching them important tools in self-talk and irrational beliefs. They can also practice taking some of their faulty self-talk examples and rephrasing them so that they reflect "productive" or "realistic" self-talk. Make sure that they learn how to revise the "faulty" self-talk into sentences that would be more "realistic" self-talk. Conversations with ourselves are often hidden and can happen very quickly. Even though they are hidden, they can make the difference between a happy and miserable life. Jumping to conclusions is one of the common ways we generate our own anger.

Example: Without any concrete evidence, Ed started worrying that his wife Carolyn was leaving him. When he thought about it, his mind would race: "Can I live without her? I don't know. I'd better be strong. She won't respect me if I'm not strong. She probably never loved me to begin with; she only wanted me to give her children."

Read the above example to the group. Ask if they can identify with these feelings. In the above example, Ed ended up feeling depressed and then angry, and he was unable to tell anyone about it. He kept asking Carolyn for signs of her love, but his constant asking began to drive her away. Find out if any of the group members had similar self-talk patterns? What are they?

HOMEWORK

Have the clients or couples practice identifying distorted self-talk and irrational beliefs during the week. Have them discuss these situations and particular examples with their partners. Have the clients review the *Using Cognitive Reframing* handout for the next session.

Faulty Self-Talk

1. **BLACK & WHITE:** This is the tendency to see things in an all-or-nothing fashion. Beware of words like "never," "always," "nothing," and "everyone."

   "Real men don't eat quiche."
   "You're either on my side or you're not."
   "You can't trust anyone over 30."

2. **MINIMIZING:** This is the tendency to downplay your achievements.

   "Even though I finally got my promotion, it's no big thing."
   "I did well, but so did a lot of other people."
   "My counselor just gives me good feedback because she's paid to say it."

3. **MIND-READING:** This is the tendency to assume that others think something without determining if this is really so.

   "I know my boss hates me . . . he gave me a dirty look."
   "She's avoiding me . . . she must be pretty mad."
   "My husband didn't call me today . . . he must not care about me."

4. **AWFULIZING:** This is the tendency to predict that things will turn out "awful" for you.

   "My brother will never trust me again."
   "I know I'm not going to make it through this place."

5. **ERROR IN BLAMING:** This is the tendency to unfairly blame yourself or others.

   "It's all my fault" or "It's all their fault."
   "It's my fault my son is shy."
   "You always mess everything up for me."

6. **PUT-DOWNS:** This is the tendency to put yourself down for having one problem or making one mistake.

   "I'm overweight, so I must be lazy and stupid."
   "I failed this test, so I must be dumb."
   "I'm in counseling, I must be a bad person."
   "She doesn't like me, I must be ugly."

7. **EMOTIONAL REASONING:** This is the tendency to conclude that if you feel a certain way about yourself, then it must be true.

   "Because I feel bad about myself, I must be a bad person."
   "I feel rejected, so everybody must be rejecting me."
   "Because I feel guilty, I must have done something wrong."

Unproductive Self-Talk

Handout

- She wants to be with someone else.

- If she's out alone, someone will pick her up.

- He never does what I want.

- No one understands.

- If I'm not tough, she'll think I'm weak.

- I need to show her I'm in control.

- If she talks to another man, it means she wants to go to bed with him.

- She does nothing but stay home, take care of the kids, and talk on the phone.

- If other women look at him, it means he is flirting with them, which demeans me.

- She is responsible for other men's reactions to her.

- He's out to make me a fool.

- She keeps the kids from respecting me.

- His wanting time for himself means he doesn't want me.

- His not being there when I want him means he doesn't care.

- I'm sick and tired of all this crap.

- No matter what I do, it won't be good enough.

- The kids are more important to her than I am.

- His family is more important to him than I am.

Adapted from *Battering: AMEND Manual for Helpers*, AMEND Program, Denver, CO.

Session 16

Changing Self-Talk

OBJECTIVES

The objectives of this session are to help the clients learn to restructure and reframe their thoughts and beliefs by changing perceptions and interpretations of events.

MATERIALS

Weekly Behavior Inventory
Using Cognitive Reframing handout
Changing Your Self-Talk handout

TASKS

1. Have group members review weekly events and irrational beliefs.
2. Have the clients role play problem areas.
3. Review *Reducing Stress and Anger* handout from Session 5.
4. Discuss cognitive reframing.
5. Role play *Using Cognitive Reframing* and have couples or clients role play.
6. Introduce *Changing Your Self-Talk*.
7. Give handouts and assign homework.

PROCEDURE

COUNSELING

As usual, have the clients complete the *Weekly Behavior Inventory*. Have the group members check in regarding any situations that occurred during the week, either positive or negative. Have them discuss their feelings about irrational beliefs and distorted thinking as they apply to them. How have these issues been useful to the group members? Role play any problem areas. Encourage the clients to share their own feelings about anger. Review the desensitization *Anger Ladder* from Session 5, and have the clients fill in new examples that may be more applicable now.

EDUCATION

Cognitive reframing is a technique that can be used for mental restructuring. It is a process of looking for positive aspects instead of negative aspects. The process that takes place is as follows:

1. Relabel events that happen so they appear in a more positive light.
2. Change self-statements to thoughts that are in conflict or opposite of negative and stressful thoughts.

Example A couple had a disagreement before going to work. When the husband returned home from work, his wife had not gotten home yet. He immediately started thinking she had left him and would not be coming home at all. He started feeling angry and started breaking things in the house. In a short time his wife got home, and he began to hit her and accuse her of planning to run away with another man.

The man in the preceding example should have reframed his thoughts. One possible way would have been the following: After returning home and not finding his wife there, he could consider that, yes, there had been a disagreement between them but he should think in a positive way how they could discuss the situation later in the evening. He could change the negative self-talk by thinking of more positive reasons for his wife being late. She may have had to work late, or she may have stopped at the grocery store. Just changing his self-talk would probably make a difference in the emotions he might feel. If there are some fears or anger, he could analyze these feelings or use other methods to deal with them. He could feel good about keeping control of his thinking and behavior. When his wife arrives, he could schedule a time to discuss the problem that led to the disagreement. After this, they could take a few minutes to relax from their busy day. During their relaxation time, they could plan or think of some pleasant things to do later in the evening or on the weekend.

SUMMARY

1. Be able to recognize and label emotions.
2. Be able to describe the situation or event that led to the emotion.
3. Identify distorted self-talk or negative perceptions.
4. Replace distorted self-talk or perceptions with rational self-talk.
5. Plan behavior based on new self-talk.
6. Recognize and label emotion after the reframing. Reward oneself for coping.

Briefly discuss the *Using Cognitive Reframing* handout. Give examples of each of these steps. The clients could talk about a situation of their own and go through the steps. Role play examples following the six steps from the handout and have the clients or couples role play their own examples. Review *Changing Your Self-Talk* handout.

HOMEWORK

Ask the clients to think of a situation in which they responded emotionally. They can follow the *Using Cognitive Reframing* handout to recognize, describe, identify, and change any distorted thinking about the situation. Have them review the *Coping Plan for Stressor Situations* handout for the next session.

RESOURCES

Beck, A. T. (1979). *Cognitive therapy and emotional disorders.* New York: New American Library.

Burns, D. D. (1980). *Feeling good: The new mood therapy.* New York: New American Library.

Edleson, J. E., & Tolman, R. (1992). *Intervention for men who batter: An ecological approach.* Newbury Park, CA: Sage.

Ellis, A. (1977). *Anger: How to live with and without it.* Secaucus, NJ: Citadel Press.

Ellis, A., & Harper, R. A. (1975). *A new guide to rational living.* North Hollywood, CA: Wilshire Book Company.

Ewing, W., Lindsey, M., & Pomerantz, J. (1984). *AMEND: Manual for helpers.* Denver, CO: AMEND Project.

McKay, M., Davis, M., & Fanning, P. (1981). *Thoughts and feelings: The art of cognitive stress intervention.* Oakland, CA: New Harbinger Publications.

Novaco, R. W. (1979). The cognitive regulation of anger and stress. In P. C. Kendall & S. D. Hollen (Eds.), *Cognitive-behavioral interventions: Theory, research, and procedure.* New York: Academic Press.

Paymar, M. (1993). *Violent no more: Helping men end domestic abuse.* Alameda, CA: Hunter House.

Rose, S. D., Hanusa, D., Tolman, R. P. M., & Hall, J. A. (1982). *A group leader's guide to assertiveness training.* Unpublished manuscript, University of Wisconsin-Madison, School of Social Work, Madison, WI.

Weisinger, H. (1985). *Anger work out book.* New York: Quill.

Wexler, D. B., & Sanders, D. G. (1993). *Navy Spouse Abuse Treatment Program: Men's group leader's manual* (rev. ed.). San Diego, CA: U.S. Navy Family Advocacy Center.

Using Cognitive Reframing

Handout

Think of a situation that you responded to emotionally. Follow the six-step method of uncovering, reframing, and changing the distorted situation to restructure your thinking.

Step 1. **Recognize and label what you were feeling.**

Step 2. **Describe the situation or experience that led to the emotions.**

Step 3. **Identify the distorted self-talk or negative perceptions.**

Step 4. **Rephrase the self-talk to be more positive and rational.**

Step 5. **Plan behavior based on new self-talk.**

Step 6. **Recognize and label your emotion after the positive self-talk. What are you feeling now? Reward yourself for coping.**

Example   A wife feels unloved and taken for granted because her husband did not call today.

Step 1.   Recognize feelings of being unloved, lonely, fearful, and angey.

Step 2.   Spouse hasn't called.

Step 3.   Distorted self-talk says that because he hasn't called, he must not love her and doesn't consider her feelings.

Step 4.   Rephrase self-talk by thinking that her spouse must have gotten involved at work and did not have time to call. She should not expect her husband to call every day. It is irrational to base her thoughts of how much her husband cares about her on whether he calls every day or not.

Step 5.   Decide to talk with spouse about taking some time for the two of them to go away together for a few days.

Step 6.   Wife feels more positive about herself and her relationship.

Changing Your Self-Talk

Handout

FOR WOMEN

Category	Faulty Self-Talk	Positive Self-Talk
Fearful and Anxious	I'm afraid I will always be alone.	I can have close relationships with others and I can depend on myself.
Anger and Frustration	There is something wrong with me for being mad—I should not feel this way.	My spouse is responsible for the abuse, and my anger is a normal response.
Guilt and Remorse	I am responsible for the abuse—I caused it.	My partner is responsible for the abuse. I was a victim.
Shame and Self-Disgust	I will always be helpless. I cannot control my life.	I can take control of my life.
Sadness	I am empty.	I am whole and I can be happy. It is up to me.

FOR MEN

Category	Faulty Self-Talk	Positive Self-Talk
Fearful and Anxious	If I don't control her she will leave me.	She is a free person. She is more likely to stay if I do not try to control her.
Anger and Frustration	I don't mean to hurt her, but she makes me do it.	I am in control of myself and I take full responsibility for my behavior.
Guilt and Remorse	She makes me hurt her and then I feel bad.	When I control my actions I feel good about myself.
Shame and Self-Disgust	I am not confident in myself. I cannot trust anyone.	I feel confident in some areas of my life. I trust myself. I can trust some people.
Sadness	I am sad. There is no hope.	I can change. I can be happy. It is up to me.

Session 17

Stress Inoculation for Anger Control

OBJECTIVES

To use the self-talk skills to prepare for anger-producing situations and to cope more effectively.

MATERIALS

Weekly Behavior Inventory
Counters handout
Coping Plan for Stressor Situations handout

TASKS

1. Review weekly events and focus on intimidation and communication patterns.
2. Have clients reframe examples and role play.
3. Discuss anger management and disagreements.
4. Discuss *Counters* and *Coping Plan for Stressor Situations*.
5. Provide examples and have clients participate.
6. Have clients generate self-statements for potential anger situations; focus on new self-talk and cognitive behavior.
7. Give handouts and assign homework.

PROCEDURE

COUNSELING

Have the clients complete the *Weekly Behavior Inventory* and note any incidents. Focus on intimidation issues in their communication patterns and how these are related to fears, insecurities, power/control, and distorted thinking. Have the group members give examples of reframing or attempts at this that they did during the week. What were the effects? How did it feel? Have them role play relevant examples in their own situations. Begin focusing on ways clients can manage anger while disagreeing.

EDUCATION

Review the *Counters* handout and give it to the clients. These are statements that can be used to counteract irrational thoughts.

Introduce the *Coping Plan for Stressor Situations* and the four-step model of Stress Inoculation for Anger Control. Use the handout to provide examples of self-statements that can be used to lower stress levels at each of these stages. The fourth step can be just as important as the others, even though it is after the fact. Be sure that they understand the importance of using realistic and supportive self-talk at this stage also. Ask each group member to identify a potential anger situation and to generate self-statements for each of the four steps. The more unique and personal statements are the best. Role play one of these situations with at least one of the group members, practicing both the old and new self-talk. Focus on the different feelings that result from the new self-talk.

Group members can help clarify the self-defeating, irrational beliefs. The counselors can model and demonstrate switching from self-defeating to self-enhancing statements, and the group members can then practice this during the cognitive rehearsal. The group can give feedback at the end of the rehearsal.

HOMEWORK

Have the clients practice the *Coping Plan* during the week. Have them review the *Dynamics of Assertion, What Is Assertive Behavior?,* and *Benefits of Assertiveness* handouts.

Counters

Handout

- ☐ These thoughts are unproductive and harmful.

- ☐ I trust her.

- ☐ She hasn't given me any reason not to trust her.

- ☐ He may be right.

- ☐ I can be assertive.

- ☐ I can take a time-out.

- ☐ I'm important to her even though it may not seem that way now.

- ☐ I'm in control.

- ☐ She/he/they can't get me upset unless I allow them to.

- ☐ It's too nice of a day to get upset.

- ☐ I need to do something for myself that's relaxing.

- ☐ It's okay that she's angry, I don't have to settle it right now.

- ☐ I can say no.

- ☐ I can negotiate and offer a compromise.

- ☐ I can ask for what I want.

Taken from *Battering: AMEND Manual for Helpers*, AMEND Program, 1984, Denver, CO.

Coping Plan for Stressor Situations

If you believe that you are being frustrated, annoyed, insulted, or attacked and begin to feel angry:

1. Don't respond immediately.
2. Take several short deep breaths to fill your chest and relax as you breathe out.
3. Think of other possible explanations for what is making you angry.
4. Think of the consequences of reacting in different ways.
5. Start to respond in some way that will control your anger and would be an alternative to aggression.

STRESS INOCULATION FOR ANGER CONTROL: COMMON COPING STATEMENTS FOR STRESSOR SITUATIONS

1. **Prepare for Stressful Situations**

   This could be a rough situation, but I know how to deal with it. I can work out a plan to handle this. Easy does it. Remember, stick to the issues and don't take it personally. There won't be any need for an argument. I know what to do.

2. **Meeting the Situation**

   As long as I keep my cool, I'm in control of the situation. I don't need to prove myself. Don't make more of this than I have to. There is no point in getting mad. Think of what I have to do. Look for the positive and do not jump to conclusions.

3. **Coping with Arousal**

   My muscles are getting tight; relax and slow things down. Time to take a deep breath. Let's take the issue point by point. My anger is a signal of what I need to do. Time for problem solving. He or she probably wants me to get angry, but I'm going to deal with it constructively.

4. **Subsequent Reflection**

   Conflict Unresolved—Forget about the mistakes now. Thinking about it only makes me upset. Try to shake it off. Do not let it interfere with my job. Remember relaxation; it is a lot better than anger. Do not take it personally. It may not be so serious.

   Conflict Resolved—I handled that one pretty well. That means I'm doing a good job. I could have gotten more upset than it was worth. My pride can get me into trouble, but I am doing better at this all the time. I actually got through this without getting angry.

Adapted from Raymond Novaco, 1979.

Session 18

Dynamics of Assertiveness

OBJECTIVES

The objective of this session is to teach the client to be more assertive through education aware-ness and cognitive restructuring.

MATERIALS

Weekly Behavior Inventory
Dynamics of Assertiveness handout
What Is Assertive Behavior? handout
Benefits of Assertiveness handout
Situations and Behaviors handout

TASKS

1. Have clients check in; go over *WBI*.
2. Review homework examples of cognitive reframing and coping plan.
3. Encourage clients to share feelings and apply techniques.
4. Describe *Dynamics of Assertiveness, What Is Assertive Behavior?*, and *Benefits of Assertiveness*.
5. Have clients give examples of assertiveness and role play.
6. Give handouts and assign homework.

PROCEDURE

COUNSELING

Have the clients fill out the *Weekly Behavior Inventory*. Check in concerning the events of the week. After bringing things up to date concerning the relationship, talk about the cognitive reframing. Discuss what each individual wrote for the situation and application of the steps. If time permits, allow the clients or couples to bring up problem areas that they feel have not been dealt with yet. The counselors can help by encouraging clients to come up with options and ways of applying techniques that they have learned to these problem areas. It is much more effective if the client comes up with his or her own answers and makes his or her own decisions about the plan of action.

EDUCATION

Review the handouts *Dynamics of Assertiveness, What Is Assertive Behavior?* and *Benefits of Assertiveness*. Discuss each one of these handouts as a way of giving basic education about assertiveness and a way of getting the client to become aware of their own degree of assertiveness. This information will also help the client to think about assertion and their degree of assertiveness in a different light.

While discussing the four types of behaviors in the first handout, encourage the clients to give possible examples for each. The counselors should give other examples. The clients and counselors can role play during the discussion of the different assertive behaviors. Then discuss the *Benefits of Assertiveness*. Encourage the clients to think of other benefits for them personally or benefits to the relationship.

HOMEWORK

For the homework assignment, give the clients the chart for *Situations and Behaviors*. Ask them to keep up with different situations during the week. They should record their body cues, behavior, feelings, what they did, and what they would like to have done concerning each situation. Ask them to bring their charts and be prepared to discuss them during the next session. Have them review *Tips on Assertiveness, Learning to Say "No,"* and *Compliments* handouts.

RESOURCES

Alberti, R. E., & Emmons, M. L. (1991) *Your perfect right: A guide to assertive living* (5th ed.). San Luis Obispo, CA: Impact Publishers.

Baer, J. (1976). *How to be an assertive (not aggressive) woman in love, life, and on the job.* New York: New American Library.

Butler, P. E. (1981). *Self-assertion for women.* San Francisco: Harper & Row.

McKay, M., Davis, M., & Fanning, P. (1983). *Messages: The communication book.* Oakland, CA: New Harbinger Publications.

Dynamics of Assertiveness

Handout

TYPES OF BEHAVIOR

1. **Assertive**   This behavior involves knowing what you feel and want. It also involves expressing your feelings and wants directly and honestly without violating the rights of others. At all times you are accepting responsibility for your feelings and actions.

Example: A person goes to the store and buys a blouse. There is a seam undone. He or she takes it back to the store and asks in a friendly but firm manner for a new blouse or a refund.

2. **Aggressive**   This type of behavior involves attacking others, being controlling, provoking, and maybe even violent. Its consequences could be harmful to others as well as yourself.

Example: Consider the same situation as the one above. The person takes the blouse back to the store and yells at the salesclerk and acts in a demanding manner.

3. **Passive**   With this behavior, the person has the tendency to withdraw, become anxious, and avoid confrontation. Passive people let others think for them, make decisions for them, and tell them what to do. Many times this causes the person to feel hurt, depressed, and lowers their self-esteem.

Example: Again, consider the same blouse scenario. The customer gets angry but does not express or deal with the anger. Depression will likely follow, he or she may believe that the salesperson sold the blouse to him or her on purpose, but does nothing about the situation.

4. **Passive-Aggressive**   With this behavior, the person is not direct in relating to people, does not accept what is happening, but will retaliate in an indirect manner. This type of behavior can cause extensive confusion because no one knows what the real issues are.

Example: When confronted with the poorly sewn blouse, the passive-aggressive person will say bad things about the store to others, mess up the merchandise on the shelves, and so on. The person never directly approaches any solution or confronts the problem, however.

What Is Assertive Behavior?

Handout

- Asking for what you want but not being demanding.
- Being able to express feelings.
- Being able to genuinely express feedback or compliments to others and being able to accept them.
- Being able to disagree without being aggressive.
- Being able to use "I" messages and "I feel" statements without being judgmental or blaming.
- Avoiding arguing just for the sake of arguing.
- Making eye contact during a conversation.

SUMMARY

Assertiveness is a way of communicating in which we make our needs, feelings, thoughts, and desires known without decreasing our rights and self-esteem, nor the rights and self-esteem of others.

Examples:

1. Honey, could we go out to eat? I'm sure tired from my day.
2. I feel embarrassed when you tease me about my weight in front of my friends.
3. I'm sorry you didn't enjoy the evening; I thought it was a lot of fun.
4. Susie, I'm having some difficulty disciplining Joey; could you give me some pointers?
5. Jerry, I feel angry when you are late and don't call.
6. Sara, could we talk about this after we've both cooled off?
7. Look the person in the eye and say, "I really care about you, let's work this out."

Benefits of Assertiveness

Handout

What benefits are there for being more assertive?

- I can be more independent.
- I can make my own decisions.
- I can have more open and honest relationships.
- Others will respect my rights and wishes.
- I can take control of my own emotions.
- I can be more relaxed and at peace with myself.
- I can get satisfaction in initiating and carrying out my own plans.
- I can get more of what I need and want.

Situations and Behaviors

Keep a record of different interpersonal situations that occur during the week. Record what your body cues were, whether your behavior was assertive, aggressive, passive, or passive/aggressive. Record how you felt. Decide if you feel good about how you responded. If not, record what you would like to have done and why you didn't do it.

Situation and date	Physical body cues	How I felt	My behavior (As., Ag., P., P-Ag.)	What I would like to have done	Why I did not do it

Session 19

Becoming More Assertive

OBJECTIVES

The objective of this session is to teach the clients specific techniques to increase assertive behaviors.

MATERIALS

Weekly Behavior Inventory
Tips on Assertiveness handout
Learning to Say "No" handout
Compliments handout
Asking for What You Want handout

TASKS

1. Check in and review *WBI*.
2. Discuss and review *Situations and Behaviors* chart.
3. Have clients role play assertiveness examples and share feelings with each other.
4. Discuss *Tips on Assertiveness* and other handouts, and role play.
5. Give handouts, explain and assign homework.

PROCEDURE

COUNSELING

The client should begin the session by filling out the *Weekly Behavior Inventory*. After checking in about the events of the week, discuss the *Situations and Behaviors* chart. Counselors should give positive reinforcement for assertive behaviors and suggest ways the clients can be more assertive in the situations that they were not assertive in this week. Let the clients talk about their awareness of body cues during these situations. Also, they should be encouraged to talk about how they felt, what they would like to have done, and why they did not act as they would have liked. The counselors should role play the situation with the clients, then have the couples or group members role play situations for their own relationships in which they need to be more assertive.

EDUCATION

Review the assertiveness handouts. Discuss the *Tips on Assertiveness* handout. Give examples where appropriate. Briefly go over the other handouts. Promote as much discussion and input from the clients as possible. Give examples and role play when appropriate.

HOMEWORK

Give the clients the *Asking for What You Want* handout for homework. Encourage them to practice the different skills they learned in the session today and to jot down some notes that they can share next time. Have them use some of the assertiveness skills at least once a day, and experiment with different techniques. They should practice giving and receiving compliments, and saying "no." Have them use the *Situations and Behaviors* chart again this week. Have the clients review the *Problem Solving* handout.

RESOURCES

Alberti, R. E., & Emmons, M. L. (1991). *Your perfect right: A guide to assertive living* (5th ed.). San Luis Obispo, CA: Impact Publishers.

Bloom, L. Z., Coburn, K., & Pearlman, J. (1975). *Stand up, speak out, talk back.* New York: Pocket Books.

Bower, S. A., & Bower, G. H. (1976). *Asserting yourself: A practical guide for positive change.* Reading, MA: Addison-Wesley.

Fensterheim, H., & Baer, J. (1975). *Don't say yes when you want to say no.* New York: David McKay.

Galassi, M. D., & Galassi, J. P. (1977). *Assert yourself: How to be your own person.* New York: Human Sciences Press.

Lazarus, A., & Fay, A. (1975). *I can if I want to.* New York: William Morrow.

Smith, M. (1975). *When I say no, I feel guilty.* New York: Bantam.

Tips on Assertiveness

Handout

- Begin statements with the pronoun "I," such as "I feel hurt when . . ."

- Do not feel that you have to justify, rationalize, or give reasons for how you feel.

- Move closer to the person with whom you are talking.

- When you do not want to do something, say "no," and do not feel that you have to apologize or make excuses. Learn to say "no" many different ways, firmly and graciously.

- Be responsible to yourself first in getting your needs met, but without attacking other's rights. You do not have to be perfect or prove how "nice" you are.

- Remember it's costly not to be assertive.

- Sometimes you may need to persist in being assertive until others realize what you want.

Learning to Say "No"

Possible reasons you say "yes" when you want to say "no."

- You want to be liked or accepted.

- It makes you feel you are a good person for helping others.

- You don't want to hurt anyone's feelings.

- What would the family think?

- You want the other person to feel obliged.

You have a right to say "no."

- When your priorities do not go along with the request.

- When the person can do it him or herself.

- When it's against your values and judgments.

- If you would feel bad doing it.

- If it would hurt you or someone else.

- If the demand is inappropriate.

- If you just don't want to do it.

- If the request is inconsiderate of you or others.

Compliments

Handout

Assertive people know how to sincerely give compliments as well as receive them.

WHAT WE COMPLIMENT

- Behavior—I appreciate you being so **attentive** when I'm feeling ill.
- Appearance—You really **look good** in that bathing suit.
- Possessions—That's a **nice tie.**

THE GOLDEN RULE

Give more compliments than criticism, more praise than punishment.

Delivery

- Be specific.
- Use the other person's name.
- Add an explanatory sentence.
- Personalize the compliment.
- Ask a question.
- Practice good nonverbal communication.

    Example: Ethel, I like the way you take the time in getting the children involved in activities.

Other ways to compliment

- **The third-person compliment:** Compliment the person within earshot or tell someone you know will repeat the compliment directly to the person.
- **The relayed compliment:** Pass on a compliment from another person; follow with an example.
- **The indirect compliment:** Words and actions can signal admiration; ask for the person's opinion or advice.
- **The nonverbal compliment:** Smiles, nods, eye contact, and other positive body language can be complimentary.

COMPLIMENT GUIDELINES

- Be honest.
- Start slowly.
- Be conservative at first.
- Avoid the hidden agenda.
- Do not repeat the exact same compliment.
- Favorably compare the person to others.
- Do not get carried away.
- Avoid being Mr./Mrs. Positive.

Compliments *(Continued)*

HOW TO ACCEPT A COMPLIMENT

- Make eye contact.
- Assume an open posture.
- Smile.
- Thank the other person.
- Use the other person's name.
- Give credit if appropriate.
- Tell the other person how you feel about the compliment.
- Self-disclose.

  Remember:
- Never discount a compliment.
- Do not return the same compliment unless appropriate.

Asking for What You Want

Handout

What are the advantages of asking for what you want? We hope the first thing you thought of was increasing the chances of getting what you want in life. Though there is no guarantee you will always get your way, the odds are more in your favor than if you do not ask, and instead expect others to read your mind. Just as with yourself, the person of whom we are making the request has the right to say no, with or without an explanation. With this in mind, let's begin by giving you some practice in asking for what you want.

ASKING FOR WHAT YOU WANT

Place two chairs facing each other. You sit in one and have your partner sit in the other. Make the following requests out loud and see how it feels to ask these questions. Are there any areas that feel more or less comfortable? Rate the difficulty of each request on a 1 to 5 scale (1 being easy and 5 being difficult). Explain why some were more difficult.

_____ 1. I would like to borrow $5.00 from you.
_____ 2. Would you be willing to help me clean the garage today?
_____ 3. I would like to be alone today.
_____ 4. I would like to have sex with you.
_____ 5. I would like to borrow $100.00.
_____ 6. Will you hold me? I'm feeling scared.
_____ 7. Will you sleep close to me tonight?
_____ 8. I would like to sleep alone tonight.
_____ 9. I would like a date with you on Friday.
_____ 10. I would like to talk quietly.
_____ 11. Will you kiss me?
_____ 12. I would like to know why you are angry with me.
_____ 13. Will you take care of the kids today?
_____ 14. How are you feeling today?
_____ 15. I would like to read the paper; can we talk later?
_____ 16. I would like to take a time-out.

ASKING FOR WHAT YOU WANT—HOMEWORK

Asking for what you want would be easier if you begin to make requests of people with whom you are comfortable or at least somewhat comfortable asserting yourself with. Choose a couple of people whom you categorized as **comfortable** and **somewhat uncomfortable** to make your requests of this week. Make three requests this week. Indicate the request, how it felt, and how you could improve the way in which you expressed it. Were you direct or in direct (escalating and/or stuffing)? Be sure to use an "I" statement followed by a clear request. Use the examples presented earlier as a guide for how to make your request.

Adapted from Sonkin and Durphy (1989). *Learning to Live Without Violence.* Volcano, CA: Volcano Press. Reprinted by permission of Volcano Press.

IV

Intimacy Issues and Relapse Prevention

Session 20

Problem Solving, Decision Making, and Negotiation

OBJECTIVES

The objective of this session is to decrease abuse in relationships by increasing the client's problem-solving and decision-making skills. The counselor will also help the clients learn to negotiate to resolve conflicts.

MATERIALS

Weekly Behavior Inventory
Problem Solving handout

TASKS

1. Review *WBI* and give feedback and positive reinforcement for clients' progress.
2. Emphasize acceptance of responsibility for behavior.
3. Have clients express feelings about previous abuse and current situations.
4. Discuss homework, assertive behavior, body cues, and role play problem areas.
5. Introduce handouts and have clients role play examples.
6. Have couples or group members role play a problem using the *Problem Solving* guidelines.
7. Have clients discuss feelings concerning problem solving.
8. Give handouts and assign homework.
9. Begin termination work.

PROCEDURE

COUNSELING

Ask the clients to fill out the *Weekly Behavior Inventory*. Look briefly at the inventories. The counselor should give feedback and positive reinforcement for the progress the clients have made in decreasing the violence. If there is still some violence occurring, discuss the situation. Have each of the clients accept responsibility for his or her behavior. Reinforce that there is never any acceptable reason for physical, verbal, emotional, or sexual abuse. Encourage each client to express his or her feelings and opinions about this. This discussion can be beneficial in bringing out the events of the week and how each client dealt with them.

After each client has had a chance to talk about the past week, discuss the *Situations and Behaviors* charts that he or she kept during the past week. Discuss assertive and nonassertive behaviors that occurred during the week. Again, take time to discuss the clients' body cues, how they felt about what they did, what they would like to have done, and why they did not. Give positive reinforcement for assertive behaviors and supportive direction for nonassertive behaviors. Discuss the other homework assignment of practicing different assertiveness skills.

EDUCATION

Review the *Problem Solving* handout. Give examples, role play, and reinforce education and techniques learned in previous sessions. Have the clients or couples role play a problem using the techniques in the *Problem Solving* handout. The group can give constructive feedback. If the techniques are followed properly and still no resolution occurs, then a value conflict exists. This must be recognized and then negotiated with compromise because there is no "solution."

Let the clients talk about their feelings, and whether they feel they are accomplishing what they intended when they entered counseling. Ask if there are other issues they feel they need to deal with. Be open to discussing these issues as they surface. Encourage expression of these feelings.

HOMEWORK

Ask the clients to think of a specific problem for which they can apply the problem-solving steps to come up with a solution. Suggest that they jot down some notes about the assignment so they can share them during the next session.

RESOURCES

Bolton, R. (1979). *People skills.* Englewood Cliffs, NJ: Prentice-Hall.

Gordon, T. (1970). *Parent effectiveness training.* New York: Peter Wyden.

McKay, M., Davis, M., & Fanning, P. (1981). *Thoughts and feelings: The art of cognitive stress intervention.* Oakland, CA: New Harbinger Publications.

McKay, M., Davis, M., & Fanning, P. (1983). *Messages: The communication book.* Oakland, CA: New Harbinger Publications.

Problem Solving

Handout

1. **Decide specifically what the problem is.**

   - Do not cast blame.
   - Use "I" messages to express your needs.
   - Verbalize the needs of others involved.
   - Listen to others' view of the problem.
   - Make sure everyone agrees on the definition of the problem.

2. **Brainstorm for possible solutions.**

   - Get possible solutions from others involved.
   - Don't evaluate or discount any solutions at this point.
   - Write down all suggested solutions.

3. **Look at the pros and cons of each possible solution.**

   - Everyone must be honest.
   - Do a lot of critical thinking about possible solutions.

4. **Decide on a solution acceptable to all.**

   - Do not push a solution on others.
   - State the solution so all will be sure they understand.
   - Write down the solution so you can check it later to make sure that it is what each agreed on.

5. **Put the solution into action.**

   - Talk about who will do what and when.
   - Trust each to carry out his or her part.
   - Promote individual responsibility by avoiding reminders, nagging, or monitoring.
   - If someone is not responsible, he or she needs to be confronted using "I" messages.

6. **Evaluate the solution.**

   - Modify the solution if necessary.
   - Check out each person's feelings about the solution.
   - If after a fair amount of time the solution is not working, try another mutually agreed on solution.

Some of the best techniques for problem solving are as follows:

- **Listen actively.**
- **Express feelings honestly.**
- **Care about the needs of others.**
- **Be open to change and revision of solutions if needed.**

Session 21

Most Violent and/or Most Frightening Incident: Part I

OBJECTIVES

To review in detail the most disturbing incident in the family, which the man has committed, so that the clients or couples can recognize the impact of this abusive behavior on both of them; also, to understand the role of power in relationships and the link between power and abusive behavior.

MATERIALS

Weekly Behavior Inventory
Power and Control handout

TASKS

1. Review homework and have clients share problem-solving techniques.
2. Mention that this is final month of therapy and get feedback.
3. Describe *Power-and-Control Wheel* and have group members discuss intimidating behavior.
4. Have the partner or an active, verbal group member discuss in detail the most disturbing incident in the relationship.
5. Focus on any denial or minimization of the description.
6. Have partner describe feelings and how it affected her.
7. Continue discussion and assign homework.
8. Continue termination work.

PROCEDURE

COUNSELING

Review homework from last session. Have any of the couples had difficulties in communication or problem solving during the week? Have them role play the situation, with group members providing feedback and constructive suggestions. Mention to the group that they need to begin preparing for closure as there is only 1 month remaining in the weekly program. Have them think about any issues they still feel unsure of. Be open to discuss any concerns the group members have; it is normal that attachments to the counselors and other members may have occurred.

EDUCATION

Have clients examine the *Power-and-Control Wheel* handout. Explain that threats to power often lead to controlling and intimidating behavior. Physical force is an obvious abuse of power. Other abuses are less obvious, but still are significant in relationships. We hope this counseling program has helped the clients transform their need to control others into control of themselves. A relationship cannot survive in the long run unless power is equally distributed between each partner so neither is threatened or intimidated. Have the clients discuss the types of controlling behavior that were previously used in their relationship.

Ask an active, verbal group member to discuss, in detail, the most disturbing abusive incident committed in the relationship. This does not necessarily mean the most physically injurious event, but rather the one that stands out as the most emotionally upsetting. Pick someone who you think will be able to do this well, providing a positive model for the others. It is very important for the group member to explain the incident as vividly as possible, as if it was happening in slow motion. If gender-specific groups are being conducted, then the partners can be invited to participate in this and the next session to provide information about the incidents. The group member should be asked to describe, at various intervals, his self-talk, emotions, and physical state during the incident. Particularly important is the client's affect during the event. The goal here is to diminish as much of the original denial and minimization as possible. This is an opportunity to go into more depth with these issues, with particular emphasis on using the new skills and information that the clients now have.

When one group member finishes, continue with his partner and have her indicate whether the incident under discussion was the most disturbing or frightening for her. Have her express her feelings concerning this even, in detail, and how it has affected her behavior and reactions. Are both partners expressing similar feelings and reactions to the incident? What techniques have they learned that will keep this from happening again in the future? What options are available to them now? Continue this discussion with other couples and group members.

HOMEWORK

Have the clients think about issues that have not been dealt with adequately, or that they still do not feel comfortable with in their relationship.

Power-and-Control Wheel

PHYSICAL ABUSE

twisting arms, tripping, biting

pushing, shoving, hitting

slapping, choking, pulling hair

punching, kicking, grabbing

PHYSICAL ABUSE

using a weapon against her

beating, throwing her down

POWER AND CONTROL

ISOLATION
Controlling what she does, who she sees and talks to, where she goes.

EMOTIONAL ABUSE
Putting partner down or making them feel bad about themselves. Calling partner names. Making partner think they are crazy. Mind games.

INTIMIDATION
Putting her in fear by: using looks, actions, gestures, loud voice, smashing things.

ECONOMIC ABUSE
Trying to keep her from getting or keeping a job. Making her ask for money, giving her an allowance, taking her money.

USING MALE PRIVILEGE
Treating her like a servant. Making all the "big" decisions. Acting like the "master of the castle."

SEXUAL ABUSE
Making her do sexual things against her will. Physically attacking the sexual parts of her body. Treating her like a sex object.

THREATS
Making and/or carrying out threats to do something to hurt partner emotionally. Threaten to take the children, commit suicide, report partner to welfare.

USING CHILDREN
Making partner feel guilty about the children. Using the children to give messages, using visitation as a way to harass partners.

Adapted from Domestic Abuse Intervention Project; Duluth, MN.

Session 22

Most Violent/Frightening Incident: Part II

OBJECTIVES

To review in detail the most disturbing incident in the family, which the man has committed, so that the clients or couples can recognize the impact of this abusive behavior on both of them; also, to understand the role of power in relationships and the link between power and abusive behavior.

MATERIALS

Weekly Behavior Inventory

TASKS

1. Have clients check in.
2. Continue discussion of most disturbing incident with other group members or other couples.
3. Explain role reversals and assign homework.
4. Continue termination work.

PROCEDURE

This session is a continuation of Session 21 so that all couples or group members can present and describe their most disturbing or frightening incident. Discuss only issues that the clients need to work on.

HOMEWORK

Have the clients do a role reversal during the next week. Have couples reverse roles for a planned event. This should be carried out in detail so that each partner can experience what it feels like to be in the "other's shoes." It is very important to make sure that power and control are reversed in this exercise, even in an exaggerated state. Give the clients the *Intimacy and Love* and *Equality* handouts to review.

Session 23

Intimacy and Love

OBJECTIVES

There are several objectives to this session. One is to provide basic education about love and intimacy. Another objective is to encourage the clients to be aware of and decide what they want in an intimate relationship as well as what they can give to an intimate relationship. The relationship among intimacy, communication, and equality is also explored.

MATERIALS

Weekly Behavior Inventory
Intimacy and Love handout
Intimacy Assignment handout
Equality handout

TASKS

1. Have clients check in and discuss problem areas.
2. Review homework and have clients share feelings.
3. Introduce *Intimacy and Love* and discuss intimacy, love, and sex issues.
4. Have couples or group members talk about expressing feelings verbally and through touch.
5. Discuss idea of marriage beliefs, and why they fell in love.
6. Introduce *Equality Wheel* and *Act of Love.*
7. Have clients share power issues and feelings.
8. Give handouts and assign homework.
9. Continue termination work.

PROCEDURE

COUNSELING

Have the clients fill out the *Weekly Behavior Inventory.* Permit each client to check in and discuss any problem areas. Ask about the homework. Let each client share a problem for which he chose to apply the steps in problem solving. After discussing the homework, discuss negotiation of value conflicts, with role playing by the clients. Have them review their progress. Have the clients discuss their feelings about the most disturbing incident descriptions during the past 2 weeks.

EDUCATION

Review the *Intimacy and Love* handout. Discuss each section, getting feedback from the clients as well as giving examples when appropriate. After completing this handout, give the group the *Intimacy Assignment* during the session. Discuss it in as much detail as time allows. Have the group discuss their marriage expectations and their original hopes and dreams. Which have been met and which have failed? What kind of touching goes on in their relationship?

Review the *Equality Wheel* handout and get feedback from the group members. Where does their relationship fit on this chart? Explain the role of self-respect and equality. What areas in the relationship need improvement in equality? Have them read the Act of Love in the *Intimacy and Love* handout and have the group members express their feelings regarding this with respect to their relationship prior to the program and now.

HOMEWORK

Have the group members complete the *Intimacy Assignment* for the next session. Have them communicate their feelings about their relationship to their partners, if available. Assign them to touch their partners nonsexually at least three times during the week to express their affection for each other gently.

RESOURCES

Barbach, L. (1982). *For each other: Sharing sexual intimacy.* Garden City, NY: Doubleday.
Burns, D. D. (1985). *Intimate connections.* New York: New American Library.
Buscaglia, L. (1984). *Loving each other.* Thorofare, NJ: Slack.
Goldberg, H. (1983). *The new male-female relationship.* New York: The New American Library.
Halpern, H. (1983). *How to break your addiction to a person.* New York: New American Library.
Kiley, D. (1983). *The Peter Pan syndrome: Men who have never grown up.* New York: Avon Books.
Lazarus, A. A. (1985). *Marital myths.* San Luis Obispo, CA: Impact Publishers.
Norwood, R. (1985). *Women who love too much.* New York: Pocket Books.
Rubin, Z. (1973). *Liking and loving.* New York: Holt, Rinehart and Winston.

Intimacy and Love

Handout

How did you get together anyway?

Why were you attracted to each other?

- **Physical Proximity**—Being together, familiarity.

- **Rewards—Anything That Satisfies A Need**—The person may treat you nicely. The benefits and reinforcement of meeting personal needs outweighs the costs.

- **Similarity**—Like backgrounds, interests, attitudes. We assume that others who are similar to us will like us. Similar others often validate our opinions or actions.

- **Opposites**—Sometimes we are attracted to opposites because they provide important needs. Sometimes the very attribute we find attractive initially is what bothers us the most later in the relationship.

  Example: She may feel that he is so strong and a real leader. After they are together for a while, she may view him as domineering and demanding.

- **Doing for Others**—Cognitive dissonance: We like someone for whom we have done a favor.

- **Physical Attractiveness**—Drawn together because of body chemistry or sexual attraction. Sometimes people confuse sexual attraction with love.

- **Self-Esteem**—Sometimes we choose less desirable people because we do not feel we deserve or can get better, or because we may want to feel superior.

STAGES IN RELATIONSHIP DEVELOPMENT

- **Sampling**—This stage involves looking over the possibilities then predicting how satisfying a relationship with this person might be.

- **Bargaining**—This stage involves negotiating mutually satisfying ways of interacting. The couple is trying to get to know each other better and trying to create a way of being together.

- **Commitment**—This stage involves making a mutual decision to spend time together as exclusive partners. This stage is more intimate.

- **Institutionalization**—This is an extension of the commitment stage. It involves some formalization of the commitment (such as marriage). This formalization varies according to cultures and individuals.

PITFALLS IN LOVE RELATIONSHIPS

Pitfalls are common problems that make it difficult to sustain love.

Intimacy and Love *(Continued)*

Handout

BEHAVIOR AT THE BEGINNING OF THE RELATIONSHIP

Individuals may present an idealized self, putting his or her "best foot forward." Other individuals may take the opposite view, however, thinking if the other person can accept his or her worst side, this will be really true love.

The individual may not know him or herself very well and may not accurately perceive the other person.

The individual may mistake sexual attraction for love and find out later they do no even like each other. Society has always glorified romantic love. This involves being wildly excited, sexually aroused, living in a fantasy, and idealizing the relationship. This type of relationship may not be very realistic or enduring.

WHAT IS LOVE?

- **Caring**—This is the feeling that the other person's well-being and satisfaction are as important as your own.

- **Attachment**—This is the need and desire to be with the other person. You want to be approved of and loved by the other person. This does not mean you are dependent on the person.

- **Intimacy**—This involves having close confidential communication and romantic love with its physiological arousal component. Intimacy involves expressing deep feelings, sharing about one's self, and showing tenderness through touching and communicating. Sexual intimacy is also a part of this.

WHAT IS INTIMACY?

Intimacy requires the freedom to be yourself without fear of rejection. It means acceptance without requirements. It is supportive rather than restrictive and combines closeness, trust, and genuine emotion, not possessiveness or control. One must have open, two-way communication, as well as tenderness, affection, warmth, and touching.

A MYTH ABOUT INTIMACY

People often believe that once you find your "one and only," you do not need anyone else. This is not true. No one person can meet all of a person's needs. It is an unrealistic and overwhelming responsibility for one person to have to be "all things" at all times. This is one of the many romantic myths we often fall prey to. We have to work at avoiding these myths.

Eric Fromm, a well-known psychologist, believes that a person's strongest need is love. We need people to listen to us, care about us, and be with us. He sees overcoming isolation and building strong relationships as one of the major tasks of life.

Intimacy and Love *(Continued)*

Handout

HOW CAN WE DEVELOP LOVE OR A LOVING RELATIONSHIP?

Learn all you can about each other. Learn to understand each other's needs. Accept each other as individuals with different needs and desires. Give the relationship time to grow slowly and constantly. Nurture more, criticize less. No one person can meet all of your needs. Give lots of positive attention to each other. Learn to love yourself, so you can love your mate more. It is okay to feel that you are **WONDERFUL!** Learn to express your needs, desires, wants, and feelings. Let your mate express his or her needs, desires, wants, and feelings.

> The act of Love
> is to say,
> "I want you to be
> who you are."
> The act of abuse
> is to say,
> "I want you to be
> who I want
> you to be."
> It is
> that simple.
>
> —James D. Gill

Intimacy Assignment

Handout

What qualities do I want in an intimate relationship?

What qualities can I contribute to an intimate relationship?

Ask your partner what qualities you bring to the relationship. List them below. How do they compare to those you listed above?

Understanding how you express feelings that create intimacy or diminish it helps toward changing or enhancing those expressions. Take a look at the feelings below and state how you express them.

Jealousy _____

Affection _____

Disagreement _____

Rejection _____

Hurt _____

Respect _____

Approval _____

Admiration _____

Anger _____

Love _____

Pride _____

Distress _____

List four people who love you, and beside each name list specific needs that each meets for you.

PEOPLE WHO LOVE ME

1. _____
2. _____
3. _____
4. _____

NEEDS THEY MEET

1. _____
2. _____
3. _____
4. _____

Intimacy Assignment *(Continued)*

Handout

There is a lot more to love than just "falling in," and being in love requires energy and a commitment to work for the relationship. Love, like a plant, needs nurturing to grow. What four actions can you take to nurture and help your love relationship grow?

1. _____

2. _____

3. _____

4. _____

Equality Wheel: Nonthreatening Behavior

Handout

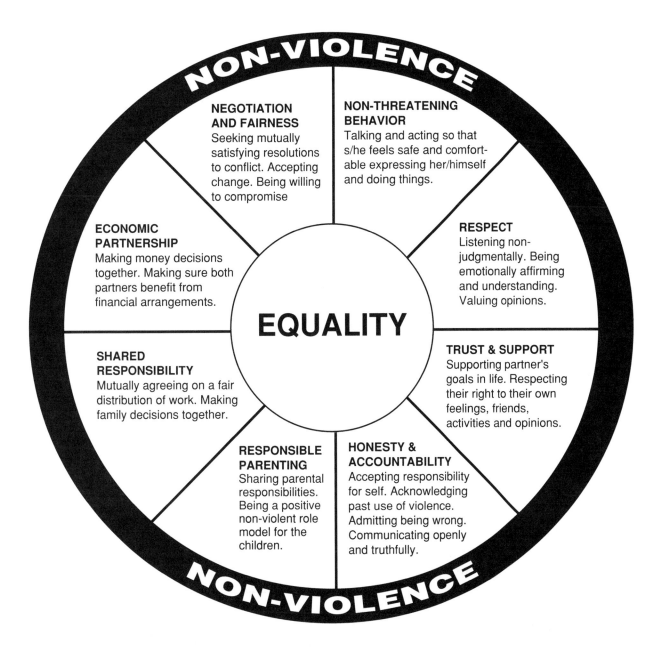

NON-VIOLENCE

NEGOTIATION AND FAIRNESS
Seeking mutually satisfying resolutions to conflict. Accepting change. Being willing to compromise

NON-THREATENING BEHAVIOR
Talking and acting so that s/he feels safe and comfortable expressing her/himself and doing things.

ECONOMIC PARTNERSHIP
Making money decisions together. Making sure both partners benefit from financial arrangements.

RESPECT
Listening non-judgmentally. Being emotionally affirming and understanding. Valuing opinions.

EQUALITY

SHARED RESPONSIBILITY
Mutually agreeing on a fair distribution of work. Making family decisions together.

TRUST & SUPPORT
Supporting partner's goals in life. Respecting their right to their own feelings, friends, activities and opinions.

RESPONSIBLE PARENTING
Sharing parental responsibilities. Being a positive non-violent role model for the children.

HONESTY & ACCOUNTABILITY
Accepting responsibility for self. Acknowledging past use of violence. Admitting being wrong. Communicating openly and truthfully.

NON-VIOLENCE

Adapted from: "Tactics of Men Who Batter," Domestic Abuse Intervention Project, Duluth, MN.

Session 24

Empathy Training
and Role Reversals

OBJECTIVES

To help group members learn skills to identify feelings of others and communicate this understanding to their partners.

MATERIALS

Weekly Behavior Inventory

TASKS

1. Review *Intimacy Assignment* homework.
2. Have couples or group members describe feelings and touching exercises.
3. Role play and point out new techniques in couples' interactions.
4. Have a couple or group members role play a specific conflict, and then have the couple or group members reverse roles.
5. Have other couples or group members practice the same exercise.
6. Discuss empathy and empathic listening.
7. Give handouts and assign homework.
8. Continue termination work.

PROCEDURE

COUNSELING

Have the clients describe the *Intimacy Assignment* homework and describe their feelings about the touching exercises. Then have them discuss their role-reversal exercises, describing their feelings during the assignment. It is important to ensure that the clients gain insight into the experiences of their partners so that empathy is established. Help the clients get "in touch" with deep feelings regarding past behaviors in the abusive relationship, and the hopefulness for improved interactions in the future. Emphasize the skills of active listening, "I" messages, congruent communication, problem solving, and expression of feelings in this counseling session. Have the group members reinforce each other and support the empathy process.

Many clients might behave quite differently if they were genuinely aware of the effect of their behavior on the people around them. At the time, they simply may not have been aware of how they were affecting someone else, or what it must have been like to be in the other person's shoes. If they knew then what they know now (or what they are now learning), they might have been in a position to have made other choices.

Have the couples or group members role play a specific interpersonal conflict. The man is then assigned to take on the woman's role. The conflict scene is role played. The man must describe exactly what his partner is thinking or feeling—without sarcasm, without editorial comments, without trying to make that person look bad. The group and partner, if present, should keep giving feedback until they think the person has played the role just right and has truly gotten inside the other person's shoes. Several couples or group members might have do this.

The goal here is not problem solving, but rather understanding. It is also important to remind people that gaining an empathic point of view does not necessarily mean agreeing with the other person, but simply understanding what it must feel like to the other person.

Let the group members know that there will be monthly follow-up sessions to monitor the relationship and maintain the skills learned in the program.

EDUCATION

Listening with empathy is extremely important in relationships. Listening with empathy means trying to understand what the person is feeling. This does not mean that you must agree with the person. A way of being a more empathetic listener is to try to understand what danger the person might be experiencing, what he or she is asking for, and what need the emotion (i.e., anger) is coming from.

Listen without judging or finding fault. Try to see the other person's point of view. Listen to the whole statement; don't make premature evaluations. How does the information being communicated fit with known facts? Listen and look for congruence of context with nonverbal expressions.

Note: Here are some keys to being a good listener: Have good eye contact, lean slightly forward, reinforce by nodding or paraphrasing, clarify by asking questions, avoid distractions, try to understand empathetically what was said.

In order to provide a better understanding of the reversal of power roles, a demonstration can be done if it is a couples group. Have all of the female group members stand on a chair and discuss the previous power issues with their partners who stand next to them. After a 5-minute discussion, have the women pretend they are at the end of the evening after a date with their partners, and have them bend down to kiss their partner. Following this exercise, discuss the feelings experienced by the group and have them share what they learned. It is important to especially focus on feelings of power, control, insecurity, and levels of comfort.

HOMEWORK

Have clients review the *Relapse-Prevention Plan* handout for the next session. They should also note any closure issues to discuss at the remaining sessions.

Session 25

Relapse-Prevention Plans

OBJECTIVES

To integrate the variety of coping skills in a rehearsal for challenging situations and to help prevent relapse under stress.

MATERIALS

Weekly Behavior Inventory
Relapse-Prevention Plan handout

TASKS

1. Review *WBI* and overall progress.
2. Have clients discuss any unresolved issues.
3. Explain *Relapse-Prevention Plan*.
4. Role play with a group member and guide through a plan.
5. Have other group members role play and practice prevention plans.
6. Give handouts and assign homework.
7. Continue termination work.

PROCEDURE

COUNSELING

Have the clients complete the *Weekly Behavior Inventory*. Because this is nearly the last session, discuss any closure issues the clients want to discuss. Have them note the changes that have occurred in abusive behavior since the beginning of the program (this can be verified by reviewing their *Weekly Behavior Inventories*). Open the discussion to the group members to focus on unresolved or difficult issues that have occurred recently in the relationship.

EDUCATION

Explain that the *Relapse-Prevention Plan* handout is based on a treatment called Cue therapy, which was originally developed to treat cocaine abusers in the Veterans Center. Clinical research showed that even though the patients were exposed to many excellent treatments, many relapsed because they could not resist the old familiar "cues" that triggered the old familiar drug pattern. Cue therapy was introduced so that they could carefully rehearse exposure to these cues while practicing many alternative coping strategies.

Ask for a volunteer to identify a difficult cue or trigger for aggression in his relationship. Then guide the client through each of the different coping strategies. At the completion, the client should have generated one strategy from each category. Now role play the cue situation and ask the volunteer to practice each of the coping strategies. Explain that in real situations it is rarely practical to use all of these. However, it is very valuable to be equipped with as many strategies as possible just in case. This is an advanced version of *The Safety-and-Control Plan* from Session 2.

Ask each group member to decide on his or her own difficult cues and to generate coping strategies for these. Rehearse as many of these as possible.

HOMEWORK

Have the clients review the *Transfer of Change* handout for the next session. Have the clients practice, discuss, and rehearse the *Relapse-Prevention Plans* for their own situations.

Relapse-Prevention Plan

Purpose To prepare you for future situations when you might be tempted to lose control over your behavior and become aggressive.

Technique Exposure to "cues" or danger signals that are very likely to lead you toward these behaviors—without letting yourself actually do them. These "cues" can be listed below and then acted out or imagined through visualization.

Cue 1._____

2._____

3._____

COPING STRATEGIES

1. **Scare yourself/Support yourself**

   a. Remember how you felt after you blew up, or remember the damage to your family.
   b. After this remembrance, focus on a positive image, such as visualizing yourself in a beautiful place and how you feel when you are able to control your reactions.

2. **Relaxation techniques**

3. **Fun**—Plan to participate in another activity that feels good whenever you notice the old urges, such as physical exercises, listening to music, and so on.

4. **Self-Talk**—Talk to yourself. Call on your supportive observer to help you. What could you say to yourself to help?

5. **Talk to a friend**—Call a friend, therapist, sponsor, crisis center, or family member who can help you cope.

Behavior I Am Trying to Manage: _____

Date _____   Name _____

Adapted from Wexler (1991).

Session 26

Future Plans

OBJECTIVES

To review the skills learned throughout the program and to make specific plans for dealing with stressful situations more effectively.

MATERIALS

Weekly Behavior Inventory
Transfer of Change handout

TASKS

1. Review prevention plan homework assignment.
2. Discuss successful uses of these plans during the week.
3. Explain "time machine" technique and practice with group member, and then repeat with other couples or clients.
4. Discuss *Transfer of Change* and have clients choose techniques they would use.
5. Have group members share their maintenance plans.
6. Discuss closure and have clients share their feelings about the program and what they have learned.
7. Continue termination work.

PROCEDURE

COUNSELING

Because this is the last session in the structured program, it is appropriate to have refreshments available to "celebrate" completion or to go out for coffee as a group as a closure ritual at the conclusion of the session.

Review the *Relapse-Prevention Plans* that each group member prepared as homework, and discuss how effective the members were at trying them throughout the past week. Discuss any significant events that occurred during the week.

EDUCATION

Use the "time machine" technique to help the group members project themselves into the future. This is a way of developing clearer goals and anticipating possible pitfalls. Ask for a volunteer. Have this client choose a date in the future, such as a year from today. Using any dramatic means with which you feel comfortable, help the group imagine that the client is being projected via time machine to that date. When she or he "wakes up," the group interviews him or her about life on this future date. Specific questions about how the client has managed to communicate better or work things out with his or her partner are very helpful. The counselor should help the client keep the material realistic. When finished, bring the client back to the present. Repeat this process with several more group members if time allows.

   Ask each group member to discuss what he or she has learned here that will have the most impact on him or her in the future, and what he or she has learned most from this program. Discuss *Transfer of Change* and follow the steps in the group.

HOMEWORK

Tell the clients that their permanent assignment is to now maintain a nonviolent, nonabusive, nonintimidating, positively reinforcing relationship. Let them know that "booster" marital therapy would be normal at times when problems or stressors arise that they have difficulty resolving. It is important for them not to wait until the problems get out of hand before contacting a counselor.

Transfer of Change

Handout

Transfer-of-change techniques help you learn to apply what you have learned in group therapy to problem situations outside of group therapy. Actually, we have already used many of the techniques you are now familiar with. Without transfer of change, what you learned in the group would have been perhaps only an interesting exercise that has **no** application to your life.

Maintenance-of-change techniques helps you preserve the level of positive gains you have made in the group. The aim is to make the skills you have learned in the group have a lasting benefit after the group is completed. Sometimes people find it hard to keep their newly learned skills sharp without an active plan for maintaining those skills.

STEPS

Keeping the skills you have learned sharp, improving your performance, and applying what you have learned in the group to other situations takes work, but it is important. The following steps can lead you to a follow-up plan:

1. Become familiar with techniques available to you. They include the following:

   - Join a self-help group.
   - Teach the assertiveness principles to others.
   - Maintain buddy contacts.
   - Join another group (not necessarily an assertiveness group).
   - Prepare for an unsympathetic environment.
   - Prepare for personal setbacks. Have back up coping statements ready for times when techniques do not work. For example, if you are backsliding say, "I slipped up but I've got the skills now."
   - Predict specific roadblocks you may face. What situations are likely to be most difficult in the future? Have a "road map" ready to handle those situations, which includes a plan of action, techniques you can use, and self-statements that would be helpful.
   - Keep a diary of successes and problem areas.
   - Periodically review the techniques you have learned and your notebook of handouts and assignments. Decide which ones could work for you.

2. Develop a specific, **realistic** plan including only those techniques you plan on using.

PURPOSE

By the end of this exercise you will have devised a personal transfer-of-change and maintenance plan.

EXERCISE

1. You should take several minutes to devise a plan.
2. Break into couples or pairs to discuss and refine plans.
3. Share plans with entire group.
4. Group helps evaluate the plan of each member. Is it complete? Realistic? How can group members help each other to maintain change?

Transfer of Change *(Continued)*

WHAT ARE YOUR MAINTENANCE PLANS FOR THE NEXT MONTH?

In relation to yourself? (e.g., "I will write down my self-talk whenever I get angry.")

_____

_____

_____

In relation to others? (e.g., " I will a set time each week to discuss problems with my partner.")

_____

_____

_____

WHAT ARE YOUR MAINTENANCE PLANS FOR THE NEXT YEAR?

In relation to yourself? (e.g., "I will practice relaxation every week so I will be ready.")

_____

_____

_____

In relation to others? (e.g., "I will encourage my partner to go out more, and will not be possessive.")

_____

_____

_____

Adapted from Wexler (1991) and Rose, Hanusa, Tolman, and Hall (1982), *A Group Leader's Guide to Assertiveness.*

© 1999 Springer Publishing Company.

Monthly Sessions Check-In for Months 7–12

OBJECTIVES

To review progress over the previous month and to provide support and new ideas for difficult family situations.

MATERIALS

Monthly Behavior Inventory

TASKS

1. Review *Monthly Behavior Inventory.*
2. Review successes of group members.
3. Review problem areas.
4. Review prior handouts relevant to problem areas.
5. Role play to improve clients' and couples' skills.
6. Rehearse anticipation situations.
7. Final Evaluations due.

PROCEDURE

1. Review the *Monthly Behavior Inventory* for the group members and discuss any problem areas.
2. Ask for group members to present situations when they have been successful in managing their reactions in new ways. Pay particular attention to examples of new self-talk and new communication skills.
3. Also review problems. Encourage group members to provide feedback based on the skills they have all learned throughout the program. Review the relevant handouts from prior sessions, discuss, and role play to improve or fine tune their skills. Review the *Prevention Plan* and edit some of the strategies if necessary.
4. Ask group members to predict possible challenging situations that may occur over the next month. Rehearse coping strategies.
5. Have clients review relevant handouts from prior sessions, practice the skills, and openly discuss strategies for improving their relationship.
6. Focus on communication techniques, assertiveness, and ways the clients can better meet each other's needs.
7. Remind the couples to continue mutually agreed on leisure activities or "dates."

Monthly Behavior Inventory

Handout

Name: _____ Date: _____

1. **MONTHLY SUCCESS.** Describe one way in the past month in which you successfully kept yourself from being aggressive or successfully used something you learned in group. The success can be large or small.

   Specifically, did you do any of the following?

   _____ Calmly stood up for my rights
   _____ Expressed my feelings appropriately
   _____ Told myself to relax
   _____ Changed my thoughts from negative to positive
   _____ Took a time-out

2. **PROBLEM SITUATION.** Describe a problem situation from the past month. What did you say or do specifically?

   How angry did you become?

1	10	20	30	40	50	60	70	80	90	100

   Not at
   all angry

   Extremely
   angry

3. **AGGRESSION.** Did you become verbally or physically aggressive toward anyone in the past month (including threats and damage to property)?

   Yes _____   No _____   If yes, what did you do?

   _____ Use of weapon   _____ Destruction of property
   _____ Slapping   _____ Choking
   _____ Kicking   _____ Sexual abuse
   _____ Punching   _____ Verbal abuse
   _____ Throwing things   _____ Emotional abuse
   _____ Threatening   _____ Other (explain): _____

   What would you do in a similar situation in the future to avoid becoming aggressive?

4. **HOMEWORK.** Did you complete Homework for the month?

   Yes _____   No _____   If yes, what did you do?

   Reviewed handouts?   Yes _____   No _____
   Completed assignment?   Yes _____   No _____
   Practiced exercise?   Yes _____   No _____
   Communicated with partner? Yes _____   No _____

© 1999 Springer Publishing Company.

Postcounseling Assessment Interpretation and Program Evaluation

Handout

OBJECTIVE

The objective of this assessment is to evaluate the counseling with a questionnaire, and the results can be compared to those prior to counseling.

POSTCOUNSELING QUESTIONNAIRE

Name _____ Client number _____

Group _____ Date _____

Counselors _____

Date that you entered counseling   _____

Date that you left or completed counseling   _____

Marital status while in the program:

Married _____ Cohabitating _____ Separated _____ Single _____

Widowed _____ Divorced _____ Other: _____

Current marital status:

Married _____ Cohabitating _____ Separated _____ Single _____

Widowed _____ Divorced _____ Other: _____

How long have you been in this relationship?

Years _____ Months _____ Don't know _____

Is this the same partner you had while you were in the program?

Yes _____ No _____ I'm not sure _____

What type of counseling format was used?

Men's Group _____ Family Counseling _____ Women's Group _____ Couples Group __

Couples Counseling _____ Individual Counseling _____

What kinds of counseling methods were used in your program?

Self-Esteem Enhancement	_____	Assertiveness Training	_____
Communication Skills	_____	Emotional Awareness Training	_____
Emotional Expression Training	_____	Problem-Solving Skills	_____
Anger Management	_____	Stress Management	_____
Explorations of Gender Roles	_____	Role Playing	_____
Tests/Evaluations	_____	Social History	_____
Support Outside Sessions (hotline, counselor access)	_____	Drug/Alcohol Intervention/ Treatment	_____
Building Social Support Systems	_____		

Postcounseling Assessment Interpretation and Program Evaluation *(Continued)*

How long were you in the program?   Months _____   Weeks _____

Did you finish the program? Yes _____   No _____

If you did not finish the program, what were your reasons?
    Did not feel it was effective _____
    Did not like the staff for the program _____
    Did not feel I needed it _____
    Time conflicted with job_____
    Other (Specify):_____

Was there violence or abuse while you were in the program?
    Yes _____   No_____

If yes, was it: Physical _____   Verbal _____   Sexual_____

If the violence was physical, compared to before you entered the program, was it?
    Less severe _____   About the same _____   More severe _____

If the abuse was verbal, compared to before you entered the program, was it?
    Less severe _____   About the same _____   More severe _____

If the abuse was sexual, compared to before you entered the program, was it?
    Less severe _____   About the same _____   More severe _____

Who was the abusive one?
    Yourself _____   Both _____   Partner _____

How often did the abuse occur?
    Once_____   Once a week_____   Once a month _____   2–3 times a week_____
    2–3 times a month _____   Daily _____   Other (Specify):_____

Did any of the techniques shown or talked about in the program help you deal more effectively with your situation?
    Yes _____   No_____   Don't Know _____   Does Not Apply _____
    If yes, which ones?_____

How much has the program helped to overcome other problems besides the abuse?
    Not Very Helpful _____   Helpful _____   Fairly Helpful_____   Very Helpful_____

How would you rate the program?
    Very Poor ____   Poor ____   Good ____   Very Good ____   Excellent ____   Don't Know ____

Postcounseling Assessment Interpretation and Program Evaluation *(Continued)*

How would you rate the program staff?
    Very Poor ____ Poor ____ Good ____ Very Good ____ Excellent ____ Don't Know ____

Would you recommend this program to others? Yes_____ No_____

Do you think your counselors understood your specific problems?
    Yes_____ No_____ Don't Know_____

Have you ever been in counseling before? Yes_____ No_____

What factors influenced your decision to enter our counseling program?

_____

_____

_____

What in the program was most beneficial to you?

_____

_____

_____

In what ways do you think the program can be improved?

_____

_____

_____

Reader Questionnaire for *Psychoeducational Approach* Manual

Dear Reader,

Please take a moment to answer a few questions about this manual to help us improve future reprints. Tear this sheet out and mail to Robert Geffner, PhD, 3215 Lower Ridge Rd., San Diego, CA 92130.

	Not Useful			Useful
Was this manual useful?	1	2	3	4	5

Was the manual written at the appropriate level of difficulty?

	Too Basic			Too Advanced
	1	2	3	4	5

Was the layout of the counseling sessions adequate?

	Needs Improvement			Excellent
	1	2	3	4	5

Please list assets and weaknesses you found in the manual.

Assets: Weaknesses:

1.   1.

2.   2.

3.   3.

General Comments:

DEMOGRAPHIC INFORMATION

Gender: M   F   Age: 19–25 _____ 26–35 _____ 36–45 _____ Over 45 _____

Ethnicity: White _____   Black _____   Hispanic _____   Native American _____
             Asian _____   Other: _____

Highest Education Completed: _____   Profession:

Reader Questionnaire
for *Psychoeducational*
Approach **Manual** *(Continued)*

How was the manual used?

Private Practice _____

Counseling Center _____   Name (Optional): _____

Shelter _____   Address: _____

Education _____   _____

Other _____   _____

Other suggestions for improving the manual or the treatment program:

Thank you for your time and effort in completing this form and providing us with valuable feedback.

    —RG

    —CM

Appendix

Case Study of a Couple (Male Batterer and Female Victim): Ray and Mary

Ray and Mary were one of many couples who completed the Spousal/Partner Abuse Program. They entered the program at a point when Mary was not sure that the abuse would stop. Ray agreed to therapy because his greatest fear was that Mary would leave him for good. Ray and Mary had been married for 12 years. They have two children. Ray has always been very possessive. He has been verbally and emotionally abusive from the beginning of the marriage. Mary uses a lot of denial concerning the abuse. She convinced herself that Ray was possessive because he "loved" her so much. She believed that he isolated her from family and friends because he wanted to be with her.

The isolation got worse, to the point that all Mary was "allowed" to do was go to work. When Mary is a few minutes late coming home, she is accused of having an affair. Ray has followed Mary numerous times to see if he can catch her with another man. He insists that Mary eat lunch with him every day. Ray has gone days without talking to Mary but expects that she will act normally toward him anyway.

The abuse has escalated through the years. Three years ago Ray started being physically violent. The violence began with an occasional shove or slap. It progressed to weekly shoves and slaps. Ray has tried to choke Mary several times. He often restrains her by pinning her to the wall or on the floor. He slams doors and drives recklessly just to frighten Mary. Ray has pulled the telephone cord out of the wall when Mary talks with friends. She is not allowed to go anywhere or talk on the phone when Ray is home. If the phone rings and the caller hangs up, Ray insists that Mary is getting calls from her boyfriend.

Ray has been verbally and emotionally abusive to the children. He is not physically violent, but the children are afraid of him. They have observed Ray's violence toward Mary numerous times. Ray has also threatened to take the children. He tells Mary that he will leave town and she will never see the children again. This is terribly upsetting to both Mary and the children.

Ray says he did not want to hurt his family. Every time, after he has been violent, he promises that it will never happen again. Mary has heard this so many times that she did not believe it anymore. After a violent incident, Ray started treating Mary and the children better. Mary and the children tried to do everything that Ray wanted. Gradually things got worse again until there was another violent incident. The abuse had become more frequent and more violent. Ray stated that if his family did not "make him mad" he would not get violent. Ray admitted that he had a problem with his temper. He feared that he was losing his wife and children. He admitted trying to control Mary to keep her from leaving. Ray had difficulty expressing these fears. He had never been able to talk about feelings or problems. He had dealt with problems by being controlling, using force, or pretending that the problems did not exist.

Ray and Mary each had three separate interviews with counselors, independently, and had been administered a battery of questionnaires and inventories. They each indicated separately that they wanted to enter a conjoint treatment program. The testing, background, and interviews indicated that this would be a reasonable option for them.

RAY'S BACKGROUND

Ray was the oldest of five children: three boys and two girls. His family had been migrant farmers. They moved often. His father was an alcoholic. He was severely abusive to Ray's mother and the children, including Ray. Ray continues to harbor intense anger toward his father. His parents divorced when Ray was 13. Ray's mother remarried a man just as abusive as Ray's father. Ray had anger toward his stepfather and toward his mother, whom he felt did not protect him. Ray was never allowed to say how he felt about anything. If he disagreed with his parents, he was beaten. Ray started working at age 14 to help support his family. He saw this as his role in life.

After Ray got married and started his own family, he worked most of the time and had little to do with Mary and the children. Mary sometimes says she does not think that Ray loves her because he works so much. Ray's perception is that Mary should know he loves her because he works all the time to provide for her. This is Ray's second marriage. He had been physically and verbally abusive during the first marriage. Ray realized that he was overly strict and sometimes spanked the children too hard. This marriage ended because of the continual and increasing abuse.

MARY'S BACKGROUND

Mary was the youngest of two children. She had three siblings who had died at birth because her alcoholic, raging father had severely battered her mother. Mary was born prematurely, when her mother was barely seven months pregnant, because her mother went into early labor after being battered. Mary's father also physically and verbally abused Mary and her brother. Mary's mother told her that there had been numerous times when Mary was a baby, that he had thrown Mary against the wall because she was crying. The only memory Mary had of her father was of her hiding behind a sofa waiting to see if he was drunk when he came home. She knew if he was drunk he would be hostile and violent.

Mary's mother was timid and insecure. She had also been abused as a child by her abusive, alcoholic father. Mary's parents separated when she was 5. Mary's mother had a sixth-grade education. She had difficulty getting employment and could not earn enough money to provide for herself and two young children. Mary and her brother lived with their grandmother for a year. They lived in an orphanage for the next 5 years. After Mary's mother remarried, they lived with her. Mary's stepfather was like a grandfather because he was twice her mother's age. He provided well financially and did not hit Mary. He was affectionate to Mary and sometimes sexually molested her. He died when Mary was 15. Mary's mother remarried a man who did not want children. Mary's brother went to live with grandparents. Mary was told daily to "get out." At age 16 she ran away from home. She lived with neighbors until she graduated from high school.

Mary had worked since she was 12. Ray did not want her to work. Mary enjoyed working and being with people. It had always been difficult for Mary to depend on anyone. She had not felt that anyone had been there for her. She had felt abandoned as a child. It was frightening to her when Ray threatened to leave and take the children. Mary also worried that if she did stay in the marriage Ray would abuse their children. It was important for Mary to have a family and for her children to have a father. This was something she never had. She tolerated Ray's abuse to keep the family together.

RAY AND MARY'S CURRENT SITUATION

Mary has low self-esteem. She feels overly responsible for keeping the family together. Mary is very sensitive and tends to internalize blame, guilt, and shame. Mary becomes depressed at times because she feels she should be able to "fix" the marriage. She has tried to do what Ray wanted but feels the expectations are constantly changing. Mary feels that she is always "walking on eggshells" to keep the peace. Mary is more verbal than Ray. She admits to nagging Ray about finances. He likes to spend money. This causes financial problems. Mary worries about their finances and feels that Ray does not seem to care. Ray's response is to not worry; his motto is, "It will work out. After all, it always does." Mary has rebelled against Ray's possessive and jealous attitude. She lies to him on occasion to keep the peace. Mary has difficulty being assertive. She feels afraid and guilty most of the time.

Ray and Mary agree on most child-rearing issues. She feared that he would be too strict. She tends to be overly protective. Ray and Mary did not want their children's lives to be like their own childhoods. They made a commitment to complete the Spouse Abuse Program so their family could be happy. Ray did not want to lose his family. He did not want to hurt his wife. Mary was afraid the abuse would continue but she loved Ray and wanted the family to stay together. All Mary ever wanted was for Ray to love her and for the abuse to stop. Mary decided to stay with Ray and not file for a divorce. They entered the Spouse Abuse Program committed to breaking the cycle of abuse.

SESSION ONE

The education module about the house of abuse helped Ray to become more aware of the different ways that he had abused Mary. He knows that hitting and pushing were violent acts. He also is beginning to realize that isolating Mary from friends and family is abusive. He had not considered that driving recklessly and slamming doors were also forms of intimidation and control.

Ray and Mary were nervous about the counseling at first. Ray was reluctant to share much with the other couples in the group. He felt that everyone thought he was "the bad guy." Mary talked about her own family background but said little about her abusive marriage. She stated in later sessions that she was concerned that Ray would get angry when they went home. During the first session, the counselors instructed Ray and Mary not to discuss the session when they went home. They were also told that initially the therapy tends to create more tension in the relationship. They were instructed to avoid arguments until they learned skills to handle the problems without violence. Each would think about the house of abuse and how it applied to their relationship. They would, however, not discuss it with each other. Ray signed a written agreement not to harm Mary in any way.

SESSION TWO

Session two started with Ray and Mary reporting that their week had been tense but there had been no violence. Mary continued to worry that the abuse could recur. The education in Session two about safety-and-control plans helped Ray and Mary learn to develop a plan for times when things might get out of control and there was a threat of violence. Ray expressed feeling threatened by this session. He feared that Mary would be planning to leave him. Ray learned about taking a "time-out" so he could cool off. He stated that he would go for a walk. This had helped him deal with his anger in the past. Ray stated that he had tried at times to leave the house when he was angry but Mary insisted he stay and talk it out. The anger increased and he ended up being abusive. Mary agreed to let Ray leave when he needed to. Each is encouraged to continue to accept responsibility for his or her own behavior. Mary's plan consisted of being able to go to the battered women's shelter if there was a threat of violence or abusiveness, and to call a friend when she needed to talk. Ray would not need to know whom Mary would be calling. Ray and Mary left the session with a safety plan to reduce the danger of another violent incident.

SESSION THREE

During Session three Ray stated that there had been one abusive incident that week. He felt that Mary was nagging him about finances. He told her he did not want to talk about it. Mary kept on griping. Ray said he kept his cool until she got right in his face, screaming at him about not writing check amounts in the checkbook. He knew he needed to take a time-out. However, he pushed Mary and left, slamming the door. Mary agreed that this was basically what had happened. Situations similar to this had occurred often. Ray stated that he knew there was no excuse for him pushing Mary. He said that it happened so quickly. Each discussed their responsibility in what happened. They discussed how they could handle these situations differently in the future. Mary realized that Ray's abuse was not her fault or her responsibility. She agreed to do her part to change her behaviors that were not helpful in these situations.

Ray is attempting to control his behavior but has a long way to go. He is beginning to accept responsibility for what he does. He agreed that even if Mary gets right in his face he does not have the right to shove her or exhibit displays of violence. The counselors used this situation to present the information about anger and appropriate ways to express anger. This module was presented by the counselors who talked about their own experiences with anger.

One counselor stated that she knows her spouse is angry when he becomes very withdrawn and quiet. Mary stated that she knows Ray is angry when his face and ears turn red. He also clenches his fists and stomps through the house. There have been times when he slammed doors. Ray said he knows Mary is angry when she will not look at him and refuses to talk. He said, "Sometimes she says there is nothing wrong but acts like there is." After talking about ways of becoming aware of when a partner is angry, the counselors discussed what they do when their partners are angry. Mary likes to talk about the problem so they can solve it. Until recently Mary had wanted to talk even if Ray was too tired or angry to talk. Mary feels that Ray just gets angry and will not talk so nothing ever gets resolved. Ray said when he feels pressured he gets frustrated and just wants to be left alone. Sometimes he just wants to run away, so he leaves the house without letting Mary know anything. He has wanted to hit the walls and sometimes has been aware that he wanted to hit Mary. He said this has made him feel awful. Ray and Mary have learned various alternatives to violence. As mentioned, Ray indicated that he likes to go for a walk so he can think more clearly and cool off. The counselors discussed the importance of personal space when someone is angry. Mary said that she likes to discuss the problem but if she knows that Ray will be willing to talk later she will be more understanding. They agreed that Ray would go for a walk but will give Mary a specific time that they can talk later. Ray and Mary agreed to try out at least two of the alternatives to violence during the next week. They will also go on a date this week. They will spend time doing a fun activity together.

SESSION FOUR

Ray stated that he was more likely to become abusive when he was under a lot of work stress. Ray said that there had been times he got abusive when his boss had been on his back that day. He would come home in a bad mood and start a fight with Mary. He took his frustration out on

Mary and the children. Ray also stated that he has a difficult time relaxing after a stressful day. Activities that are relaxing to Ray are fishing and walking. There had been limited time available for these activities. Mary likes to read or take a hot bath when she feels stressed. Mary stated that a good "foot rub" helps her relax.

Ray and Mary agreed to be aware of a stressful situation during the week. They would apply some of the stress-control techniques discussed during the session. They would also continue doing an enjoyable activity. Giving each other a back rub was discussed.

SESSION FIVE

Ray became angry during the week when Mary was late coming home from work. He stated that "the later she is the angrier I get." At times he has thought she was with another man. His thinking had been extreme to the point of thinking she was at a motel with another man. He had gone looking for her car at local motels. He had seen her talking with male coworkers and believed that she was having an affair. Ray was encouraged to use his relaxation techniques to calm down when he has these thoughts and feelings. He also developed a step-by-step method to help him feel more comfortable and more secure even when he sees Mary with one of her male coworkers. This step-by-step desensitization method consisted of:

1. Using a relaxation technique.
2. Thinking about Mary having lunch with a male coworker.
3. Using his relaxation technique.
4. Looking at pictures of Mary with a male coworker.
5. Using his relaxation technique.
6. Actually observing Mary having lunch with a male coworker.
7. Using his relaxation technique.

The *Anger Ladder* handout was discussed. Ray and Mary made a list of situations that ranged from low intensity to high intensity that caused them to feel angry. They practiced relaxation techniques with each of these situations. Ray and Mary were debriefed by counselors before leaving the session to assure that they would not take the anger home with them. The cycle of violence was discussed. Ray and Mary had expressed early in their relationship that the tension would continue to build and Ray would become violent. He would be sorry about the abuse and promise that it would not happen again. Everything would go well for a while; then the tension would build again. Ray and Mary are now more aware of the cycle of violence. Ray has learned other skills to reduce the tension.

SESSION SIX

The session about the roots of aggression and alcoholism issues was of special interest to both Ray and Mary. They came from a long history of aggressive role models. Ray and Mary were both abused by fathers and stepfathers. They were both raised in an era when abuse of children was socially acceptable. Men were considered to be the "king of the castle." No one interfered even when they witnessed the abuse. Ray and Mary saw their mothers being abused. They grew up not realizing that many forms of violent behavior were abuse. They had viewed aggression as normal behavior. Ray and Mary were also raised in homes where there was extreme alcohol abuse. Many times the alcohol was used to justify severe aggression.

Ray and Mary were not alcohol users but continued to be influenced by the effects of family alcoholism, especially learned aggression and submissiveness to aggressors. Ray and Mary realized they did not want to raise their children the way they were raised. Ray said, "It's scary sometimes when I get angry. I sound just like my father." Ray and Mary have learned how to and continue to practice expressing anger appropriately in their relationship and toward their children. Accepting full responsibility for their behavior had continually been reinforced during counseling sessions. Understanding the effects of aggressive role models and growing up with alcoholism and family violence has increased Ray and Mary's awareness and the way they react to potentially violent situations. They continue to increase their ability to break the cycle of abuse.

SESSION SEVEN

Ray and Mary used some of the alternatives to violence last week. Ray had gone for a walk on several occasions and had worked out at the gym. Mary had gotten upset with Ray and had talked with a friend about the situation. She also took care of her own relaxation needs by going fishing.

One situation that had come up during the week was a disagreement about the children. Mary wanted to talk about it "right now." Ray recognized he was getting angry and told Mary he needed time to think. Mary was proud of herself because she did not push Ray to talk. They talked about the problem later and were able to come up with some solutions. Both were amazed that they had actually solved a problem without violence and had been assertive in doing so. There had been another situation that did not go as well. Ray said Mary had a habit of meeting him at the door with problems when he came home from work. This particular problem also involved the children. They had been difficult that day and Mary wanted Ray to discipline them immediately on his arrival. Ray was tired and did not want to deal with the children. Mary felt that he was dumping all the responsibility of the children on her. She also said all he does is come home and pile up on the couch. She feels she has to do all the cooking, cleaning, and child care. She reminded him that she works outside the home too. Ray stated that she does not work as hard as he does. Both kept adding ammunition to the fight and soon were fighting about numerous situations instead of the original problem. There was no physical violence but they came to no solutions either.

This situation leads to the counselors discussing the fair-fighting education module. Mary agreed to give Ray at least 30 minutes to rest after he got home before they would handle the problems of the day. Ray agreed that he would handle the situation after he relaxed for a few minutes. Both agreed to make a list of the household chores and divide them up. The children could also be included in doing some of the chores. Ray's feelings about working harder than Mary were discussed. Mary was able to express her feelings also. Counselors were able to use these situations to help Ray and Mary become aware of the dirty fighting in their relationship. Examples discussed were Mary's wanting to solve problems immediately and Ray "hitting below the belt," when he says that he works harder than Mary. They discussed fair-fighting techniques that could be used in these situations.

SESSION EIGHT

Ray and Mary continued to discuss fair-fighting and dirty-fighting techniques during Session eight. Ray reported that Mary is always analyzing him and playing psychiatrist. He also said that sometimes she says so much that he forgets what the real problem is. This has been frustrating to him because he does not know what he needs to "fix." Mary pointed out that Ray is so jealous that he tries to set her up to make her look bad. He spies on her during the day. At the end of her day he asks her questions about her day trying to trip her up. If she does not give him exact details, he accuses her of being unfaithful. Ray also goes through Mary's purse looking for telephone numbers or he listens in on her telephone conversations. When she tells him the truth about telephone numbers and any other situations, he does not believe her and continues to accuse her until they get into a fight. Mary said she told Ray about a coworker flirting with her. Ray continues to throw this up to her making it sound like she encouraged it. Mary feels that Ray has a hard time putting things in the past. When they do get into a fight over these kinds of situations, Ray does not apologize. He expects Mary to just act like nothing ever happened. This has made it difficult for Mary to feel close to Ray or want to be sexually intimate. She is hurt and angry. These situations are discussed during the counseling. Ray and Mary realize that this is dirty fighting and that it is creating barriers in their communication. Specific rules for effective communication are discussed. Two other barriers to their communication were explored. These were "mind reading" and "putting the other person in a double bind." During the session Mary stated that Ray never tells her he loves her. Ray said, "She should know I love her. After all I work day and night so she can have things." Mary is able to let Ray know that she needs to hear him verbalize his feelings for her. He agrees to start telling Mary how he feels instead of expecting her to read his mind. Another situation that had occurred during the week was an example of Ray putting Mary in a double bind. Ray had become angry, stomped out of the house, and slammed the door. Mary thought he needed a time-out so she did not go after him. He became angrier and angrier and accused her of not caring about his feelings.

Mary was confused about this because she thought that Ray wanted a time-out. Ray thought Mary should have known when to come after him to give him comfort by how hard he slammed the door. Mary could have been in danger if she followed him outside. Ray realized that this was a mixed message and was setting Mary up to lose either way. Mary did not think she could tell the difference in how hard Ray slammed the door. Ray agreed to make more of an effort to verbalize what he needed from Mary and not expect that she read his mind or tell by nonverbal cues. Direct methods of communication were discussed. Ray will tell Mary in a more direct way when he needs a hug or to be comforted. Ray and Mary role played this same situation using these methods.

SESSION NINE

Ray and Mary reported that their communication was much better during the past week. Mary said that one problem that she and Ray have had is that Ray sometimes talks "mean" to her. Ray denied this. The counselors decided to tape the session so Ray and Mary could hear themselves communicate. After discussing several issues that had come up during the week and hearing Ray and Mary disagree about those events the counselors replayed the tape. Ray was surprised that he did sound gruff and critical when he talked to Mary. Mary also realized that she did sound like she was nagging Ray. Each accepted responsibility in how he or she was expressing his or her opinions and feelings.

There had been another verbally abusive incident during the week. Ray's jealousy had come up again. Mary was 30 minutes late getting home from work. Ray immediately started questioning Mary and demanded to know where she had been. When Ray began accusing her of being with another man, Mary knew things were getting out of control. She suggested they take a time-out and talk in an hour. Ray agreed to this. When Ray and Mary did talk, Ray was able to express that he worries about Mary when she is late. He begins to fear that she has been hurt and that he was not there to protect her. What Ray really wanted was to be able to ask Mary to call if she is going to be late. Mary said she would call next time if at all possible. Ray also agreed to not overreact when Mary is a few minutes late. The counselors used this situation to discuss expressing feelings and listening to each other. One of Ray's gripes about Mary was that he feels that she does not let him talk. Ray said that Mary interrupts when he is talking and sometimes finishes his sentences for him. Ray said that he just backs off and does not say anything. Mary gets upset when Ray clams up. She feels that he just does not care. Mary feels that Ray tunes her out and does not listen to how she feels. Mary stated that when she talks to him he has his nose in the TV or newspaper. The counselors shared two other extreme situations with the group. One situation was about a wife who had become frustrated and violent because she did not feel that her husband was listening. This woman was trying to tell her husband what had happened to the children while he was gone. He did not respond to anything she had said. She became angry and deliberately turned a bowl of soup upside down on the table. This got his attention but ended up with his beating her. Another wife became upset because her husband had been giving her the silent treatment for over a week. When he went to take a shower, she tried to stab him with a kitchen knife. Ray and Mary's situation was not this extreme but because of their difficulty talking with each other and the feeling that the other was not listening it could escalate. Ray and Mary role played their situation using more positive methods. They were given lots of reinforcement by counselors and other group members for a job well done.

SESSION TEN

There were two major issues that tended to get Mary upset with Ray. One was that Ray works so much he does not have much time with Mary. The other is that Ray does not handle finances very well. Ray accuses Mary of nagging him about these problem areas. Mary sees it as a problem that needs to be discussed and solved. The counselors used these issues to teach Ray and Mary about learning to give and handle criticism effectively.

Ray considers that he is showing his love to Mary by being a hard worker. Mary appreciates how well he provides for the family but gets angry because they have no time left for each other. Ray and Mary are encouraged to see the other's point of view. They are also encouraged to accept their part in the problem but to also consider some solutions to these problems. The following solutions were discussed:

1. Agree to spend more time together.
2. Take advantage of the time together by making it quality time.
3. Talk more about finances.
4. Agree on spending and record keeping.

Ray also had some criticisms of Mary. One criticism was that she does not want to visit with his family. Another is that he feels she is always late to pick him up from work. Mary admits that she is uncomfortable around Ray's family. She feels that they are critical of her. When she has gone to visit in the past, his mother asked if she had gained weight. Ray agrees that Mary does not have to go with him all of the time to visit his family but he would like her to come some of the time. Mary states that she is not always late to pick him up but she is late sometimes. Mary will make more of an effort to be on time to pick Ray up, but Ray will not expect her to be on time every day.

SESSION ELEVEN

Ray was not allowed to express his feelings when he was growing up. He was beaten and put down for being weak or disrespectful. He grew up keeping feelings inside, eventually blowing up in a rage. The only feeling that he could identify was anger. In reality he was sensitive and caring. He was frightened sometimes but usually expressed this as anger. Mary was raised to be submissive. She was accused of being aggressive when she tried to express how she felt or asked for what she needed. Many times she heard, "Mary, that's not ladylike."

Ray and Mary both had a difficult time identifying what they felt. This had affected their being able to have open communication with each other. Many times they had to mind read to try to understand what the other was feeling. This guessing was inaccurate and either caused more distance in their relationship or an argument.

SESSION TWELVE

Ray reported getting angry at Mary this week. She had invited one of her friends over to their home. Ray said, "I feel so angry when Mary invites her friends over and they sit at the kitchen table talking and laughing. I'm usually sitting in the living room by myself." Mary said Ray gets mad and goes in the bedroom and slams the door. Mary gets embarrassed. Her friends feel uncomfortable and leave. They will not come over again. After this happens, the fight is on. The counselors discuss the emotional-awareness and cognitive-reframing education to assess this recurring situation. Ray is asked what he is feeling before the anger and his reaction. Ray says, "I feel that she does not care about me." Ray is asked what he is feeling physically. Ray says his stomach feels sick and he begins to get restless and tense. As he remembered how his body felt he was encouraged to think about how he could have done something differently in a similar situation. He said he could also join in the conversation with Mary and her friend. Ray said he did not mind if Mary has friends. He does not like to feel excluded. Ray is encouraged to view this situation in a different way. Just because Mary has friends does not mean that she cares less about him. It was also emphasized that it is important for Ray to have friends to talk to and do things with. Ray and Mary role play a situation similar to what happened during the week. Both are encouraged to express their feelings and to be aware of physiological responses to those feelings. As they become more aware of what happens physiologically they will have more control to stop and think about an appropriate reaction to the situation. This does not mean they will always react appropriately, but it will increase their ability to do so.

SESSION THIRTEEN

It was evident that Ray and Mary both have low self-esteem. Ray realized that his lack of self-confidence affected his relationship with Mary and with others. He is jealous and fears losing Mary to someone who is better looking, has a better job, or has more money. Sometimes he even doubts his sexual adequacy. His fear of losing Mary has made him extremely possessive. He tries to keep Mary isolated from everyone. Mary had been told by her stepfather that she was no good and would never amount to anything. She thinks of this often. She hesitates about doing anything new for fear that she will fail. This, along with her feeling rejected, and the childhood abuse had increased her low self-esteem. This lack of self-confidence was a part of putting up with Ray's abuse. She feared that no one else would want her. She also feared she would be unable to make a living for herself and the children. Ray and Mary's feelings about themselves are discussed while the counselors present the dynamics of self-esteem. This module has helped Ray and Mary to view themselves in a more positive way.

SESSION FOURTEEN

Ray and Mary thought more about why they had low self-esteem. Ray said that Mary was always putting herself down. He also admitted to being very critical of Mary. He called her stupid on numerous occasions. He became aware of how this had reinforced Mary's low self-esteem. The counselors presented the module about the techniques for building self-esteem, indicating ways to stop negative self-talk and verbal self-criticism. An example of this was Mary saying, "I'm stupid." Replacing this with positive statements could change this way of thinking.

Ray had no trouble saying positive things about others but had difficulty accepting compliments. Mary said that Ray is very intelligent. Ray quickly discounted this compliment by saying that he only finished high school. Ray shared that he felt inferior to Mary and others who have college degrees. Ray worked at a highly skilled job. He supervised and trained other men. Ray was encouraged to see that these skills are just as much a part of intelligence as taking college courses. The dangers of comparing oneself with others were discussed. Ray and Mary were encouraged to continue looking at their strengths and to continue building each other up.

SESSIONS FIFTEEN AND SIXTEEN

Ray and Mary had another incident that involved Ray getting angry because Mary was late getting home. Mary said she had been talking on the phone at work and had not noticed that she left work late. She had not called Ray to let him know she would be late. When she got home, Ray met her at the door accusing her of being with someone else. Ray said he did not really believe that Mary was with anyone else. Ray was encouraged to really think about what he was thinking and feeling when Mary was late. Ray and Mary both said this situation comes up often. Mary thought that Ray was extremely jealous and too possessive. Ray said that when he gets home and no one is there he becomes restless. If Mary does not come home soon after he does, it really bothers him. Sometimes he feels all alone and gets scared that Mary will not come home. At this point, he gets angry at himself and starts feeling that he is weak. Ray has realized that this is irrational thinking and he gets caught up in the negative self-talk. His thoughts about losing Mary are negative self-talk that gets him upset and angry. He ends up taking his anger out on Mary. This session helped him to recognize negative self-talk. He also learned skills to change the self-talk and to think about the situation differently. He had learned to replace the negative thinking with positive self-talk. When he starts fearing that Mary will leave him, he will recognize this as irrational and negative self-talk. Ray will change his thinking to see the situation in a positive way so he will not get all upset when Mary is getting home.

SESSION SEVENTEEN

It has always been upsetting for Ray when Mary had a friend over to visit when he was home. This came up again in the past week. Ray started feeling left out. He began to fall into negative self-talk and irrational thinking. He thought that Mary enjoyed being with her friend more than with him. He continued this negative thinking until he got himself all worked up and angry. He thought that he would just show Mary. He did not need her either. The more he thought this way, the angrier he got. He thought at one time that he would just storm out and slam the door. He knew she would know he was angry and the friend would get upset and leave. Then it came to his mind that he was thinking negatively and trying to control Mary. He learned to recognize negative self-talk. He began to reframe his thinking, using counters and relaxation techniques to manage his anger. He knew that he should approach this in a more assertive manner to get his needs met. He went into the kitchen and asked if he could join in the conversation with Mary and her friend. He talked for a while and then told Mary he was going to go over to a friend's house to visit for a while.

Ray learned that he did not need to feel threatened by Mary's friendships. He started to make plans to engage in activities with his friends and family and not expect that Mary should be there. Ray and Mary practiced ways that they can respond when they start thinking negatively in these situations. They have learned to react more appropriately to stressful situations that could lead to violence.

SESSION EIGHTEEN

Ray's violence toward Mary caused her to be fearful. She had a difficult time expressing feelings, thoughts, and needs in an assertive way. She admitted to being manipulative and passive-aggressive in dealing with Ray. Mary said the relationship had improved since they have been in counseling but she still had a lot of fear. Mary stated that Ray's unwillingness to voluntarily help around the house continues to be a problem for her. In a previous session Ray had agreed that he would help Mary but had not consistently followed through. He says he forgets. She has difficulty asking for his help because she is afraid he will get angry. This situation was used to point out that Mary has difficulty being assertive with Ray. Mary said at times she slams and bangs things around, such as dishes, to let Ray know that she is upset. Mary said that she could ask Ray for help if she was not afraid he would get angry. Ray says he will not get angry if Mary asks for help with the household chores. Mary stated that she would like for Ray to help without being asked. Ray and Mary agree that they will make a chore list and each will accept the responsibility to do the chores he or she has agreed to. They will also work together on some neither wants to do. Ray will begin accepting more responsibility around the house. He has realized that Mary works hard on her job and has a lot of responsibility at home. Ray had grown up thinking that household duties were "women's work." He has developed a different attitude since Mary brought this to his attention. Ray and Mary feel much better about their relationship when they work together, even if it's cleaning toilets.

SESSION NINETEEN

Ray and Mary continued to think about situations that needed more assertive action. Mary thought of one situation in which it had been difficult for her to say no. This situation involved her church friends asking her to do things in the church that she did not want to do. Mary would go ahead and say yes and then be angry. Ray gripes at her for getting overly involved when she really does not want to. Ray says he has a difficult time saying no when his buddies ask him to go out. He thinks they might think he is henpecked if he does not go. Ray and Mary role play these situations and practice saying no to requests from others that they really do not want to do.

SESSION TWENTY

Ray and Mary are communicating more effectively now. They are both more assertive and direct with each other. They are now able to talk about their feelings and the problems they have regarding feeling threatened or becoming violent. Their finances, for example, had caused a lot of stress in their relationship. This problem was discussed in relationship to problem-solving and decision-making skills.

According to Mary, Ray pretends there is no problem. This is upsetting to Mary because she feels he does not care. She feels it is left up to her to see that the bills are paid. There have been times that Ray wrote checks and did not record them. He had also written checks knowing that the money was not in the bank to cover the checks. This ended up causing bounced checks that Mary had to explain. This was embarrassing as well as costly. Ray believes that Mary worries too much about finances. He admitted that he does cause additional financial expense because of his neglect in record keeping. This situation caused both Ray and Mary to get upset. Some possible solutions are discussed. Mary suggested that they work together to pay bills so Ray can be more aware of their financial obligations. They also decided to develop a budget. Both agreed to discuss any additional financial endeavors with the other prior to spending the money. Ray agreed not to write checks unless there was sufficient money in the bank to cover them. He would also take the time to record the check properly. They believe their debt is large enough to consult with the local consumer-credit counselor for advice. Ray and Mary have been able to look at a specific problem and come up with several solutions. Compromising and working together have been the key points of emphasis.

SESSIONS TWENTY-ONE AND TWENTY-TWO

Ray shared an abusive incident with the group that he thought was the most violent in his relationship with Mary. He stated that he had come home from a very stressful day at work and Mary was on the phone talking with one of her coworkers. He can not explain why he gets so angry when Mary is on the phone. He reported feeling his stomach tighten and his body getting more tense. This all happened very quickly. He remembered grabbing the phone out of her hand and pulling the cord out of the wall. He said he could not believe that he was suddenly out of control. He grabbed Mary and started choking her. He remembered how frightened she looked. To top it all off, his daughter came into the room and saw what he was doing. She began crying and telling him he was hurting mommy. He let go of Mary and asked if she was okay. Mary continued to look frightened and took their daughter to another room. Ray stated that he could not believe that it was he who had actually done this. He went to the bedroom door telling Mary he was sorry. Ray now realizes that he has a lot of rage that tends to jump out when he gets angry. Ray talked about how Mary must have felt through this violent incident. He has realized that just his size and nonverbal, hostile attitude is very intimidating to Mary. He now accepts responsibility for his behavior and does not blame his reactions on Mary. He has also learned to slow his thinking when he becomes angry. This has helped him to react in a more appropriate way.

Mary stated that she can tell when Ray comes home what mood he is in. She said when he gets an angry look on his face, stomps in the door, and just gives her a "certain look" she becomes frightened and fears that there will be trouble. Mary stated that one of the most frightening incidents to her had been Ray's threat to leave and take the children. She felt that Ray did this to control her. Ray stated that he knew that if Mary left him she would come back if he had the children. The *Power-and-Control Wheel* is discussed in relationship to these incidents. Mary stated that Ray has taken more control of his behavior. He was relating to her on a more assertive and equal level. She has become more relaxed and intimate in the relationship because of these changes. Mary also talked about her feelings during and after the incident that Ray described. This had a strong impact on Ray and the others in the group.

SESSION TWENTY-THREE

Progress in the counseling is evaluated during this session. Ray and Mary are communicating openly about problems and feelings. They are dealing with anger appropriately and learning to be less fearful. They have learned to talk about solutions to problems as the problems come up. These changes have already brought about more openness and intimacy in the relationship. They report feeling much closer to each other.

During this session it is discussed that Ray and Mary both need to have other people in their lives. Neither one needs to feel threatened because they have other friends. Each partner should have his or her own friends, family, and activities that he or she enjoys. They also need couples with whom they can do things. It is discussed that no one person can meet all of a person's needs. Ray has learned to deal with his fear of losing Mary so he is more open to her having friends. Mary is also becoming less fearful about reaching out to make friends. Ray no longer demands that Mary do everything with him. He goes fishing with his buddies without insisting that she go. He also goes to visit family without Mary.

Ray and Mary have become more assertive in expressing their likes and needs when it comes to intimacy. Mary says she feels more desire for sexual intimacy because she is less frightened and angry. Ray said he does not feel rejected when Mary does not want to be sexually intimate. He no longer fears that he is not pleasing her. He no longer fears that she might look for another man who might please her more. His increased self-esteem and confidence have added strength to the marriage.

SESSION TWENTY-FOUR

Ray has become more aware of the effects of his behavior on Mary and the children. The counselors encouraged Ray to put himself in Mary's place and describe how he would feel if he were the one being controlled, frightened, and abused. Mary has described how frightened she was when Ray threatened to leave and take the children. He had said she would never see them again. Ray described that he would have been terrified if Mary had said that to him. Ray seems to be more empathetic toward Mary. He has made an effort to use positive communication to get his needs met. He and Mary have learned to listen to each other as well as talk openly and honestly. Mary no longer feels that she has to agree with Ray just to keep the peace.

SESSIONS TWENTY-FIVE AND TWENTY-SIX

Ray and Mary have benefitted tremendously from the Spouse Abuse Program. There has been no physical violence in several months. Other forms of abuse have decreased. Ray and Mary are more aware of the repetitive nature of situations. They have learned the cues and triggers that have led to violence in the past. They have learned to quickly resort to more positive, nonviolent ways to handle these situations. Ray and Mary have enjoyed having fun together. They have learned to participate in activities that feel good and that have brought the intimacy back into their relationship. They each plan to continue in individual counseling to work on some of their childhood traumas. They have realized the effect that the past has had on their relationship. They also plan to continue to be in contact with other group members who have been part of their "buddy system." Ray and Mary know that even though they have made good progress, the future will not be perfect. They will expect setbacks and deal with them as they come up. They will call the counselors immediately if they are unable to handle a situation. They will also attend refresher courses that will be offered by their counselors. They look forward to group gatherings and reunions in the future. They also decided to enter marital counseling to continue to work on the issues raised in this program, and to improve their skills.

References

Beck, A. T. (1978). *Beck Depression Inventory*. Philadelphia: Center for Cognitive Therapy.

Beck, A. T. (1979). *Cognitive therapy and emotional disorders*. New York: New American Library.

Briere, J. (1985). *Trauma Symptom Inventory (TSI)*. Odessa, FL: Psychological Assessment Resources.

Burns, D. D. (1989). *Feeling good: The new mood therapy*. New York: New American Library.

Campbell, J. C. (Ed.). (1995). *Assessing dangerousness: Violence by sexual offenders, batterers, and child abusers*. Newbury Park, CA: Sage.

Coolidge, F. L. (1994). *Coolidge Axis II Inventory*. Colorado Springs, CO: University of Colorado.

Cull, J. G., & Gill, W. S. (1982). *Suicide Probability Scale (SPS)*. Los Angeles: Western Psychological Services.

Derogatis, L. R. (1975). *Symptom Checklist—90 Revised (SCL-90 R)*.

Ellis, A., & Harper, R. A. (1975). *A new guide to rational living*. North Hollywood, CA: Wilshire Book Company.

Geffner, R., Jordan, K., Hicks, D., & Cook, S. (1985, August). Psychological characteristics of violent couples. In R. Geffner (Chair), *Violent couples: Current research and new directions for family psychologists*. Symposium conducted at the annual convention of the American Psychological Association, Los Angeles.

Geffner, R., Mantooth, C., Franks, E. D., & Patrick, T. (1992). *Aggressive Behavior Inventory*. Unpublished manuscript.

Geffner, R., & Pagelow, M. (1989). *The Spouse Abuse Identification Questionnaire*. Tyler, TX: The Family Violence & Sexual Assault Institute.

Gondolf, E. W. (1998). *Assessing woman battering in mental health services*. Thousand Oaks, CA: Sage Press.

Hathaway, S. R., & McKinley, J. C. (1989). *The Minnesota Multiphasic Personality Inventory 2 (MMPI 2)*. Minneapolis, MN: National Computer Systems.

Hudson, W. W., & McIntosh, S. R. (1981). The assessment of spouse abuse: Two quantifiable dimensions. *Journal of Marriage & the Family, 43*, 873–885.

Jaffe, P. G., & Geffner, R. (1998). Child custody disputes and domestic violence: Critical issues for mental health, social service, and legal professionals. In G. Holden, R. Geffner, & E. Joureles (Eds.), *Children exposed to marital violence: Theory, research and applied issues*. Washington, DC: American Psychological Association.

Mantooth, C., Geffner, R., Patrick, J., & Franks, A. D. (1987). *Family preservation: A treatment program for reducing couple violence*. Tyler, TX: University of Texas at Tyler Press.

Mauger, P. D., Adkinson, R. R., Zoss, S. K., Firestone, G., & Hook, D. (1980). *Interpersonal Behavior Survey (IBS)*. Los Angeles: Western Psychological Services.

Millon, T. (1987). *Millon Clinical Multiaxial Inventory II (MCMI-II)*. Minneapolis, MN: National Computer Systems.

Olson, D. H., Portner, J., & Lavee, Y. (1985). *Faces III: Family Adaptability and Cohesion Evaluation Scales*. St. Paul, MN: University of Minnesota.

Riza, R. R., Stacey, W. A., & Schupe, A. (1985). *An evaluation of the effect of the Family Preservation Program in Tyler, Texas (Vol. 35)*. Arlington, TX: University of Texas at Arlington, Department of Sociology, Anthropology, and Social Work, Center for Social Research.

Saunders, D. G. (1980). *Alternatives to aggression: A curriculum developed for the Alaskan prison system*. Ann Arbor, MI: University of Michigan School of Social Work.

Saunders, D. G., Lynch, A. E., Grayson, M., & Linz, D. (1987). The inventory of beliefs about wife beating. *Violence and Victims, 2*, 39–57.

Schinka, J. A. (1985). *Personal Problems Checklist for Adults.* Odessa, FL: Psychological Assessment Resources.

Schinka, J. A. (1989). *Personal History Checklist for Adults.* Odessa, FL: Psychological Assessment Resources.

Selzer, M. (1971). The Michigan Alcohol Screening Test: The quest for a new diagnostic instrument. *American Journal of Psychiatry, 127,* 1653–1658.

Shupe, A., Stacey, W. A., & Hazelwood, L. R. (1987). *Violent men, violent couples: The dynamics of domestic violence.* Boston: Lexington Books.

Snyder, D. K. (1997). *Marital Satisfaction Inventory—Revised (MSI).* Los Angeles: Western Psychological Services.

Stacey, W. A., & Schupe, A. (1983). *The family secret: Domestic violence in America.* Boston: Beacon Press.

Straus, M. A. (1979). Measuring intrafamily conflict and violence: The Conflict Tactics (CT) Scales. *Journal of Marriage and the Family, 41,* 75–88.

Tolman, R. M. (1989). The initial development of a measure of psychological maltreatment of women by their male partners. *Violence and Victims, 4,* 159–178.

SP *Springer Publishing Company*

Crisis Intervention and Trauma Response
Theory and Practice

Barbara Rubin Wainrib, EdD and **Ellin L. Bloch,** PhD

"The authors have eminently succeeded in developing effective and well-grounded theoretical approaches towards helping people in crisis situations . . . an important contribution to the field of crisis intervention . . . actively helps restore the feelings of self that has been damaged by trauma. I highly recommend this book."

—**Martin Symonds**, M.D.
Deputy Chief Surgeon (Psychiatrist)
New York City Police Department, Clinical Associate Professor of
Psychiatry, New York University-School of Medicine

Crisis Intervention and Trauma Response
THEORY AND PRACTICE
Barbara Rubin Wainrib
Ellin L. Bloch
Springer Publishing Company

"This book is very special in its integration of solid conceptualization and compassionate practice. Covering an unusually wide spectrum of crises and traumas, it places them in a context well-suited for the practice-oriented student. Through the use of well-integrated exercises and introspections, it successfully conveys the message that 'helping' is a personal—not just an academic—experience."

—**John A. Clizbe**, PhD
Management and Consulting Psychologist

Written in a lively and informative style, the book presents a successful general crisis response model for intervention. Using real-life case examples and exercises to develop techniques for building verbal and nonverbal skills, the authors encourage therapists to help clients cope by focusing on clients' inner strengths rather than on pathologies that need to be fixed.

The authors' down-to-earth approach to this topic will appeal to crisis intervention professionals, teachers, students, and volunteer workers.

Contents:
- Crisis, Trauma, and You: Theories of Crisis and Trauma
- How We Respond to Crisis and Trauma
- Principles and Models of Intervention
- Assessment for Crisis and Trauma
- Suicide and Violence: Assessment and Intervention
- Putting it all Together: The Pragmatics

1998   224pp   0-8261-1175-0   softcover   www.springerpub.com

536 Broadway, New York, NY 10012 • (212) 431-4370 • Fax: (212) 941-7842

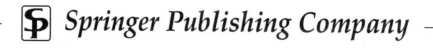

The Heart of Intimate Abuse
New Interventions in Child Welfare, Criminal Justice, and Health Settings

Linda G. Mills, PhD, LCSW, JD

"This delightfully readable book is a must for all child welfare workers. Through her strength of scholarship and critical analysis, Mills has produced a groundbreaking work that will be the basis of redirecting future research, training and professional practice. She is truly a pioneer."

—**Duncan Lindsey,** author of **The Welfare of Children**
Editor, *Children and Youth Services Review*

This startling analysis of patterns of violence in intimate relationships contends that every abusive relationship has a paradoxical "heart" of its own. This dynamic emotional field must be understood in order for family violence interventions to be successful.

Mills takes a critical view of broad current case practices in criminal justice, social work and medical systems especially those that meet family violence with coercive interventions such as mandatory arrest—strategies which often ignore the interpersonal bonds hidden within abusive relationships. Mills introduces new intervention strategies which build on the emotional strengths of the battered woman as an individual, and go to the heart of her abusive relationship to find an intervention that works.

Here at last is a bold vision of the core causes of intimate abuse on which professionals and policymakers can build strategies—a new ground of theory that at least reaches the heart of the problem of family violence.

Partial Contents:
- The Criminal Justice System's Response to Domestic Violence
- The Public Child Welfare System's Response to Domestic Violence
- The Health Care System's Response to Domestic Violence
- Engaging the Battered Mother: Empowerment and Affective Advocacy
- Systems Strategies for Working with Battered Mothers and Their Children
- Empowerment and Affective Strategies I: Meetings in Criminal Justice
- Empowerment and Affective Strategies II: Meetings in Public Child Welfare
- Empowerment and Affective Strategies III: Meetings in Health Care
- Treating Domestic Violence
- An Empowerment Model for Battered Women and Their Children

Springer Series on Family Violence
1998   296pp   0-8261-1216-1   hardcover   www.springerpub.com

536 Broadway, New York, NY 10012 • (212) 431-4370 • Fax: (212) 941-7842

SP Springer Publishing Company

Education Groups for Men Who Batter
The Duluth Model
Ellen Pence and Michael Paymar
with Contributions by: Tineke Ritmeester and Melanie Shepard

"Pence and Paymar are right on target again. Their analysis of battering is excellent and their approach...is straightforward, useful and clear. [The book] tells you what to do with abusive men and how to do it well. [The authors] challenge practitioners to do their work in a manner that is compassionate yet never colluding. Accountability and safety to battered women and creating a process of change for abusive men are central to its success."

-Susan Schechter, author of *Women and Male Violence*

"Drawing upon years of experience . . . Pence and Paymar have written a practical and conceptually sound curriculum for batterers' groups. This book offers an effective guide to both the beginning facilitator and the experienced clinician for engaging batterers in the lifelong process of changing their intimate relationships, from those based on coercive control to those based on equality. [They] accomplish this task without compromising their commitment to advocacy with battered women."

-Anne L. Ganley, PhD, Domestic Violence Program,
Seattle Veterans Administration Medical Center

*"**Education Groups for Men Who Batter** is a curriculum and a methodology which unequivocally identifies the exercise of violent and coercive tactics against women in intimate relationships as intentional, strategic behavior . . . [It] is an essential training tool for all actors in the justice and human services systems. Only when tactics of control are seen as intentional intimate terrorism can these systems construct responses effectively to end violence."*

-Barbara J. Hart, Esq., Pennsylvania Coalition Against Domestic Violence

Contents:
- Contributors; Acknowledgements; Introduction
- Theoretical Framework for Understanding Battering
- The Project Design
- The Curriculum
- Role of the Facilitator
- A Facilitator's Guide to Weekly Sessions
- Evaluation of Domestic Abuse Intervention Programs, *Melanie Shepard*
- Batterers' Programs, Battered Women's Movement,
  and Issues of Accountability, *Tineke Ritmeester*
- Ending the Violence; Appendices; Index

1993 212pp. 0-8261-7990-8 www.springerpub.com

536 Broadway, New York, NY 10012 • (212) 431-4370 • Fax: (212) 941-7842